# Internet of Things Programming Projects

Build modern IoT solutions with the Raspberry Pi 3
and Python

**Colin Dow**

BIRMINGHAM - MUMBAI

# Internet of Things Programming Projects

**Commissioning Editor:** Vijin Boricha
**Acquisition Editor:** Prachi Bisht
**Content Development Editor:** Deepti Thore
**Technical Editor:** Varsha Shivhare
**Copy Editor:** Safis Editing
**Project Coordinator:** Kinjal Bari
**Proofreader:** Safis Editing
**Indexer:** Mariammal Chettiyar
**Graphics:** Jisha Chirayil
**Production Coordinator:** Aparna Bhagat

First published: October 2018

Production reference: 1301018

Published by Packt Publishing Ltd.
Livery Place
35 Livery Street
Birmingham
B3 2PB, UK.

ISBN 978-1-78913-480-3

www.packtpub.com

mapt.io

Mapt is an online digital library that gives you full access to over 5,000 books and videos, as well as industry leading tools to help you plan your personal development and advance your career. For more information, please visit our website.

## Why subscribe?

- Spend less time learning and more time coding with practical eBooks and Videos from over 4,000 industry professionals

- Improve your learning with Skill Plans built especially for you

- Get a free eBook or video every month

- Mapt is fully searchable

- Copy and paste, print, and bookmark content

## Packt.com

Did you know that Packt offers eBook versions of every book published, with PDF and ePub files available? You can upgrade to the eBook version at www.packt.com and as a print book customer, you are entitled to a discount on the eBook copy. Get in touch with us at customercare@packtpub.com for more details.

At www.packt.com, you can also read a collection of free technical articles, sign up for a range of free newsletters, and receive exclusive discounts and offers on Packt books and eBooks.

# Contributors

## About the author

**Colin Dow** is the owner and chief engineer of Sigma Rockets and Aerospace Inc., a model aerospace business. He has enjoyed working with numerous educational facilities and hobbyists in delivering product sales, presentations, and aerospace workshops over the years.

Colin has extensive experience of creating website content, educational documentation, and instructional videos.

He has been a programmer since early home computers first caught his eye. He has worked as a software developer for some of Canada's largest companies, using technologies such as Python, Java, J2EE, PHP, Pearl, Ruby on Rails, Apache, and SOAP web services.

*I would like to thank my wife Constance for her encouragement, support and assistance; and my sons Maximillian and Jackson for their inspiration and optimism. I am forever grateful to them for this unique opportunity.*
*I would also like to thank Deepti Thore and Varsha Shivhare at Packt for their guidance and expertise throughout the whole process. Without their assistance and patience this book would not have been possible.*

# About the reviewer

**Arvind Ravulavaru** is a platform architect at Ubiconn IoT Solutions, with over 9 years of experience of software development and 2 years experience of hardware and product development. For the last 5 years, he has been working extensively on JavaScript, both on the server side and the client side. Over the past couple of years, his focus has been on IoT, building a platform for rapidly developing IoT solutions named The IoT Suitcase. Prior to that, Arvind worked on big data, cloud computing, and orchestration.

# Packt is searching for authors like you

If you're interested in becoming an author for Packt, please visit authors.packtpub.com and apply today. We have worked with thousands of developers and tech professionals, just like you, to help them share their insight with the global tech community. You can make a general application, apply for a specific hot topic that we are recruiting an author for, or submit your own idea.

# Table of Contents

**Preface**      1

**Chapter 1: Installing Raspbian on the Raspberry Pi**      9
  **A brief history of the Raspberry Pi**      9
  **A look at operating systems for the Raspberry Pi**      12
  **Project overview**      13
  **Getting started**      13
  **Installing the Raspbian OS**      13
    Formatting a microSD card for Raspbian      14
    Copying the NOOBS files to the microSD RAM      14
    Running the installer      15
  **A quick overview of the Raspbian OS**      22
    The Chromium web browser      22
    The home folder      23
    The Terminal      24
    Mathematica      26
    Sonic Pi      27
    Scratch and Scratch 2.0      28
    LibreOffice      29
  **Summary**      30
  **Questions**      30
  **Further reading**      31

**Chapter 2: Writing Python Programs Using Raspberry Pi**      33
  **Project overview**      33
  **Technical requirements**      34
  **Python tools for Raspberry Pi**      34
    The Terminal      34
    Integrated Development and Learning Environment      35
    Thonny      35
  **Using the Python command line**      37
  **Writing a simple Python program**      41
    Creating the class      41
    Creating the object      42
    Using the object inspector      43
    Testing your class      44
    Making the code flexible      45
      Example one      45
      Example two      45
  **Summary**      46

**Questions** 46
**Further reading** 47
**Chapter 3: Using the GPIO to Connect to the Outside World** 49
**Project overview** 49
**Technical requirements** 50
**Python libraries for the Raspberry Pi** 50
picamera 52
Pillow 53
sense-hat and sense-emu 53
**Accessing Raspberry Pi's GPIO** 56
Pibrella 57
RPi.GPIO 60
GPIO zero 61
**Setting up the circuit** 61
Fritzing 62
Building our circuit 64
**Hello LED** 66
Blink LED using gpiozero 66
Morse code weather data 66
**Summary** 70
**Questions** 71
**Further reading** 72
**Chapter 4: Subscribing to Web Services** 73
**Prerequisites** 73
**Project overview** 74
**Getting started** 74
**Cloud services for IoT** 74
Amazon Web Services IoT 74
IBM Watson platform 76
Google Cloud platform 77
Microsoft Azure 78
Weather Underground 78
**A basic Python program to pull data from the cloud** 79
Accessing the web service 79
Using the Sense HAT Emulator 82
**Summary** 84
**Questions** 85
**Further reading** 85
**Chapter 5: Controlling a Servo with Python** 87
**Knowledge required to complete this chapter** 87
**Project overview** 87
**Getting started** 88

**Wiring up a servo motor to the Raspberry Pi** 88
Stepper motors 88
DC motors 90
Servo motors 91
Connecting the servo motor to our Raspberry Pi 93
**Control the servo through the command line** 95
**Write a Python program to control the servo** 97
**Summary** 100
**Questions** 100
**Further reading** 100

**Chapter 6: Working with the Servo Control Code to Control an Analog Device** 101
**Knowledge required to complete this chapter** 101
**Project overview** 102
**Getting started** 103
**Accessing weather data from the cloud** 103
**Controlling the servo using weather data** 106
Correcting for servo range 106
Changing the position of the servo based on weather data 108
**Enhancing our project** 110
Printing out the main graphic 111
Adding the needle and LED 112
**Summary** 114
**Questions** 115
**Further reading** 115

**Chapter 7: Setting Up a Raspberry Pi Web Server** 117
**Knowledge required to complete this chapter** 117
**Project overview** 117
**Getting started** 118
**Introducing CherryPy – a minimalist Python web framework** 118
What is CherryPy? 118
Who uses CherryPy? 118
Installing CherryPy 119
**Creating a simple web page using CherryPy** 120
Hello Raspberry Pi! 120
Say hello to myFriend 122
What about static pages? 124
HTML weather dashboard 125
**Summary** 132
**Questions** 133
**Further reading** 133

**Chapter 8: Reading Raspberry Pi GPIO Sensor Data Using Python** 135

**Project overview** 135
**Getting started** 136
**Reading the state of a button** 136
Using GPIO Zero with a button 136
Using the Sense HAT emulator and GPIO Zero button together 138
Toggling an LED with a long button press 141
**Reading the state from an infrared motion sensor** 143
What is a PIR sensor? 144
Using the GPIO Zero buzzer class 147
Building a basic alarm system 150
**Modifying Hello LED using infrared sensor** 152
Configuring a distance sensor 153
Taking Hello LED to another level 155
**Summary** 157
**Questions** 158
**Further reading** 158

**Chapter 9: Building a Home Security Dashboard** 159
**Knowledge required to complete this chapter** 159
**Project overview** 159
**Getting started** 160
**Creating our dashboard using CherryPy** 160
Using the DHT11 to find temperature and humidity 160
Using the Pi camera to take a photo 165
Creating our dashboard using CherryPy 166
**Displaying sensory data on our dashboard** 171
Home security dashboard with a temperature sensor 172
Home security dashboard with quick response 181
**Summary** 189
**Questions** 189
**Further reading** 190

**Chapter 10: Publishing to Web Services** 191
**Project overview** 191
**Getting started** 191
**Publishing sensory data to cloud-based services** 192
Install the MQTT library 192
Set up an account and create a device 192
Reading sensory data and publishing to ThingsBoard 195
Creating a dashboard in ThingsBoard 198
Sharing your dashboard with a friend 201
**Setting up an account for text message transmission** 202
Setting up a Twilio account 203
Installing Twilio on our Raspberry Pi 207
Sending a text through Twilio 207

Creating a new home security dashboard                                     208
**Summary**                                                                219
**Questions**                                                              219
**Further reading**                                                        220

**Chapter 11: Creating a Doorbell Button Using Bluetooth**                 221
**Project overview**                                                       221
**Getting started**                                                        222
**Introducing Blue Dot**                                                   222
Installing the bluedot library on the Raspberry Pi                         224
Pairing Blue Dot with your Raspberry Pi                                    224
**Wiring up our circuit**                                                  225
What is an RGB LED?                                                        226
Testing our RGB LED                                                        226
Completing our doorbell circuit                                            229
**Reading our button state using Bluetooth and Python**                    232
Reading button information using Python                                    232
Creating a Bluetooth doorbell                                              234
Creating a secret Bluetooth doorbell                                       237
**Summary**                                                                238
**Questions**                                                              238
**Further reading**                                                        239

**Chapter 12: Enhancing Our IoT Doorbell**                                 241
**Project overview**                                                       242
**Getting started**                                                        243
**Sending a text message when someone is at the door**                     243
Creating a simple doorbell application with text messaging                 244
Creating a secret doorbell application with text messaging                 249
**Summary**                                                                255
**Questions**                                                              255
**Further reading**                                                        255

**Chapter 13: Introducing the Raspberry Pi Robot Car**                     257
**The parts of the robot car**                                             258
**Building the robot car**                                                 260
Step 1 – Adafruit 16-Channel PWM/Servo HAT for Raspberry Pi               260
Step 2 – Wiring up the motors                                              262
Step 3 – Assembling the servo camera mount                                 265
Step 4 – Attaching the head                                                270
Step 5 – Assembling the DC motor plate                                     274
Step 6 – Attaching the motors and wheels                                   282
Step 7 – Wiring up the motors                                              284
Step 8 – Attaching the camera mount, Raspberry Pi, and Adafruit servo
board                                                                      285

Step 9 – Attaching the buzzer and voltage divider    289
Step 10 – Wiring up T.A.R.A.S                         292
**Learning how to control the robot car**            295
Configuring our Raspberry Pi                          295
Python library for Adafruit Servo HAT                296
**Summary**                                           297
**Questions**                                         298

**Chapter 14: Controlling the Robot Car Using Python**    299
**Knowledge required to complete this chapter**       299
**Project overview**                                  300
**Getting started**                                   300
**Taking a look at the Python code**                  301
Controlling the drive wheels of the robot car         301
Moving the servos on the robot car                    302
Taking a picture                                       303
Making a beep noise                                    304
Making the LEDs blink                                  304
**Modifying the robot car Python code**               307
Move the wheels                                        307
Move the head                                          308
Make sounds                                            310
**Enhancing the code**                                312
Stitching our code together                            312
**Summary**                                           314
**Questions**                                          314
**Further reading**                                   315

**Chapter 15: Connecting Sensory Inputs from the Robot Car to the Web**    317
**Knowledge required to complete this chapter**       317
**Project overview**                                  318
**Getting started**                                   318
**Identifying the sensor on the robot car**           318
Taking a closer look at the HC-SR04                    319
**Reading robot car sensory data with Python**        322
**Publishing robot car sensory data to the cloud**    323
**Create a ThingsBoard device**                       324
**Summary**                                            330
**Questions**                                          330
**Further reading**                                   330

**Chapter 16: Controlling the Robot Car with Web Service Calls**    331
**Knowledge required to complete this chapter**       331
**Project overview**                                  332
**Technical requirements**                            332

**Reading the robot car's data from the cloud** 332
Changing the look of the distance gauge 332
Changing the range on the distance gauge 335
Viewing the dashboard outside of your account 337
**Using a Python program to control a robot car through the cloud** 338
Adding a switch to our dashboard 340
Controlling the green LED on T.A.R.A.S 342
Using the internet to make T.A.R.A.S dance 345
**Summary** 347
**Questions** 347
**Further reading** 348

**Chapter 17: Building the JavaScript Client** 349
**Project overview** 349
**Getting started** 350
**Introducing JavaScript cloud libraries** 350
Google Cloud 350
AWS SDK for JavaScript 351
Eclipse Paho JavaScript client 351
**Connecting to cloud services using JavaScript** 351
Setting up a CloudMQTT account 352
Setting up an MQTT Broker instance 354
Writing the JavaScript client code 356
Running the code 359
Understanding the JavaScript code 362
Publishing MQTT messages from our Raspberry Pi 365
**Summary** 366
**Questions** 367
**Further reading** 367

**Chapter 18: Putting It All Together** 369
**Project overview** 370
**Getting started** 371
**Building a JavaScript client to connect to our Raspberry Pi** 371
Writing the HTML code 372
Writing the JavaScript code to communicate with our MQTT Broker 376
**Creating a JavaScript client to access our robot car's sensory data** 382
Writing the code for T.A.R.A.S 383
Livestreaming videos from T.A.R.A.S 387
**Enhancing our JavaScript client to control our robot car** 389
Nipple.js 390
HTML5 Gamepad API 390
Johnny-Five 390
**Summary** 391
**Questions** 391

**Further reading** 392

**Assessments** 393

**Other Books You May Enjoy** 413

**Index** 417

# Preface

The **Internet of Things (IoT)** promises to unlock the real world the way that the internet unlocked millions of computers just a few decades ago. First released in 2012, the Raspberry Pi computer has taken the world by storm. Originally designed to give newer generations the same excitement to programming that personal computers from the 1980s did, the Raspberry Pi has gone on to be a staple of millions of makers everywhere.

In 1991, Guido van Rossum introduced the world to the Python programming language. Python is a terse language and was designed for code readability. Python programs tend to require fewer lines of code than other programming languages. Python is a scalable language that can be used for anything from the simplest programs to massive large-scale projects.

In this book, we will unleash the power of Raspberry Pi and Python to create exciting IoT projects.

The first part of the book introduces the reader to the amazing Raspberry Pi. We will learn how to set it up and jump right into Python programming. We will start our foray into real-world computing by creating the "Hello World" app for physical computing, the flashing LED.

Our first project takes us back to an age when analog needle meters ruled the world of data display. Think back to those old analog multimeters and endless old sci-fi movies where information was controlled and displayed with buttons and big flashing lights. In our project, we will retrieve weather data from a web service and display it on an analog needle meter. We will accomplish this using a servo motor connected to our Raspberry Pi through the GPIO.

Home security systems are pretty much ubiquitous in modern life. Entire industries and careers are based on the installation and monitoring of them. Did you know that you could easily create your own home security system? In our second project, we do just that, as we build a home security system using Raspberry Pi as a web server to display it.

The humble doorbell has been with us since 1831. In our third project, we will give it a 21st century twist and have our Raspberry Pi send a signal to a web service that will text us when someone is at the door.

In our final project, we take what we've learned from our previous two projects and create an IoT robot car we call T.A.R.A.S (This Amazing Raspberry-Pi Automated Security Agent).

In years to come, driverless cars will become the rule instead of the exception, and ways of controlling these cars will be needed. This final project gives the reader insight and knowledge into how someone would go about controlling cars devoid of a human driver.

# Who this book is for

This book is geared toward those who have had some sort of exposure to programming and are interested in learning about the IoT. Knowledge of the Python programming language would be a definite asset. An understanding of, or a keen interest in, object-oriented programming will serve the reader well with the coding examples used in the book.

# What this book covers

Chapter 1, *Installing Raspbian on the Raspberry Pi*, sets us off on our Raspberry Pi IoT journey by installing the Raspbian OS on our Raspberry Pi. We will then take a look at some of the programs that come pre-installed with Raspbian.

Chapter 2, *Writing Python Programs Using Raspberry Pi*, covers how Windows, macOS, and Linux are operating systems that are familiar to developers. Many a book on developing the Raspberry Pi involves using one of these operating systems and accessing the Raspberry Pi remotely. We will take a different approach in this book. We will use our Raspberry Pi as a development machine. In this chapter, we will get our feet wet with using the Raspberry Pi as a development machine.

Chapter 3, *Using the GPIO to Connect to the Outside World*, explains how, if the Raspberry Pi was just a $35 computer, that would be enough for many of us. However, the real power behind the Raspberry Pi is the ability of the developer to access the outside world through the use of the **General Purpose Input Output** (**GPIO**) pins. In this chapter, we will delve into the GPIO and start to connect the Raspberry Pi to the real world. We will create a Morse code generator for our project using an outside LED and then use this generator to blink out simulated weather information.

Chapter 4, *Subscribing to Web Services*, explores a few web services offered by some of the biggest companies in the world. Our project will use the virtual version of the Raspberry Pi Sense HAT as a ticker to display current weather information from the Yahoo! Weather web service.

Chapter 5, *Controlling a Servo with Python*, introduces the concept of creating an analog meter needle using a servo motor connected to the Raspberry Pi.

Chapter 6, *Working with the Servo Control Code to Control an Analog Device*, continues the theme of working with servo motors as we build our first real IoT device, a weather dashboard. Not only will this weather dashboard feature an analog needle; it will use the needle to point to a picture of a suggested wardrobe based on the weather conditions.

Chapter 7, *Setting Up a Raspberry Pi Web Server*, goes into how to install and configure the web framework CherryPy. We will conclude the chapter by building a local website that displays weather information.

Chapter 8, *Reading Raspberry Pi GPIO Sensor Data Using Python*, covers how to read the state of a button before moving on to a PIR sensor and distance sensor. We will conclude the chapter by building simple alarm systems.

Chapter 9, *Building a Home Security Dashboard*, explains how to build a home security dashboard using the Raspberry Pi as a web server serving up HTML content containing sensory data collected from the GPIO.

Chapter 10, *Publishing to Web Services*, goes into how to measure room temperature and humidity and publish these values to the web through the use of an IoT dashboard. We will also set up and run a text messaging alert using the service Twilio.

Chapter 11, *Creating a Doorbell Button Using Bluetooth*, turns our focus to using Bluetooth in this chapter. Bluetooth is a wireless technology that allows for transmission of data over short distances. For our project we will explore the BlueDot app from the Android Play Store. We will use this app to build a simple Bluetooth connected doorbell.

Chapter 12, *Enhancing Our IoT Doorbell*, will take the simple doorbell we created in Chapter 11, *Creating a Doorbell Button Using Bluetooth*, and turn it into an IoT doorbell using the knowledge we learned in Chapter 10, *Publishing to Web Services*.

Chapter 13, *Introducing the Raspberry Pi Robot Car*, starts us off on our journey into the IoT robot car by introducing This Amazing Raspberry-Pi Automated Security Agent (T.A.R.A.S). This chapter will begin by outlining the components we need to build T.A.R.A.S and then we will proceed to putting it all together.

Chapter 14, *Controlling the Robot Car Using Python*, goes into how to write Python code for our robot car. We will utilize the GPIO Zero library to make the car wheels move forward, move the servo motors holding the camera, and light up the LEDs at the back of the robot car.

Chapter 15, *Connecting Sensory Inputs from the Robot Car to the Web*, helps us understand that in order to turn our robot car into a true IoT device we have to connect it to the internet. In this chapter we will connect the distance sensor from our robot car to the internet.

Chapter 16, *Controlling the Robot Car with Web Service Calls*, continues to turn our robot car into an Internet of Things device by taking a deeper look at the internet dashboard we created for the robot car.

Chapter 17, *Building the JavaScript Client*, moves our attention away from Python, switching our focus to JavaScript instead. We will use JavaScript to build a web-based client that communicates over the internet using the MQTT protocol.

Chapter 18, *Putting It All Together*, covers how we will connect our robot car, T.A.R.A.S, to a JavaScript client, and control it over the internet using the MQTT protocol.

# To get the most out of this book

To get the most out of this book, I will assume the following:

- You have purchased, or will purchase, a Raspberry Pi Computer, preferably a 2015 model or newer.
- You have had some exposure to the Python programming language, or are eager to learn it.
- You have a basic familiarity with electronic components and how to use a breadboard.
- You have purchased, or are willing to purchase, basic electronic components.

In terms of hardware requirements, you will need at least the following:

- A Raspberry Pi Model 3 (2015 model or newer)
- A USB power supply
- A computer monitor
- A USB keyboard
- A USB mouse
- A microSD RAM card
- A breadboard and breadboard jumpers

Additional pieces of hardware will be introduced at the beginning of every chapter.

In terms of software requirements, you will require the Raspberry Pi NOOBS image
(`https://www.raspberrypi.org/downloads/noobs/`). Additional software, accounts, and
Python packages will be presented along the way. Any piece of software, web service, or
Python package we use in this book is free of charge.

# Download the example code files

You can download the example code files for this book from your account
at `www.packt.com`. If you purchased this book elsewhere, you can
visit `www.packt.com/support` and register to have the files emailed directly to you.

You can download the code files by following these steps:

1. Log in or register at `www.packt.com`.
2. Select the **SUPPORT** tab.
3. Click on **Code Downloads & Errata**.
4. Enter the name of the book in the **Search** box and follow the onscreen
   instructions.

Once the file is downloaded, please make sure that you unzip or extract the folder using the
latest version of:

- WinRAR/7-Zip for Windows
- Zipeg/iZip/UnRarX for Mac
- 7-Zip/PeaZip for Linux

The code bundle for the book is also hosted on GitHub at `https://github.com/
PacktPublishing/Internet-of-Things-Programming-Projects`. In case there's an update
to the code, it will be updated on the existing GitHub repository.

We also have other code bundles from our rich catalog of books and videos available
at `https://github.com/PacktPublishing/`. Check them out!

# Download the color images

We also provide a PDF file that has color images of the screenshots/diagrams used in this book. You can download it here: https://www.packtpub.com/sites/default/files/downloads/9781789134803_ColorImages.pdf.

# Conventions used

There are a number of text conventions used throughout this book.

CodeInText: Indicates code words in text, database table names, folder names, filenames, file extensions, pathnames, dummy URLs, user input, and Twitter handles. Here is an example: "In order to access Python 3, we type the python3 command in a Terminal window."

A block of code is set as follows:

```
wind_dir_str_len = 2
if currentWeather.getWindSpeed()[-2:-1] == ' ':
    wind_dir_str_len = 1
```

Any command-line input or output is written as follows:

```
pip3 install weather-api
```

**Bold**: Indicates a new term, an important word, or words that you see on screen. For example, words in menus or dialog boxes appear in the text like this. Here is an example: "From the **View** menu, select **Object inspector** and **Variables**."

Warnings or important notes appear like this.

Tips and tricks appear like this.

# Get in touch

Feedback from our readers is always welcome.

**General feedback**: If you have questions about any aspect of this book, mention the book title in the subject of your message and email us at customercare@packtpub.com.

**Errata**: Although we have taken every care to ensure the accuracy of our content, mistakes do happen. If you have found a mistake in this book, we would be grateful if you would report this to us. Please visit www.packt.com/submit-errata, selecting your book, clicking on the Errata Submission Form link, and entering the details.

**Piracy**: If you come across any illegal copies of our works in any form on the internet, we would be grateful if you would provide us with the location address or website name. Please contact us at copyright@packt.com with a link to the material.

**If you are interested in becoming an author**: If there is a topic that you have expertise in, and you are interested in either writing or contributing to a book, please visit authors.packtpub.com.

# Reviews

Please leave a review. Once you have read and used this book, why not leave a review on the site that you purchased it from? Potential readers can then see and use your unbiased opinion to make purchase decisions, we at Packt can understand what you think about our products, and our authors can see your feedback on their book. Thank you!

For more information about Packt, please visit packt.com.

# 1
# Installing Raspbian on the Raspberry Pi

The Raspberry Pi is marketed as a small and affordable computer that you can use to learn programming. At least that was its initial goal. As we will see in this book, it is much more than that.

The following topics will be covered in this chapter:

- A brief history of the Raspberry Pi
- A look at operating systems for the Raspberry Pi
- Installing the Raspbian OS
- A quick overview of the Raspbian OS

## A brief history of the Raspberry Pi

First released in 2012, the first Raspberry Pi featured a 700 MHz single core processor and 256 MB of RAM. The Raspberry Pi 2 was released in February of 2015 with a 900 MHz quad core processor and 1 GB of RAM. Released in February of 2016, the Raspberry Pi 3 increased the processor speed to 1.2 GHz. This model was also the first one to include wireless LAN and Bluetooth.

Here is an image of a Raspberry Pi 3 B (2015):

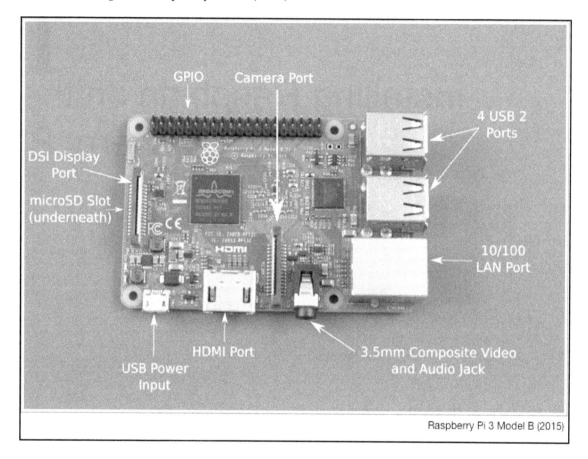

Raspberry Pi 3 Model B (2015)

This version of the Raspberry Pi features the following parts:

- Four USB 2 ports
- A LAN port
- A 3.5 mm composite video and audio jack
- An HDMI port for video and audio
- An OTG USB port (which we will use to connect the power)
- A microSD slot (to hold our operating system)

- A DSI display port for the Raspberry Pi touchscreen
- A **General Purpose Input Output** (**GPIO**) pins
- A camera port for a special Raspberry Pi camera

The Raspberry Pi Zero was released in November of 2015. Here is an image of it:

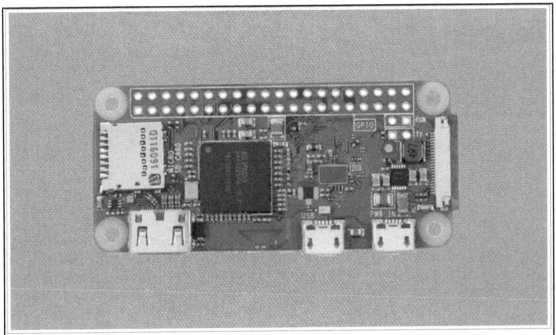

Raspberry Pi Zero W

Although not as powerful as the previous Raspberry Pis, the Zero featured a smaller size (65 mm X 30 mm), perfect for projects with limited physical space (namely, wearable projects). Plus, the Raspberry Pi zero was priced at $5 USD, making it very affordable. The Raspberry Pi zero W was released on February 28, 2017 at double the price ($10 USD) with built-in Wi-Fi and Bluetooth capabilities.

The latest model, as of the time of writing, is the Raspberry Pi 3 B+, which was released on March 14, 2018. The processor speed has been upgraded to 1.4 GHz as well as the wireless LAN now supporting both 2.4 GHz and 5 GHz bands. Another upgrade is the addition of Bluetooth low energy, a technology built for applications that do not require large amounts of data to be exchanged but are required to have a long battery life.

Creators of the Raspberry Pi initially believed that they would sell at most 1,000 units. Little did they know that their invention would explode in popularity. As of March 2018, sales of Raspberry Pi computers has passed the 19 million mark.

# A look at operating systems for the Raspberry Pi

There are various operating systems (or system images) that may be installed on the Raspberry Pi. These range from application-specific operating systems, such as audio players, to various general purpose operating systems. The power behind Raspberry Pi is the way it can be used for various applications and projects.

The following is a list of just a few of the operating systems (system images) available for the Raspberry Pi:

- **Volumio**: Do you have a desire to set up a networked audio system where you access your music list using a computer or cell phone? Volumio may be what you are looking for. Installing it on a Raspberry Pi creates a headless audio player (a system that does not require a keyboard and mouse) that connects to your audio files either over USB or a network. A special audio **Hardware Added on Top** (**HAT**) may be added to your Pi to provide a pristine audio connection to an amplifier and speakers. There is even a plugin to add Spotify so that you can set up your Raspberry Pi to access this service and play music over your sound system.
- **PiFM radio transmitter**: The PiFM radio transmitter turns your Raspberry Pi into an FM transmitter, which you can use to send audio files over the air to a standard FM radio receiver. Using a simple wire connected to one of the GPIO pins (we will learn more about GPIO later), you can create an antenna for the transmitted FM signal, which is surprisingly strong.
- **Stratux**: ADS-B is the new standard in aviation where geo-location and weather information are shared with ground controllers and pilots. The Stratux image with additional hardware turns the Raspberry Pi into an ADS-B receiver of this information.
- **RetroPie**: RetroPie turns your Raspberry Pi into a retro game console by emulating gaming consoles and computers from the past. Some of the emulations include Amiga, Apple II, Atari 2600, and the Nintendo Entertainment System of the early 1980s.

- **OctoPi**: OctoPi turns your Raspberry Pi into a server for your 3D printer. Through OctoPi, you may control your 3D printer over the network, including viewing the status of your 3D printer using a webcam.
- **NOOBS**: This is arguably the easiest way to install an operating system on the Raspberry Pi. NOOBS stands for New Out-Of-the Box Software, and we will be using NOOBS to install Raspbian.

# Project overview

In this project, we will install the Raspbian operating system onto our Raspberry Pi. After installation, we will take a quick tour of the operating system to familiarize ourselves with it. We will start by formatting a microSD card to store our installation files. We will then run the installation from the microSD card. After Raspbian has been installed, we will take a quick look at it in order to familiarize ourselves with it.

This project should take about two hours to complete, as we install the Raspbian operating system and take a quick look at it.

# Getting started

The following is required to complete this project:

- A Raspberry Pi Model 3 (2015 model or newer)
- A USB power supply
- A computer monitor
- A USB keyboard
- A USB mouse
- A microSD RAM card
- A Raspberry Pi NOOBS image (`https://www.raspberrypi.org/downloads/noobs/`)

# Installing the Raspbian OS

The Raspbian OS is considered the default or go-to operating system for the Raspberry Pi. In this section, we will install Raspbian using the NOOBS image.

# Formatting a microSD card for Raspbian

Raspberry Pi uses a microSD card to store the operating system. This allows you to easily switch between different operating systems (system images) for your Raspberry Pi. We will be installing the default Raspbian OS for our projects using the NOOBS image.

Start by inserting the microSD card into a USB adapter and plug it into your computer:

Inserting the microSD card into a USB adapter

You may need to format the microSD card. If so, use the utilities appropriate for your computer's operating system to format the card to FAT32. It is recommended that you use a card with a capacity of 8 GB or greater. For Windows OS and cards with 64 GB of capacity or greater, a third-party tool such as FAT32 format should be used for formatting.

# Copying the NOOBS files to the microSD RAM

Unzip the NOOBS image that you downloaded. Open up the unzipped directory and drag the files over to the microSD card.

The files should look the same as in the following screenshot:

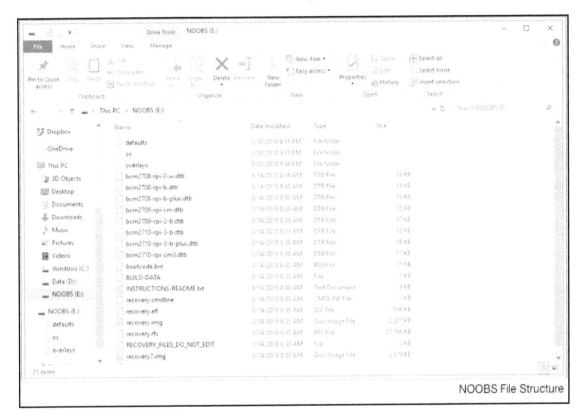

NOOBS File Structure

# Running the installer

We will now install Raspbian on our Raspberry Pi. This step should be familiar to those that have previous experience installing operating systems such as Windows or macOS. The Raspbian operating system will be installed and will run off of our microSD card.

To install Raspbian onto our microSD card, do the following:

1. Start by inserting the microSD card into the appropriate slot on the Raspberry Pi. Be sure to install it so that the label side (opposite side of the exposed contacts) is facing up. Insert it with the metal contacts facing the board. The microSD card should have a slight ridge at the top of the label side, which is good for easy removal using a fingernail.

2. Insert a keyboard and mouse into the USB slots on the side, a monitor into the HDMI port, and lastly, a USB power cable into the power port. The Raspberry Pi does not have an on/off switch and will power up as soon as the power cable is connected:

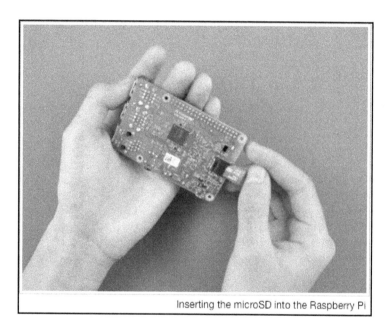

Inserting the microSD into the Raspberry Pi

3. After an initial black screen with rolling white text, you should see the following dialog:

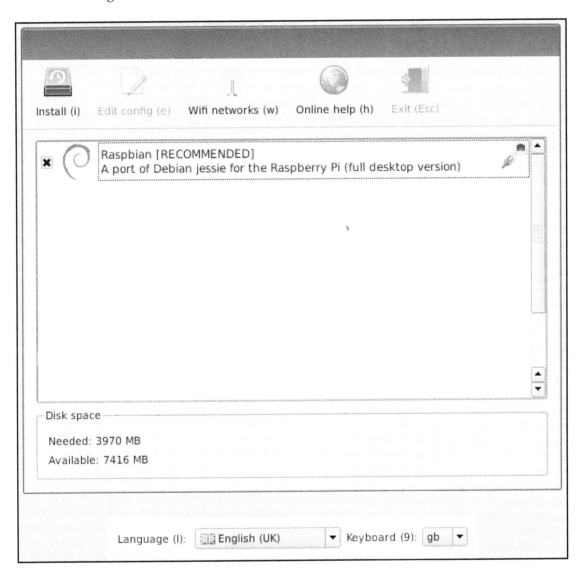

4. In the previous screenshot, we clicked on the **Language** option. For our purposes, we will keep the default of **English (UK)**. We will also keep the keyboard at the standard **gb**.

5. As the Raspberry Pi 3 has wireless LAN, we can set up our Wi-Fi (for older boards, please plug a Wi-Fi dongle into a USB port or use the wired LAN port and skip the next step):

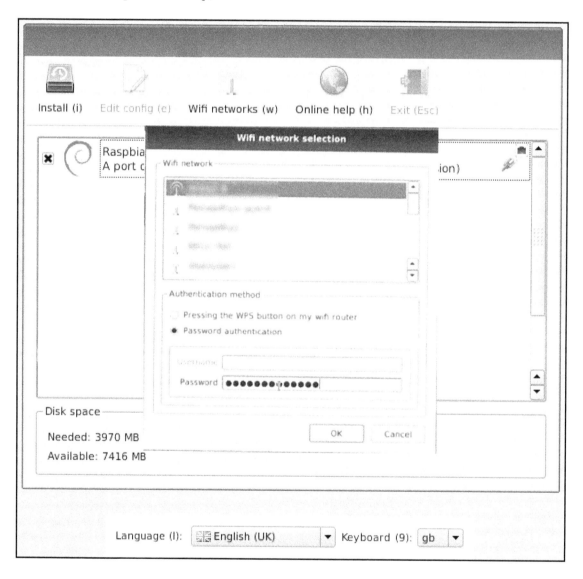

6. Click on the **Wifi networks (w)** button. Choose the **Authentication method** using the radio buttons. Some routers are equipped with a **WPS** button that allows you to connect directly to the router. To use the `password` method, choose the **Password authentication** radio button and enter the password for your network. After connecting to your network, you will notice that there are now more operating system options to select from:

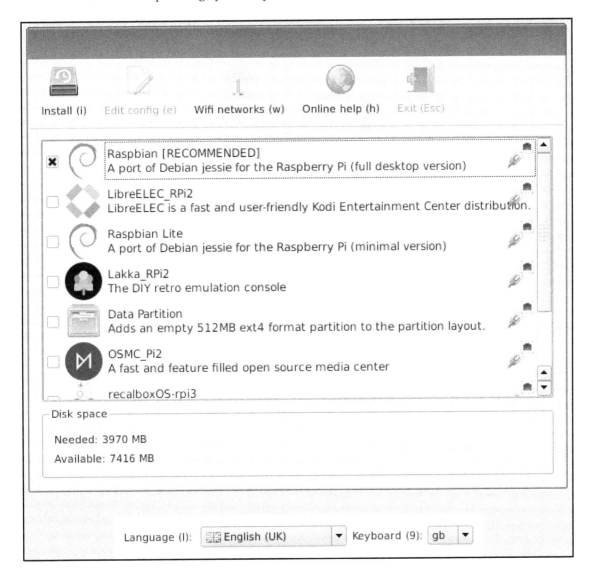

7. We will go with the top option, **Raspbian**. Check the box beside **Raspbian [RECOMMENDED]** and then click on the **Install (i)** button at the top-left corner of the dialog. Raspbian will start installing on your Raspberry Pi. You will see a progress bar with previous graphics, describing various features of the Raspbian operating system:

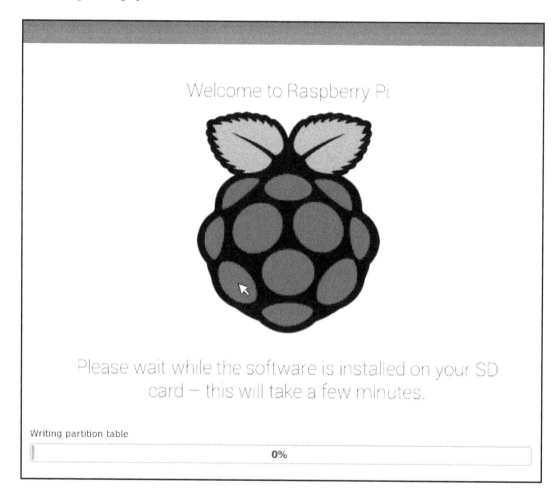

8. After the progress bar hits 100%, the computer will reboot and you will see a screen with text before the default desktop loads up:

# A quick overview of the Raspbian OS

The Raspbian desktop is similar to the desktops of other operating systems such as Windows and macOS. Clicking the top-left button drops down the application menu where you may access the various pre-installed programs. We may also shut down the Raspberry Pi from this menu:

# The Chromium web browser

The second button from the left loads the Google Chromium web browser for the Raspberry Pi:

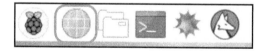

The Chromium browser is a lightweight browser that runs remarkably well on the Raspberry Pi:

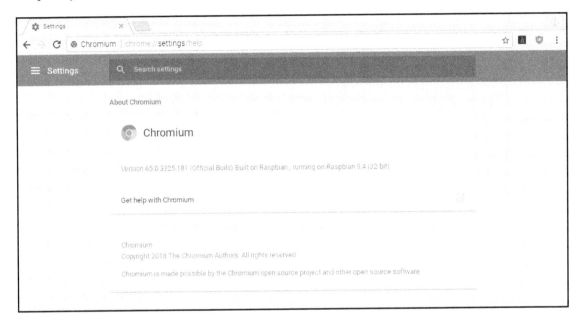

# The home folder

The two-folders button opens up a window showing the home folder:

The home folder is a great place to start when looking for files on your Raspberry Pi. In fact, when you take screenshots using either the scrot command or the **Print Screen** button, the file is automatically stored in this folder:

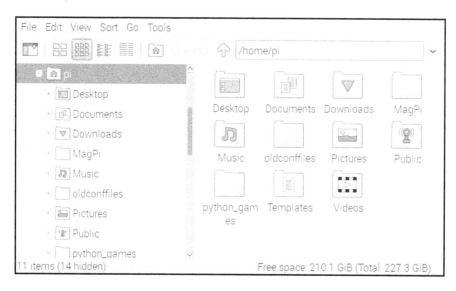

# The Terminal

The third button from the left opens up the Terminal. The Terminal permits command-line access to Raspberry Pi's files and programs:

It is from the command line where you may update the Raspberry Pi using the sudo apt-get update and sudo apt-get dist-upgrade commands.

`apt-get` updates the packages list, and `apt-get dist-upgrade` updates the packages:

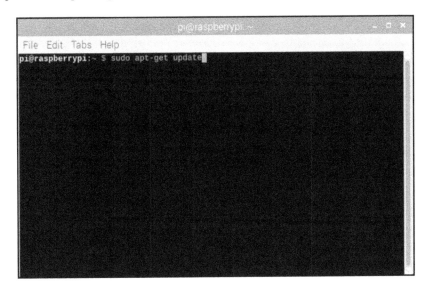

It's a good idea to run both of these commands right after installing Raspbian using the `sudo` command. The default user for Raspbian on the Raspberry Pi is `pi`, which is part of the Super Users group in Raspbian, and thus must use the `sudo` command (the default password for the `pi` user is `raspberry`):

Mastering the command line is a virtue that many a programmer aspires to acquire. Being able to rapidly type command after command looks so cool that even movie makers have picked up on it (when was the last time you saw the computer wiz in a movie clicking around the screen with a mouse?). To assist you in becoming this uber cool computer wiz, here are some basic Raspbian commands for you to master using the Terminal:

ls: Command to see the contents of the current directory
cd: Command to change directories. For example, use cd to move up a directory from where you currently are
pwd: Command to display the directory you are currently in
sudo: Allows the user to perform a task as the super user
shutdown: Command that allows the user to shut down the computer from the Terminal command line

# Mathematica

The third and fourth buttons are for Mathematica, and a terminal to access the Wolfram language, respectively:

Mathematica spans all areas of technical computing and uses the Wolfram language as the programming language. The areas in which Mathematica is used include machine learning, image processing, neural networks and data science:

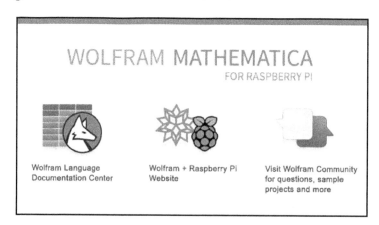

Mathematica, a proprietary software first released in 1988, can be used free for individuals on the Raspberry Pi through a partnership that was announced in late 2013.

Now let's take a look at some of the programs that are accessed from the main drop-down menu.

# Sonic Pi

Sonic Pi is a live coding environment for creating electronic music. It is accessed from the **Programming** menu option. Sonic Pi is a creative way to create music as the user programs loops, arpeggios, and soundscapes in real time by cutting and pasting code from one part of the app to another. Synthesizers in Sonic Pi may be configured on a deep level, providing a customized experience for the music coder:

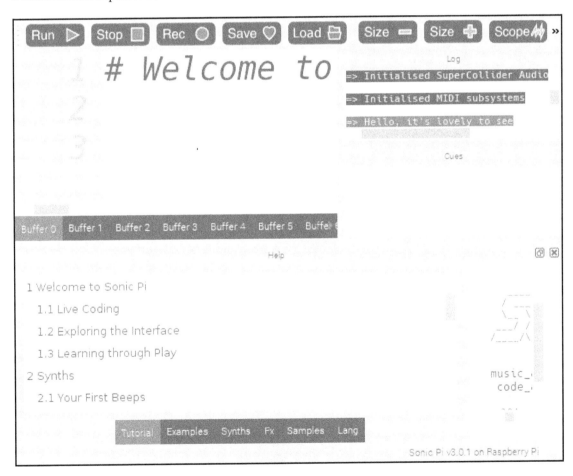

Geared toward an EDM style of music, Sonic Pi may also be used to compose classical and jazz styles of music.

# Scratch and Scratch 2.0

Scratch and Scratch 2.0 are visual programming environments designed for teaching programming to children. Using Scratch, the programmer creates their own animations with looping and conditional statements.

Games may be created within the program. The first version of Scratch was released in 2003 by the Lifelong Kindergarten group at the MIT media lab. Scratch 2.0 was released in 2013, and development is currently underway with Scratch 3.0:

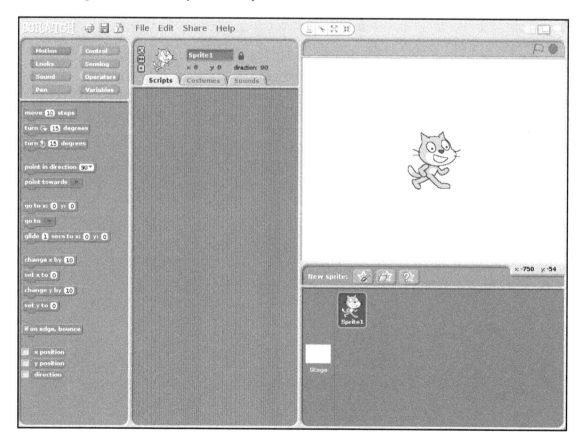

Scratch and Scratch 2.0 may be accessed under the **Programming** menu option.

# LibreOffice

LibreOffice is a free and open source office suite that forked over from OpenOffice in 2010. The LibreOffice suite consists of a word processor, a spreadsheet program, a presentation program, a vector graphics editor, a program for creating and editing mathematical formulae, and a database management program. The LibreOffice suite of programs may be accessed through the **LibreOffice** menu option:

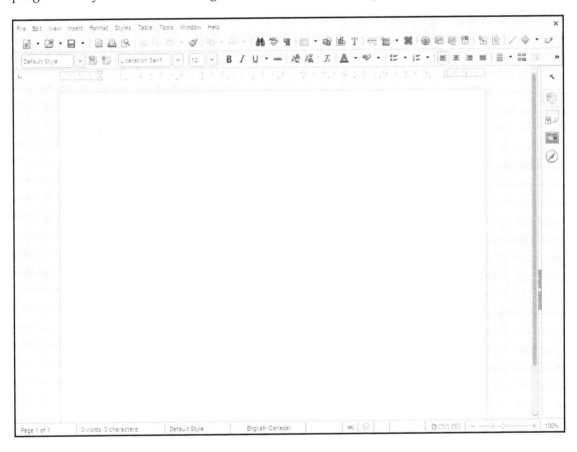

# Summary

We started this chapter with a look at the history of the Raspberry Pi. What started as an initiative to promote programming to a new generation has grown into a global phenomenon. We then downloaded the NOOBS image and installed the Raspbian OS, the default operating system for the Raspberry Pi. This involved formatting and preparing a microSD card for the NOOBS files.

It's easiest to think that a computer as inexpensive and small as the Raspberry Pi is not all that powerful. We demonstrated that the Raspberry Pi is indeed a very capable computer, as we took a look at some of the applications that come pre-installed with the Raspbian OS.

In Chapter 2, *Writing Python Programs Using Raspberry Pi*, we will begin Python coding using the Raspberry Pi and some of the development tools available in Raspbian.

# Questions

1. What year did the first Raspberry Pi come out?
2. What upgrades did the Raspberry Pi 3 Model B+ have over the previous version?
3. What does NOOBS stand for?
4. What is the name of the pre-installed application that allows for creating music with Python code?
5. Where is the operating system stored for the Raspberry Pi?
6. What is the name of the visual programming environment designed for children that comes pre-installed with Raspbian?
7. What is the name of the language used in Mathematica?
8. What is the default username and password for Raspbian?
9. What does GPIO stand for?
10. What is RetroPie?
11. True or false? Clicking on the two-folders icon on the main bar loads the home folder.
12. True or false? The microSD card slot is located at the bottom of the Raspberry Pi.
13. True or false? To shutdown the Raspberry Pi, select **Shutdown** from the **Application** menu.
14. True or false? You may only install the Raspbian OS with NOOBS.
15. True or false? Bluetooth low energy refers to people that eat too many blueberries and have a hard time waking up in the morning.

# Further reading

For more information on the Raspberry Pi, please consult the main Raspberry Pi website at `www.raspberrypi.org`.

# Writing Python Programs Using Raspberry Pi

**2**

In this chapter, we will start writing python programs with Raspberry Pi. Python is the official programming language for Raspberry Pi and is represented by the Pi in the name.

The following topics will be covered in this chapter:

- Python tools for Raspberry Pi
- Using the Python command line
- Writing a simple Python program

Python comes pre-installed on Raspbian in two versions, versions 2.7.14 and 3.6.5 (as of this writing) representing Python 2 and Python 3, respectively. The differences between the two versions are beyond the scope of this book. We will use Python 3 in this book unless otherwise stated.

## Project overview

In this project, we will become comfortable with Python development on Raspberry Pi. You may be used to development tools or **Integrated Development Environments** (**IDEs**) on other systems such as Windows, macOS, and Linux. In this chapter, we will get our feet wet in terms of using Raspberry Pi as a development machine. We will start off slowly with Python as we get our development juices flowing.

# Technical requirements

The following is required to complete this project:

- Raspberry Pi Model 3 (2015 model or newer)
- USB power supply
- Computer monitor
- USB keyboard
- USB mouse

# Python tools for Raspberry Pi

The following are pre-installed tools that we may use for Python development on Raspberry Pi using Raspbian. This list is by no means the only tools that we may use for development.

## The Terminal

As Python comes pre-installed with Raspbian, an easy way to launch it is to use the Terminal. As we can see in the following screenshot, the Python interpreter can be accessed by simply typing `python` as the command prompt in a Terminal window:

We may test it out by running the simplest of programs:

```
print 'hello'
```

Notice the Python version in the line after the command, 2.7.13. The `python` command in Raspbian is tied to Python 2. In order to access Python 3, we must type the `python3` command in a Terminal window:

```
pi@raspberrypi: ~

File  Edit  Tabs  Help

pi@raspberrypi:~ $ python3
Python 3.5.3 (default, Jan 19 2017, 14:11:04)
[GCC 6.3.0 20170124] on linux
Type "help", "copyright", "credits" or "license" for more information.
>>>
```

# Integrated Development and Learning Environment

The **Integrated Development and Learning Environment** (IDLE) has been the default IDE for Python since version 1.5.2. It is written in Python itself using the Tkinter GUI toolkit and is intended to be a simple IDE for beginners:

```
Python 3.5.3 Shell

File  Edit  Shell  Debug  Options  Window  Help

Python 3.5.3 (default, Jan 19 2017, 14:11:04)
[GCC 6.3.0 20170124] on linux
Type "copyright", "credits" or "license()" for more information.
>>>
```

IDLE features a multi-window text editor with auto-completion, syntax highlighting, and smart indent. IDLE should be familiar to anyone that has used Python. There are two versions of IDLE in Raspbian, one for Python 2 and the other for Python 3. Both programs are accessed from **Application Menu | Programming**.

# Thonny

Thonny is an IDE that comes packaged with Raspbian. With Thonny, we may evaluate expressions by using the `debug` function. Thonny is also available for macOS and Windows.

To load Thonny, go to **Application Menu** | **Programming** | **Thonny**:

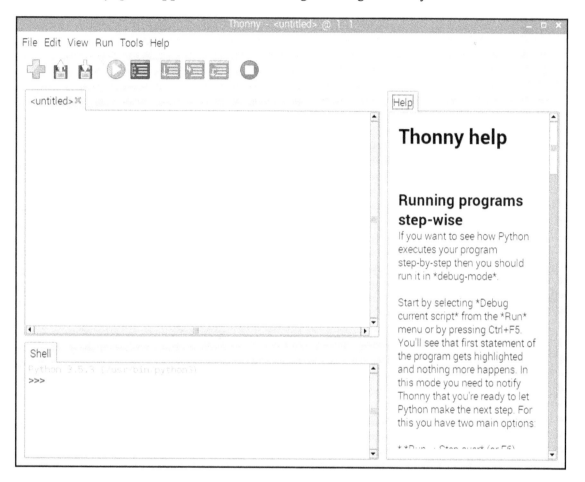

Above is the default screen for Thonny. Panels to view variables in your program, as well as a panel to view the filesystem, are toggled on and off from the **View** menu. Thonny's compact structure makes it ideal for our projects.

We will be learning a bit more about Thonny as we go through the rest of this book.

# Using the Python command line

Let's start doing some coding. Whenever I start using a new operating system for development, I like to go through some basics just to get my mind back into it (I'm speaking particularly to those of us who are all too familiar with coding into the wee hours of the morning).

The simplest way to access Python is from the Terminal. We will run a simple program to get started. Load the Terminal from the main toolbar and type `python3` at the prompt. Type the following line and hit *Enter*:

```
from datetime import datetime
```

This line loads the `datetime` object from the `datetime` module into our instance of Python. Next type the following and hit *Enter*:

```
print(datetime.now())
```

You should see the current date and time printed to the screen:

Let's try another example. Type the following into the shell:

```
import pyjokes
```

This is a library that's used to tell programming jokes. To have a joke printed out, type the following and hit *Enter*:

```
pyjokes.get_joke()
```

You should see the following output:

```
pi@raspberrypi:~ $ python3
Python 3.5.3 (default, Jan 19 2017, 14:11:04)
[GCC 6.3.0 20170124] on linux
Type "help", "copyright", "credits" or "license" for more information.
>>> import pyjokes
>>> pyjokes.get_joke()
'Java: Write once, run away.'
>>>
```

OK, so this may not be your cup of tea (or coffee, for the Java programmers out there). However, this example demonstrates how easy it is to import a Python module and utilize it.

If you receive an ImportError, it is because pyjokes did not come pre-installed with your version of the OS. Similar to the following example, typing sudo pip3 install pyjokes will install pyjokes onto your Raspberry Pi.

What these Python modules have in common is their availability for our use. We simply need to import them directly into the shell in order to use them, as they are pre-installed with our Raspbian operating system. However, what about libraries that are not installed?

Let's try an example. In the Python shell, type the following and hit *Enter*:

```
import weather
```

You should see the following:

```
                           pi@raspberrypi ~                    _ □ x

 File  Edit  Tabs  Help
 pi@raspberrypi:~ $ python3
 Python 3.5.3 (default, Jan 19 2017, 14:11:04)
 [GCC 6.3.0 20170124] on linux
 Type "help", "copyright", "credits" or "license" for more information.
 >>> import weather
 Traceback (most recent call last):
   File "<stdin>", line 1, in <module>
 ImportError: No module named 'weather'
 >>> █
```

Since the `weather` package is not installed on our Raspberry Pi we get an error when trying to import. In order to install the package, we use the Python command-line utility `pip`, or in our case, `pip3` for Python 3:

1. Open up a new Terminal (make sure that you're in a Terminal session and not a Python shell). Type the following:

   ```
   pip3 install weather-api
   ```

2. Hit *Enter*. You will see the following:

```
                           pi@raspberrypi ~                    _ □ x

 File  Edit  Tabs  Help
 Collecting urllib3<1.23,>=1.21.1 (from requests->weather-api)
   Downloading https://files.pythonhosted.org/packages/63/cb/6965947c13a94236f6d4
 b8223e21beb4d576dc72e8130bd7880f600839b8/urllib3-1.22-py2.py3-none-any.whl (132k
 B)
     100% |                                | 133kB 1.2MB/s
 Collecting certifi>=2017.4.17 (from requests->weather-api)
   Downloading https://files.pythonhosted.org/packages/7c/e6/92ad559b7192d846975f
 c916b65f667c7b8c3a32bea7372340bfe9a15fa5/certifi-2018.4.16-py2.py3-none-any.whl
 (150kB)
     100% |                                | 153kB 1.1MB/s
 Collecting idna<2.7,>=2.5 (from requests->weather-api)
   Downloading https://files.pythonhosted.org/packages/27/cc/6dd9a3869f15c2edfab8
 63b992838277279ce92663d334df9ecf5106f5c6/idna-2.6-py2.py3-none-any.whl (56kB)
     100% |                                | 61kB 1.9MB/s
 Collecting chardet<3.1.0,>=3.0.2 (from requests->weather-api)
   Downloading https://files.pythonhosted.org/packages/bc/a9/01ffebfb562e4274b648
 7b4bb1ddec7ca55ec7510b22e4c51f14098443b8/chardet-3.0.4-py2.py3-none-any.whl (133
 kB)
     100% |                                | 143kB 1.5MB/s
 Installing collected packages: urllib3, certifi, idna, chardet, requests, weathe
 r-api
 Successfully installed certifi-2018.4.16 chardet-3.0.4 idna-2.6 requests-2.18.4
 urllib3-1.22 weather-api-1.0.3
 pi@raspberrypi:~ $ █
```

3. After the process is finished, we will have the `weather-api` package installed on our Raspberry Pi. This package will allow us to access weather information from Yahoo! Weather.

Now let's try out a few examples:

1. Type `python3` and hit *Enter*. You should now be back in the Python shell.
2. Type the following and hit *Enter*:

```
from weather import Weather
from weather import Unit
```

3. What we have done is imported `Weather` and `Unit` from `weather`. Type the following and hit *Enter*:

```
weather = Weather(unit=Unit.CELSIUS)
```

4. This instantiates a `weather` object called `weather`. Now, let's make use of this object. Type the following and hit *Enter*:

```
lookup = weather.lookup(4118)
```

5. We now have a variable named `lookup` that's been created with the code `4118`, that corresponds to the city Toronto, Canada. Type the following and hit *Enter*:

```
condition = lookup.condition
```

6. We now have a variable called `condition` that contains the current weather information for the city of Toronto, Canada via the `lookup` variable. To view this information, type the following and hit *Enter*:

```
print(condition.text)
```

7. You should get a description of the weather conditions in Toronto, Canada. When I ran it, the following was returned:

```
Partly Cloudy
```

Now that we've seen that writing Python code on the Raspberry Pi is just as easy as writing it on other operating systems, let's take it a step further and write a simple program. We will use Thonny for this.

A Python module is a single Python file containing code that may be imported for use. A Python package is a collection of Python modules.

# Writing a simple Python program

We will write a simple Python program that contains a class. To facilitate this, we will use Thonny, a Python IDE that comes pre-installed with Raspbian and has excellent debug and variable introspection functionalities. You will find that its ease of use makes it ideal for the development of our projects.

# Creating the class

We will begin our program by creating a class. A class may be seen as a template for creating objects. A class contains methods and variables. To create a class in Python with Thonny, do the following:

1. Load Thonny through **Application Menu** | **Programming** | **Thonny**. Select **New** from the top left and type the following code:

```python
class CurrentWeather:
    weather_data={'Toronto':['13','partly sunny','8 km/h NW'],
                  'Montreal':['16','mostly sunny','22 km/h W'],
                  'Vancouver':['18','thunder showers','10 km/h NE'],
                  'New York':['17','mostly cloudy','5 km/h SE'],
                  'Los Angeles':['28','sunny','4 km/h SW'],
                  'London':['12','mostly cloudy','8 km/h NW'],
                  'Mumbai':['33','humid and foggy','2 km/h S']
                  }

    def __init__(self, city):
        self.city = city

    def getTemperature(self):
        return self.weather_data[self.city][0]

    def getWeatherConditions(self):
        return self.weather_data[self.city][1]

    def getWindSpeed(self):
        return self.weather_data[self.city][2]
```

As you can see, we've created a class called `CurrentWeather` that will hold weather conditions for whichever city we instantiated the class for. We are using a class as it will allow us to keep our code clean and prepare us for using outside classes later on.

# Creating the object

We will now create an object from our `CurrentWeather` class. We will use `London` as our city:

1.  Click on the **Run Current Script** button (a green circle with a white arrow) in the top menu to load our code into the Python interpreter.
2.  At the command line of the Thonny shell, type the following and hit *Enter*:

    ```
    londonWeather = CurrentWeather('London')
    ```

    We have just created an object in our code called `londonWeather` from our `CurrentWeather` class. By passing `'London'` to the constructor (`init`), we set our new object to only send weather information for the city of `London`. This is done through the class attribute city (`self.city`).

3.  Type the following at the shell command line:

    ```
    weatherLondon.getTemperature()
    ```

    You should get the answer `'12'` on the next line.

4.  To view the weather conditions for `London`, type the following:

    ```
    weatherLondon.getWeatherConditions()
    ```

    You should see `'mostly cloudy'` on the next line.

5.  To get the wind speed, type the following and hit *Enter*:

    ```
    weatherLondon.getWindSpeed()
    ```

You should get `8 km/h NW` on the next line.

Our `CurrentWeather` class simulates data coming from a web service for weather data. The actual data in our class is stored in the `weather_data` variable.

> In future code, whenever possible, we will wrap calls to web services in classes in order to keep things organized and make the code more readable.

# Using the object inspector

Let's do a little analysis of our code:

1. From the **View** menu, select **Object inspector** and **Variables**. You should see the following:

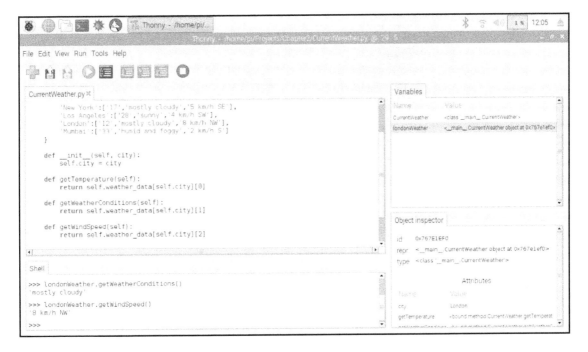

2. Highlight the `londonWeather` variable under the Variables tab. We can see that `londonWeather` is an object of type `CurrentWeather`. In the Object inspector, we can also see that the attribute city is set to `'London'`. This type of variable inspection is invaluable in troubleshooting code.

# Testing your class

It is very important to test your code as you write it so that you can catch errors early on:

1. Add the following function to the `CurrentWeather` class:

   ```
   def getCity(self):
       return self.city
   ```

2. Add the following to the bottom of `CurrentWeather.py`. The first line should have the same indentation as the class definition as this function is not part of the class:

   ```
   if __name__ == "__main__":
       currentWeather = CurrentWeather('Toronto')
       wind_dir_str_len = 2

       if currentWeather.getWindSpeed()[-2:-1] == ' ':
           wind_dir_str_len = 1

       print("The current temperature in",
               currentWeather.getCity(),"is",
               currentWeather.getTemperature(),
               "degrees Celsius,",
               "the weather conditions are",
               currentWeather.getWeatherConditions(),
               "and the wind is coming out of the",
               currentWeather.getWindSpeed()[-(wind_dir_str_len):],
               "direction with a speed of",
               currentWeather.getWindSpeed()
               [0:len(currentWeather.getWindSpeed())
               -(wind_dir_str_len)]
               )
   ```

3. Run the code by clicking on the **Run current script** button. You should see the following:

   ```
   The current temperature in Toronto is 13 degrees Celsius, the
   weather conditions are partly sunny and the wind is coming out of
   the NW direction with a speed of 8 km/h
   ```

   The `if __name__ == "__main__":` function allows us to test the class in the file directly as the `if` statement will only be true if the file is run directly. In other words, imports of `CurrentWeather.py` will not execute the code following the `if` statement. We will explore this method more as we work our way through this book.

# Making the code flexible

Code that is more generic is more flexible. The following are two examples of how we can make the code less specific.

## Example one

The `wind_dir_str_len` variable is used to determine the length of the string for wind direction. For example, a direction of `S` would only use one character, whereas NW would use two. This is done so that an extra space is not included in our output when the direction is represented by only one character:

```
wind_dir_str_len = 2
if currentWeather.getWindSpeed()[-2:-1] == ' ':
    wind_dir_str_len = 1
```

By looking for a space using `[-2:-1]`, we can determine the length of this string and change it to 1 if there is a space (as we are parsing back two characters from the end of the string).

## Example two

By adding the `getCity` method to our class, we are able to create classes with more generic names like `currentWeather` as opposed to `torontoWeather`. This makes it easy to reuse our code. We can demonstrate this by changing the following line:

```
currentWeather = CurrentWeather('Toronto')
```

We will change it to this:

```
currentWeather = CurrentWeather('Mumbai')
```

If we run the code again by clicking on the **Run** button, we get different values for all the conditions in the sentence:

```
The current temperature in Mumbai is 33 degrees Celsius, the weather
conditions are humid and foggy and the wind is coming out of the S
direction with a speed of 2 km/h
```

# Summary

We began this chapter by discussing the various tools that are available for Python development in Raspbian. The quickest and easiest way to run Python is from the Terminal window. Since Python comes pre-installed in Raspbian, the `python` command in the Terminal prompt loads Python (Python 2, in this case). There is no need to set environment variables in order to have the command find the program. Python 3 is run from the Terminal by typing `python3`.

We also took a brief look at IDLE, the default IDE for Python development. IDLE stands for Integrated Development and Learning Environment and is an excellent tool for beginners to use when learning Python.

Thonny is another Python IDE that comes pre-installed with Raspbian. Thonny has excellent debug and variable introspection functionalities. It too is designed for beginning Python developers, however, its ease of use and object inspector make it ideal for the development of our projects. We will be using Thonny more as we progress through the book.

We then jumped right into programming in order to get our development juices flowing. We started out with simple expressions using the Terminal and concluded with a weather data example designed to emulate objects that are used to call web services.

In `Chapter 3`, *Using the GPIO to Connect to the Outside World*, we will jump right into the most powerful feature of programming on Raspberry Pi, the GPIO. The GPIO allows us to interact with the real world through the use of devices connected to this port on Raspberry Pi. GPIO programming will take our Python skills to a whole new level.

# Questions

1. Which operating systems is Thonny available for?
2. How do we enter Python 2 from the Terminal command line?
3. Which tool in Thonny do we use to view what is inside an object?
4. Give two reasons as to why we are using an object in our weather example code.
5. What is the advantage of adding a method called `getCity` to the `CurrentWeather` class?
6. What language is IDLE written in?

7. What are the two steps taken in order to print the current date and time?
8. In our code, how did we compensate for wind speed directions that are represented by only one letter?
9. What does the `if __name__ =="__main__"` statement do?
10. What does IDLE stand for?

# Further reading

*Python 3 - Object Oriented Programming* by Dusty Phillips, Packt Publishing.

# Using the GPIO to Connect to the Outside World

In this chapter we will start unlocking the real power behind the Raspberry Pi—the GPIO, or General Purpose Input Output. The GPIO allows you to connect your Raspberry Pi to the outside world through the use of pins that may be set to input or output, and are controlled through code.

The following topics will be covered in this chapter:

- Python libraries for the Raspberry Pi
- Accessing Raspberry Pi's GPIO
- Setting up the circuit
- Hello LED

## Project overview

In this chapter, we start by exploring Raspberry Pi-specific libraries for Python. We will demonstrate these with a few examples by using the Raspberry Pi camera module and Pibrella HAT. We will try a few coding examples with the Sense Hat emulator before moving on to designing a physical circuit using the Fritzing program. Using a breadboard, we will set up this circuit and connect it to our Raspberry Pi.

We will finish off this chapter by building a Morse code generator that transmits weather data in Morse code from the class we created in Chapter 2, *Writing Python Programs Using Raspberry Pi*. This chapter should take an afternoon to complete.

# Technical requirements

The following is required to complete this project:

- A Raspberry Pi Model 3 (2015 model or newer)
- A USB power supply
- Computer monitor
- A USB keyboard
- A USB mouse
- A Raspberry Pi camera module (optional)—`https://www.raspberrypi.org/products/camera-module-v2/`
- A Pribrella HAT (optional)—`www.pibrella.com`
- A Sense HAT (optional, as we will be using the emulator in this chapter)—`https://www.raspberrypi.org/products/sense-hat/a`
- A breadboard
- Male-to-female jumper wires
- An LED

# Python libraries for the Raspberry Pi

We will turn our attention to the Python libraries or packages that come pre-installed with Raspbian. To view these packages from Thonny, click on **Tools** | **Manage Packages**. After a short delay, you should see many packages listed in the dialog:

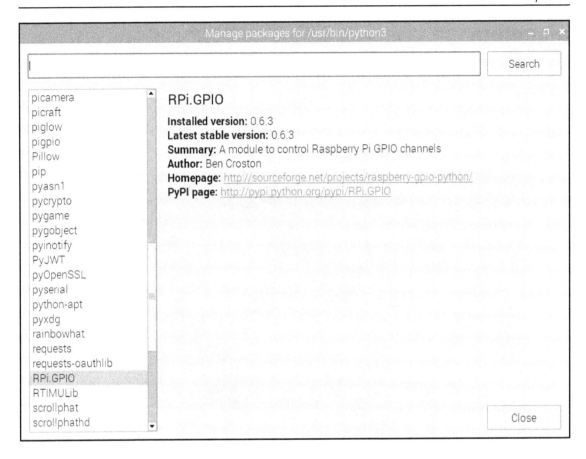

Let's explore a few of these packages.

# picamera

The camera port, or CSI, on the Raspberry Pi allows you to connect the specially designed Raspberry Pi camera module to your Pi. This camera can take both photos and videos, and has functionality to do time-lapse photography and slow-motion video recording. The `picamera` package gives us access to the camera through Python. The following is a picture of a Raspberry Pi camera module connected to a Raspberry Pi 3 Model B through the camera port:

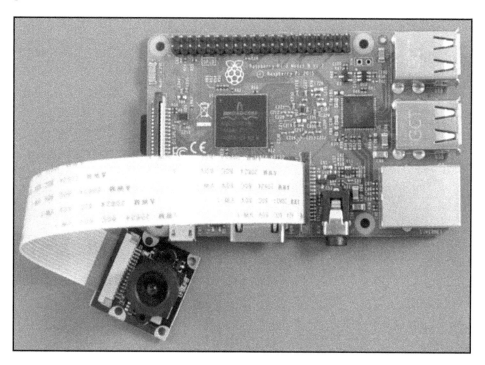

Connect your Raspberry Pi camera module to your Pi, open up Thonny, and type in the following code:

```
import picamera
import time

picam = picamera.PiCamera()
picam.start_preview()
time.sleep(10)
picam.stop_preview()
picam.close()
```

This code imports the `picamera` and `time` packages, and then creates a `picamera` object called `picam`. From there, we start the preview and then sleep for `10` seconds, before stopping the preview and then closing the camera. After running the program, you should see a `10` second preview from the camera on your screen.

# Pillow

The Pillow package is used for image processing with Python. To test this out, download an image to the same directory as your project files. Create a new file in Thonny and type in the following:

```
from PIL import Image

img = Image.open('image.png')
print(img.format, img.size)
```

You should see the format and size of the image (in brackets) printed at the commandline that follows.

# sense-hat and sense-emu

The Sense HAT is a sophisticated add-on board for the Raspberry Pi. The Sense HAT is the main component in the Astro Pi kit, part of a program to have young students program a Raspberry Pi for the International Space Station.

The Astro Pi competition was officially opened in January of 2015 to all primary and secondary school-aged children in the United Kingdom. During a mission to the International Space Station, British astronaut Tim Peake deployed Astro Pi computers on board the station.

The winning Astro Pi competition code was loaded onto an Astro Pi while in orbit. The data generated was collected and sent back to Earth.

The Sense HAT contains an array of LEDs that can be used as a display. The Sense HAT also has the following sensors onboard:

- Accelerometer
- Temperature sensor
- Magnetometer
- Barometric pressure sensor
- Humidity sensor
- Gyroscope

We can access the sensors and LEDs on the Sense HAT through the `sense-hat` package. For those that do not have a Sense HAT, the Sense HAT emulator in Raspbian may be used instead. We use the `sense-emu` package to access the emulated sensors and LED display on the Sense HAT emulator.

To demonstrate this, perform the following steps:

1. Create a new file in Thonny and name it `sense-hat-test.py`, or something similar.
2. Type in the following code:

   ```
   from sense_emu import SenseHat

   sense_emulator = SenseHat()
   sense_emulator.show_message('Hello World')
   ```

3. Load the Sense HAT Emulator program from **Application Menu | Programming | Sense HAT Emulator**.
4. Arrange your screen so that you can see the LED display of the Sense HAT emulator and the full window of Thonny (see the following screenshot):

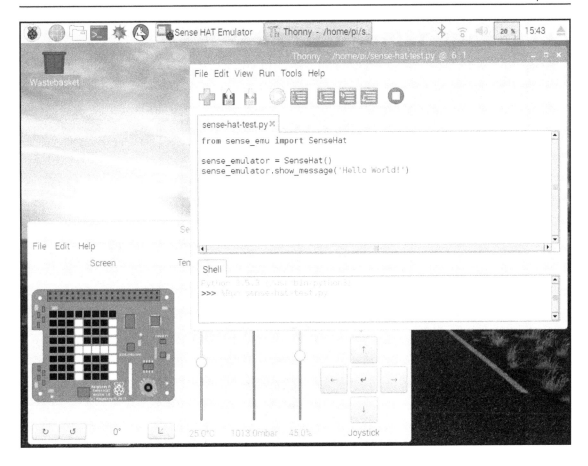

5. Click on the **Run current script** button.
6. You should see the `Hello World!` message scroll across the LED display of the Sense HAT emulator one letter at a time (see the previous screenshot).

# Accessing Raspberry Pi's GPIO

Through the GPIO, we are able to connect to the outside world. Here is a diagram of the Raspberry Pi GPIO pins:

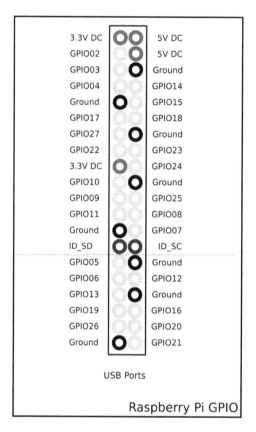

The following is an explanation of these pins:

- Red pins represent power coming out of the GPIO. The GPIO provides 3.3 Volts and 5 Volts.
- Black pins represent pins used for electrical ground. As you can see, there are 8 ground pins on the GPIO.

- Blue pins are used for Raspberry Pi **Hardware Added on Top** (**HATs**). They allow communication between the Raspberry Pi and the HAT's **Electrical Erasable Programmable Read-Only Memory** (**EEPROM**).
- Green pins represent the input and output pins that we may program for. Please note that some of the green GPIO pins double up with additional functionality. We will not be covering the additional functionality for this project.

The GPIO is what lies at the heart of the Raspberry Pi. We can connect LEDs, buttons, buzzers, and so on to the Raspberry Pi through the GPIO. We can also access the GPIO through HATs designed for the Raspberry Pi. One of those, called `Pibrella`, is what we will use next to explore connecting to the GPIO through Python code.

Raspberry Pi 1 Models A and B only have the first 26 pins (as shown by the dotted line). Models since then, including Raspberry Pi 1 Models A+ and B+, Raspberry Pi 2, Raspberry Pi Zero and Zero W, and Raspberry Pi 3 Model B and B+, have 40 GPIO pins.

# Pibrella

Pibrella is a relatively inexpensive Raspberry Pi HAT that makes connecting to the GPIO easy. The following are the components on-board of Pibrella:

- 1 red LED
- 1 yellow LED
- 1 green LED
- Small speaker
- Push button
- 4 inputs
- 4 outputs
- Micro USB power connector for delivering more power to the outputs

Pibrella was designed for early Raspberry Pi models and thus only has a 26-pin input. It can, however, be connected to later models through the first 26 pins.

To install the Pibrella Hat, line up the pin connectors on the Pibrella with the first 26 pins on the Raspberry Pi, and push down. In the following picture, we are installing Pibrella on a Raspberry Pi 3 Model B:

Pibrella should fit snugly when installed:

The libraries needed to connect to Pibrella do not come pre-installed with Raspbian (as of the time of writing), so we have to install them ourselves. To do that, we will use the `pip3` command from the Terminal:

1. Load the Terminal by clicking on it on the top tool bar (fourth icon from the left). At the Command Prompt, type the following:

   **sudo pip3 install pibrella**

2. You should see the package load from the Terminal:

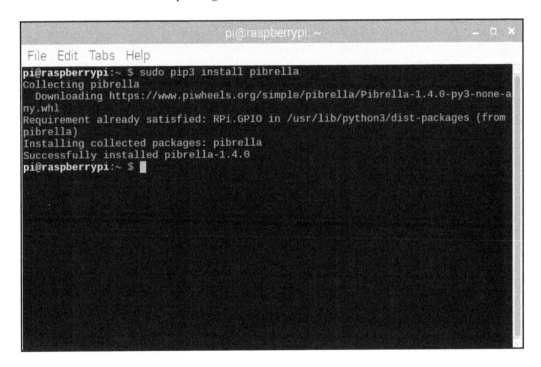

3. With the `Pibrella` library, there is no need to know the GPIO pin numbers in order to access the GPIO. The functionality is wrapped up in the `Pibrella` object we import into our code. We will do a short demonstration.

4. Create a new file in Thonny called `pibrella-test.py`, or name it something similar. Type in the following code:

```
import pibrella
import time

pibrella.light.red.on()
time.sleep(5)
```

```
pibrella.light.red.off()
pibrella.buzzer.success()
```

5. Run the code by clicking on the **Run current script** button. If you typed everything in correctly, you should see the red light on the Pibrella board turn on for 5 seconds before a short melody is played over the speaker.

Congratulations, you have now crossed the threshold into the world of physical computing.

# RPi.GPIO

The standard Python package for accessing the GPIO is called RPi.GPIO. The best way to describe how it works is with some code (this is for demonstration purposes only; we will be running code to access the GPIO in the upcoming section):

```
import RPi.GPIO as GPIO
import time

GPIO.setmode(GPIO.BCM)
GPIO.setup(18, GPIO.OUT)
GPIO.output(18, GPIO.HIGH)
time.sleep(5)
GPIO.output(18, GPIO.LOW)
```

As you can see, this code seems a little bit confusing. We will step through it:

1. First, we import the RPi.GPIO and time libraries:

   ```
   import RPi.GPIO as GPIO
   import time
   ```

2. Then, we set the mode to BCM:

   ```
   GPIO.setmode(GPIO.BCM)
   ```

3. In BCM mode, we access the pin through GPIO numbers (the ones shown in our Raspberry Pi GPIO graphic). The alternative is to access the pins through their physical location (GPIO.BOARD).

4. To set GPIO pin 18 to an output, we use the following line:

   ```
   GPIO.setup(18, GPIO.OUT)
   ```

5. We then set GPIO `18` to `HIGH` for 5 seconds before setting it to `LOW`:

```
GPIO.output(18, GPIO.HIGH)
time.sleep(5)
GPIO.output(18, GPIO.LOW)
```

If we had set up the circuit and run the code, we would see our LED light for 5 seconds before turning off, similar to the Pibrella example.

# GPIO zero

An alternative to `RPi.GPIO` is the GPIO Zero package. As with `RPi.GPIO`, this package comes pre-installed with Raspbian. The zero in the name refers to zero boilerplate or setup code (code that we are forced to enter every time).

To accomplish the same task of turning an LED on and off for 5 seconds, we use the following code:

```
from gipozero import LED
import time

led = LED(18)
led.on()
time.sleep(5)
led.off()
```

As with our `RPi.GPIO` example, this code is for demonstration purposes only as we haven't set up a circuit yet. It's obvious that the GPIO Zero code is far simpler than the `RPi.GPIO` example. This code is pretty self-explanatory.

In the following sections, we will start building a physical circuit on a breadboard with an LED, and use our code to turn it on and off.

# Setting up the circuit

The Pibrella HAT gave us a simple way of programming the GPIO, however, the ultimate goal of Raspberry Pi projects is to create a customized working circuit. We will now take the steps to design our circuit, and then create the circuit using a breadboard.

The first step is to design our circuit on the computer.

# Fritzing

Fritzing is a free circuit design software available for Windows, macOS, and Linux. There is a version in the Raspberry Pi store that we will install on our Raspberry Pi:

1. From the **Application Menu**, choose **Preferences | Add / Remove Software**. In the **Search** box, type in `Fritzing`:

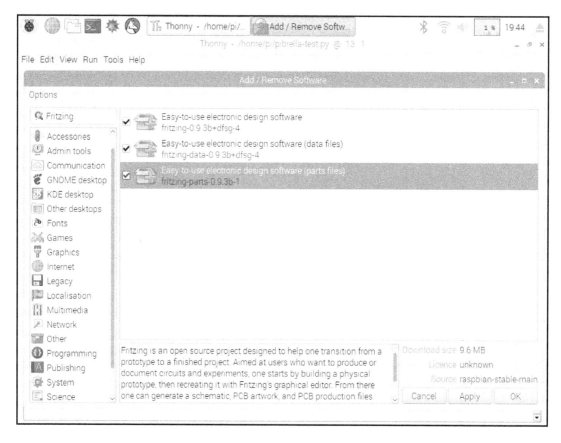

2. Select all three boxes and click on **Apply**, and then **OK**. After installation, you should be able to load Fritzing from **Application Menu | Programming | Fritzing**.

3. Click on the **Breadboard** tab to access the breadboard design screen. A full size breadboard dominates the middle of the screen. We will make it smaller as our circuit is small and simple.

4. Click on the breadboard. In the **Inspector** box, you will see a heading called **Properties**.
5. Click on the **Size** dropdown and select **Mini**.
6. To add a Raspberry Pi to our circuit, type in `Raspberry Pi` in the search box. Drag a Raspberry Pi 3 under our breadboard.
7. From here, we may drag and drop components onto our breadboard.
8. Add an LED and 330 Ohm resistor to our breadboard, shown in the following diagram. We use the resistor to protect both the LED and Raspberry Pi from excessive currents that may cause damage:

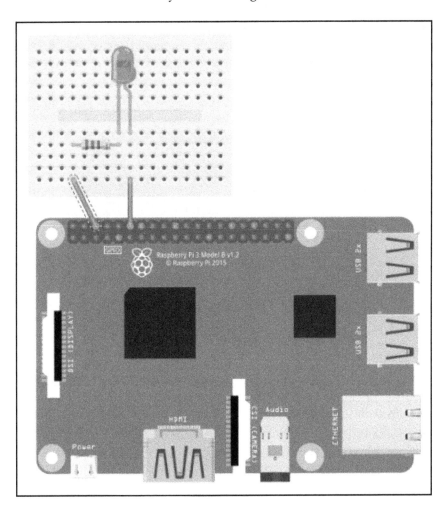

9. You will notice that as we hover our mouse over each pin on our Raspberry Pi component, a yellow tip will pop up with the pin's BCM name. Click on **GPIO 18** and drag a line over to the positive leg of our LED (the longer one).
10. Do the same to drag a GND connection to the left-hand side of the resistor.

This is the circuit we will build for our Raspberry Pi.

# Building our circuit

To build our physical circuit, start by inserting components into our breadboard. Referring to our diagram from before, we can see that some of the holes are green. This indicates continuity in the circuit. For example, we connect the negative leg of the LED to the 330 Ohm resistor through the same vertical column. Thus, the two component legs are connected together through the breadboard.

We take this into account as we start to place our components on the breadboard:

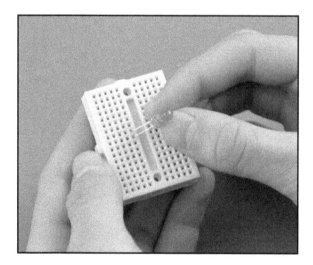

1. Insert the LED into our breadboard, as shown in the preceding picture. We are following our Fritzing diagram and have the positive leg in the lower hole.
2. Follow our Fritzing diagram and wire up the 330 Ohm resistor. Using female-to-male jumper wires, connect the Raspberry Pi to our breadboard.
3. Refer to our Raspberry Pi GPIO diagram to find GPIO 18 and GND on the Raspberry Pi board.

It is a good practice to have the Raspberry Pi powered off when connecting jumpers to the GPIO.

As you can see in the following image, the complete circuit resembles our Fritzing diagram (only our breadboard and Raspberry Pi are turned sideways):

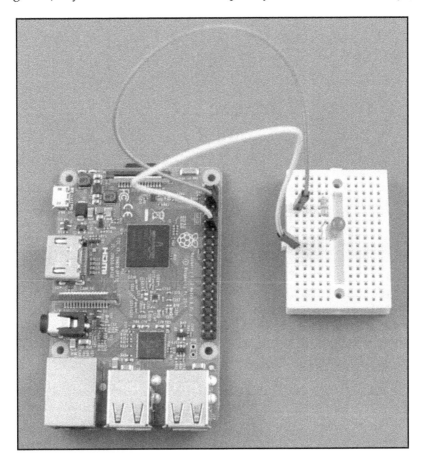

4. Connect the Raspberry Pi back up to the monitor, power supply, keyboard, and mouse.

We are now ready to program our first real GPIO circuit.

# Hello LED

We will jump right into the code:

1.  Create a new file in Thonny, and call it `Hello LED.py` or something similar.
2.  Type in the following code and run it:

```
from gpiozero import LED

led = LED(18)
led.blink(1,1,10)
```

# Blink LED using gpiozero

If we wired up our circuit and typed in our code correctly, we should see our LED blink for 10 seconds in 1 second intervals. The blink function in the `gpiozero LED` object allows us to set `on_time` (the length of time in seconds that the LED stays on), `off_time` (the length of time in seconds that the LED is turned off for), n or the number of times the LED blinks, and `background` (set to `True` to allow other code to run while the LED is flashing).

The `blink` function call with its default parameters looks like this:

```
blink(on_time=1, off_time=1, n=none, background=True)
```

Without parameters passed into the function, the LED will blink non-stop at 1 second intervals. Notice how we do not need to import the `time` library like we did when we used the `RPi.GPIO` package for accessing the GPIO. We simply pass a number into the `blink` function to represent the time in seconds we want the LED on or off.

# Morse code weather data

In `Chapter 2`, *Writing Python Programs Using Raspberry Pi*, we wrote code that simulates calls to a web service that supplies weather information. Taking what we learned in this chapter, let's revisit that code and give it a physical computing upgrade. We will use our LED to flash a Morse code representation of our weather data.

Many of us believe that the world only started to become connected in the 1990s with the World Wide Web. Little do we realize that we already had such a world beginning in the 19th century with the introduction of the telegraph and trans-world telegraph cables. The language of this so-called Victorian Internet was Morse code, with the Morse code operator as its gate keeper.

The following are the steps for flashing Morse code representation of our weather data:

1. We will first start by creating a `MorseCodeGenerator` class:

```python
from gpiozero import LED
from time import sleep

class MorseCodeGenerator:
    led = LED(18)
    dot_duration = 0.3
    dash_duration = dot_duration * 3
    word_spacing_duration = dot_duration * 7
    MORSE_CODE = {
        'A': '.-', 'B': '-...', 'C': '-.-.',
        'D': '-..', 'E': '.', 'F': '..-.',
        'G': '--.', 'H': '....', 'I': '..',
        'J': '.---', 'K': '-.-', 'L': '.-..',
        'M': '--', 'N': '-.', 'O': '---',
        'P': '.--.', 'Q': '--.-', 'R': '.-.',
        'S': '...', 'T': '-', 'U': '..-',
        'V': '...-', 'W': '.--', 'X': '-..-',
        'Y': '-.--', 'Z': '--..', '0': '-----',
        '1': '.----', '2': '..---', '3': '...--',
        '4': '....-', '5': '.....', '6': '-....',
        '7': '--...', '8': '---..', '9': '----.',
        ' ': ' '
    }
    def transmit_message(self, message):
        for letter in message:
            morse_code_letter = self.MORSE_CODE[letter.upper()]
            for dash_dot in morse_code_letter:
                if dash_dot == '.':
                    self.dot()
                elif dash_dot == '-':
                    self.dash()
                elif dash_dot == ' ':
                    self.word_spacing()
            self.letter_spacing()
    def dot(self):
        self.led.blink(self.dot_duration, self.dot_duration, 1, False)
```

```
        def dash(self):
    self.led.blink(self.dash_duration,self.dot_duration,1,False)
        def letter_spacing(self):
            sleep(self.dot_duration)
        def word_spacing(self):
            sleep(self.word_spacing_duration-self.dot_duration)

if __name__ == "__main__":
    morse_code_generator = MorseCodeGenerator()
    morse_code_generator.transmit_message('SOS')
```

2. After importing the `gpiozero` and `time` libraries into our `MorseCodeGenerator` class, we define GPIO 18 as our LED with the line `led=LED(18)`

3. We set the duration of how long a `dot` lasts with the line `dot_duration = 0.3`

4. We then define the duration of the dash and spacing between words based on the `dot_duration`

5. To speed up or slow down our Morse code transmutation, we may adjust `dot_duration` accordingly

6. We use a Python dictionary with the name `MORSE_CODE`. We use this dictionary to translate letters to Morse code

7. Our `transmit_message` function steps through each letter of the message, and then each character in the Morse code, which is equivalent to using the `dash_dot` variable

8. The magic of our class happens in the `dot` and `dash` methods by using the `blink` function from the `gpiozero` library:

```
        def dot(self):
                self.led.blink(self.dot_duration,
        self.dot_duration,1,False)
```

In the `dot` method, we can see that we turn the LED on for the duration set in `dot_duration`, and then we turn it off for the same amount of time. We only blink it once as set it by the number 1 in the `blink` method call. We also set the background parameter to `False`.

This last parameter is very important, as if we leave it to the default of `True`, the code will continue to run before the LED has a chance to blink on and off. Basically, the code won't work unless the background parameter is set to `False`.

We forgo the usual `Hello World` for our test message and instead use the standard `SOS`, which is familiar to the most casual of Morse code enthusiasts. We may test our class by clicking on the **Run** button and, if all is set up correctly, we will see the LED blink SOS in Morse code.

Now, let's revisit our `CurrentWeather` class from `Chapter 2`, *Writing Python Programs Using Raspberry Pi*. We will make a few minor modifications:

```python
from MorseCodeGenerator import MorseCodeGenerator

class CurrentWeather:
    weather_data={
        'Toronto':['13','partly sunny','8 NW'],
        'Montreal':['16','mostly sunny','22 W'],
        'Vancouver':['18','thunder showers','10 NE'],
        'New York':['17','mostly cloudy','5 SE'],
        'Los Angeles':['28','sunny','4 SW'],
        'London':['12','mostly cloudy','8 NW'],
        'Mumbai':['33','humid and foggy','2 S']
    }
    def __init__(self, city):
        self.city = city
    def getTemperature(self):
        return self.weather_data[self.city][0]
    def getWeatherConditions(self):
        return self.weather_data[self.city][1]
    def getWindSpeed(self):
        return self.weather_data[self.city][2]
    def getCity(self):
        return self.city
if __name__ == "__main__":
    current_weather = CurrentWeather('Toronto')
    morse_code_generator = MorseCodeGenerator()
    morse_code_generator.transmit_message(current_weather.
    getWeatherConditions())
```

We start by importing our `MorseCodeGenerator` class (make sure that both files are in the same directory). As we do not have a Morse code equivalent of /, we take out the km/h in the `weather_data` data set. The rest of the class remains the same as it did in Chapter 2, *Writing Python Programs Using Raspberry Pi*. In our test section, we instantiate both a `CurrentWeather` class and a `MorseCodeGenerator` class. Using the `CurrentWeather` class, we pass the weather conditions for Toronto into the `MorseCodeGenerator` class.

If there aren't any mistakes made in entering the code, we should see our LED blink `partly sunny` in Morse code.

# Summary

A lot was covered in this chapter. By the end of it, you should be feeling pretty good about developing applications on the Raspberry Pi.

The `picamera`, `Pillow`, and `sense-hat` libraries make it easy to communicate with the outside world with your Raspberry Pi. Using the Raspberry Pi camera module and `picamera`, we open up a whole new world of possibilities with our Pi. We only touched on a small part of what `picamera` can do. Additionally, we only scratched the surface of image processing with the `Pillow` library. The Sense HAT emulator allowed us to save spending money on buying the actual HAT and test out our code. With `sense-hat` and the Raspberry Pi Sense HAT, we truly expand our reach into the physical world.

The inexpensive Pibrella HAT provided an easy way to jump into the physical computing world. By installing the `pibrella` library, we are giving our Python code access to an assortment of LEDs, a speaker, and a button, all neatly packaged into a Raspberry Pi HAT.

However, the true ultimate goal with physical computing is to build electronic circuits that bridge the gap between our Raspberry Pi and the outside world. We started our journey of building electronic circuits with the Fritzing circuit builder, available from the Raspberry Pi store. From there, we built our first circuit on a breadboard with an LED and resistor.

We concluded this chapter by creating a Morse code generator with our Raspberry Pi and LED circuit. In a twist of old meets new, we were able to transmit weather data in Morse code via a blinking LED.

In `Chapter 4`, *Subscribing to Web Services*, we will incorporate web services into our code, thereby connecting the internet world with the real world in a concept called the Internet of Things.

# Questions

1. What is the name of the Python package that allows you access to the Raspberry Pi camera module?
2. True or false? A Raspberry Pi with code written by students was deployed on the international space station.
3. What are the sensors included with Sense HAT?
4. True or false? We do not need to buy a Raspberry Pi Sense HAT for development, as an emulator of this HAT exists in Raspbian.
5. How many ground pins are there on the GPIO?
6. True or false? Raspberry Pi's GPIO has pins that supply both 5V and 3.3V.
7. What is a Pibrella?
8. True or false? You may only use a Pibrella on early Raspberry Pi computers.
9. What does BCM mode mean?
10. True or false? BOARD is the alternative to BCM.
11. What does the Zero in `gpiozero` refer to?
12. True or false? Using Fritzing, we are able to design a GPIO circuit for our Raspberry Pi.
13. What is the default background parameter in the `gpiozero` LED `blink` function set to?
14. True or false? It is far easier to use the `gpiozero` library to access the GPIO than it is to use the `RPi.GPIO` library.
15. What is the Victorian Internet?

# Further reading

A lot of concepts were covered in this chapter, with the assumption that the skills needed were not beyond the average developer and tinkerer. To further solidify understanding of these concepts, please Google the following:

- How to install the Raspberry Pi camera module
- How to use a breadboard
- An introduction to the Fritzing circuit design software
- Python dictionaries

For those of you that are as fascinated about technology of the past as I am, the following is a great book to read on the age of the Victorian Internet: *The Victorian Internet,* by Tom Standage.

# Subscribing to Web Services 4

Many of us take the technologies that the internet is built on top of for granted. When we visit our favorite websites, we care little that the web pages we are viewing are crafted for our eyes. However, lying underneath is the internet protocol suite of communication protocols. Machines can also take advantage of these protocols and communicate machine to machine through web services.

In this chapter, we will continue our journey toward connecting devices through the **Internet of Things** (**IoT**). We will explore web services and the various technologies behind them. We will conclude our chapter with some Python code where we call a live weather service and extract information in real time.

The following topics will be covered in this chapter:

- Cloud services for IoT
- Writing a Python program to extract live weather data

## Prerequisites

The reader should have a working knowledge of the Python programming language to complete this chapter as well as an understanding of basic object-oriented programming. This will serve the reader well, as we will be separating our code into objects.

# Project overview

In this project, we will explore the various web services that are available and touch on their core strengths. We will then write code that calls the Yahoo! Weather web service. We will conclude by having a "ticker" display of real-time weather data using the Raspberry Pi Sense HAT emulator.

This chapter should take a morning or afternoon to complete.

# Getting started

To complete this project, the following will be required:

- A Raspberry Pi Model 3 (2015 model or newer)
- A USB power supply
- A computer monitor (with HDMI support)
- A USB keyboard
- A USB mouse
- Internet access

# Cloud services for IoT

There are many cloud services that we may use for IoT development. Some of the biggest companies in technology have thrown their weight behind IoT and in particular IoT with artificial intelligence.

The following are the details of some of these services.

## Amazon Web Services IoT

The Amazon Web Services IoT is a cloud platform that allows connected devices to securely interact with other devices or cloud applications. These are offered as pay-as-you-go services without the need for a server, thereby simplifying deployment and scalability.

**Amazon Web Services** (**AWS**) services that may be used by the AWS IoT Core are as follows:

- AWS Lambda
- Amazon Kinesis
- Amazon S3
- Amazon Machine Learning
- Amazon DynamoDB
- Amazon CloudWatch
- AWS CloudTrail
- Amazon Elasticsearch Service

AWS IoT Core applications allow for the gathering, processing, and analysis of data generated by connected devices without the need to manage infrastructure. Pricing is per messages sent and received.

The following is a diagram of how AWS IoT may be used. In this scenario, road conditions data from a car is sent to the cloud and stored within an S3 Cloud Storage service. The AWS service broadcasts this data to other cars, warning them of potential hazardous road conditions:

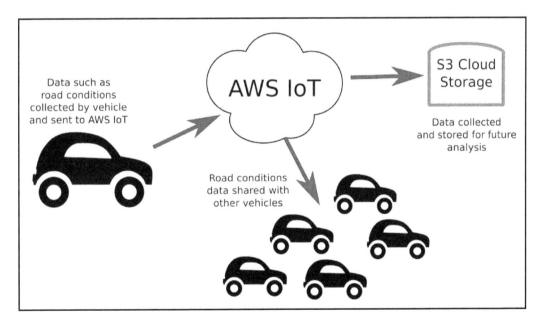

# IBM Watson platform

IBM Watson is a system capable of answering questions posted in natural language. Originally designed to compete on the TV game show *Jeopardy!*, Watson was named after IBM's first CEO, Thomas J. Watson. In 2011, Watson took on *Jeopardy!* champions Brad Rutter and Ken Jennings and won.

Applications using the IBM Watson Developer Cloud may be created with API calls. The potential for processing IoT information with Watson is immense.

To put it bluntly, Watson is a supercomputer from IBM that may be accessed over the web through API calls.

One such use of Watson with IoT is the IBM Watson Assistant for Automotive, an integrated solution provided to manufacturers for use in cars. Through this technology, the driver and passengers may interact with the outside world for such things as booking reservations at restaurants and checking on appointments in their calendars. Sensors in the car may be integrated, providing IBM Watson Assistant with information on the state of the car such as tire pressure. The following is a diagram illustrating a scenario where Watson warns the driver of low tire pressure, suggests having it fixed, and then books an appointment at the garage:

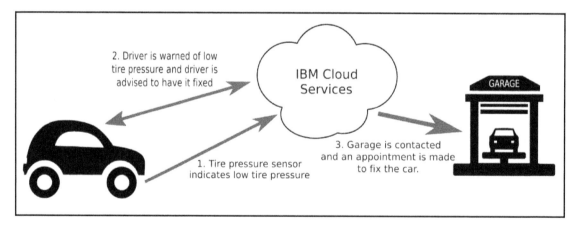

IBM Watson Assistant for Automotive is sold as a white-label service so that manufacturers may label it to suit their needs. The success of IBM Watson Assistant for Automotive will depend on how well it competes with other AI assistant services such as Amazon's Alexa and Google's AI assistant. Integration with popular services such as Spotify for music and Amazon for shopping will also play a role in future success.

# Google Cloud platform

Although not as extensive and well-documented as AWS IoT, Google is taking on IoT with a lot of interest. A developer may take advantage of Google's processing, analytics, and machine intelligence technologies through the use of Google Cloud Services.

The following is a list of some of the services offered through Google Cloud Services:

- **App engine**: Application hosting service
- **BigQuery**: Large-scale database analytics service
- **Bigtable**: Scalable database service
- **Cloud AutoML**: Machine learning services that allow developers access to Google's Neural Architecture Search technology
- **Cloud machine learning engine**: Machine learning service for TensorFlow models
- **Google video intelligence**: Service to analyze videos and create metadata
- **Cloud Vision API**: Service to return data on images through the use of machine learning

The following is a diagram of how the Google Cloud Vision API may be used. An image of a dog standing next to an upside-down flowerpot is passed to the service through the API. The image is scanned and, using machine learning, objects are identified in the photo. The returning JSON file contains the results in percentages:

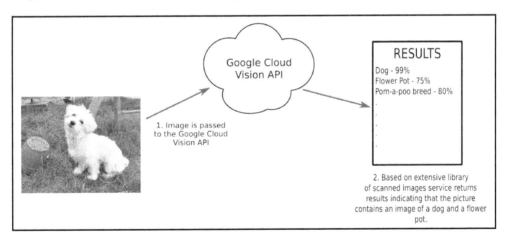

Google's focus on keeping things easy and fast gives developers access to Google's own private global network. Pricing for the Google Cloud Platform is lower than AWS IoT.

# Microsoft Azure

Microsoft Azure (known formerly as Windows Azure) is a cloud-based service from Microsoft that allows developers to build, test, deploy, and manage applications using Microsoft's vast array of data centers. It supports many different programming languages, which are both Microsoft-specific and from outside third parties.

Azure Sphere, part of the Microsoft Azure framework, was launched in April of 2018 and is Azure's IoT solution. The following is a scenario where Azure Sphere (or Azure IoT, as shown in the diagram) may be used. In this scenario, a robot arm located in a remote factory is monitored and controlled by a cellphone app somewhere else:

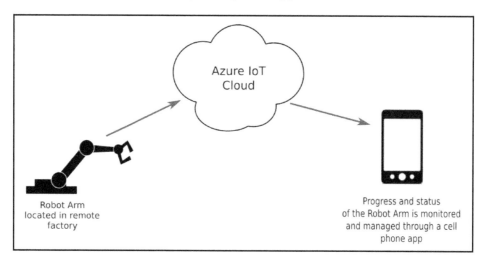

You may have noticed that the previous examples could be set up with any of the competing cloud services, and that really is the point. By competing with each other, the services become better and cheaper, and as a result, more accessible.

With these large companies such as IBM, Amazon, Google, and Microsoft taking on the processing of IoT data, the future of IoT is boundless.

# Weather Underground

Although not heavyweight like the Googles and IBMs of the world, Weather Underground offers a web service of weather information that developers may tie their applications into. Through the use of a developer account, IoT applications utilizing current weather conditions may be built.

At the time of writing this chapter, the Weather Underground network offered APIs for developers to use to access weather information. An end-of-service notice has been posted to the Weather Underground API site since. To keep up to date on the state of this service, visit `https://www.wunderground.com/weather/api/`.

# A basic Python program to pull data from the cloud

In `Chapter 2`, *Writing Python Programs Using Raspberry Pi*, we introduced a package called `weather-api` that allows us to access the Yahoo! Weather web service. In this section, we will wrap up the `Weather` object from the `weather-api` package in our own class. We will reuse the name `CurrentWeather` for our class. After testing out our `CurrentWeather` class, we will utilize the Sense Hat Emulator in Raspbian and build a weather information ticker.

## Accessing the web service

We will start out by modifying our `CurrentWeather` class to make web service calls to Yahoo! Weather through the `weather-api` package:

1. Open up Thonny from **Application Menu** | **Programming** | **Thonny Python IDE**.
2. Click on the **New** icon to create a new file.
3. Type the following:

```
from weather import Weather, Unit

class CurrentWeather:
    temperature = ''
    weather_conditions = ''
    wind_speed = ''
    city = ''

    def __init__(self, city):
        self.city = city
        weather = Weather(unit = Unit.CELSIUS)
        lookup = weather.lookup_by_location(self.city)
        self.temperature = lookup.condition.temp
        self.weather_conditions = lookup.condition.text
```

```
            self.wind_speed = lookup.wind.speed

        def getTemperature(self):
            return self.temperature

        def getWeatherConditions(self):
            return self.weather_conditions

        def getWindSpeed(self):
            return self.wind_speed

        def getCity(self):
            return self.city

    if __name__=="__main__":
            current_weather = CurrentWeather('Montreal')
            print("%s %sC %s wind speed %s km/h"
            %(current_weather.getCity(),
            current_weather.getTemperature(),
            current_weather.getWeatherConditions(),
            current_weather.getWindSpeed()))
```

4. Save the file as `CurrentWeather.py`.
5. Run the code.
6. You should see weather information from the web service printed to the shell in Thonny. When I ran the program, I saw the following:

```
Toronto 12.0C Clear wind speed 0 km/h
```

7. Now, let's take a closer look at the code to see what is going on. We start off by importing the resources from packages we need for our program:

```
from weather import Weather, Unit
```

8. We then define our class name, `CurrentWeather`, and set the class variables (`temperature`, `weather_conditions`, `wind_speed`, and `city`) to initial values:

```
class CurrentWeather:
    temperature = ''
    weather_conditions = ''
    wind_speed = ''
    city = ''
```

9. In the init method, we set our class variables based on the city that is passed into the method. We do this by instantiating a variable we call weather as a Weather object with the unit set to CELSIUS. The lookup variable is created based on the city name we pass in. From there, it is a simple matter of setting our class variables (temperature, weather_conditions, and wind_speed) from values we extract from lookup. The weather-api does all of the heavy lifting for us as we are able to access values with dot notation. There is no need for us to parse XML or JSON data:

```
def __init__(self, city):
    self.city = city
    weather = Weather(unit = Unit.CELSIUS)
    lookup = weather.lookup_by_location(self.city)
    self.temperature = lookup.condition.temp
    self.weather_conditions = lookup.condition.text
    self.wind_speed = lookup.wind.speed
```

10. With the class variables set in the init method, we use method calls to return these class variables:

```
def getTemperature(self):
    return self.temperature

def getWeatherConditions(self):
    return self.weather_conditions

def getWindSpeed(self):
    return self.wind_speed

def getCity(self):
    return self.city
```

11. Since we are running CurrentWeather.py as a program in Thonny, we are able to use the if __name__=="__main__" method and utilize the CurrentWeather class. Note that the if __name__=="__main__" method has the same indentation as the class name. It would not work if it didn't.

With every module in Python, there is an attribute called __name__. If you were to check this attribute for a module you have imported into your program, you would get the name of the module returned. For example, if we were to put the line print(Weather.__name__) in the preceding code, we would get the name Weather returned. Checking for __name__ in a file we are running returns the __main__ value.

12. In the `if __name__=="__main__"` method, we create an object called `current_weather` of type `CurrentWeather`, passing in the city name `Montreal`. We then print out the values for `city`, `temperature`, `weather conditions`, and `wind speed` using the appropriate method calls:

```
if __name__=="__main__":
    current_weather = CurrentWeather('Montreal')
    print("%s %sC %s wind speed %s km/h"
    %(current_weather.getCity(),
    current_weather.getTemperature(),
    current_weather.getWeatherConditions(),
    current_weather.getWindSpeed()))
```

# Using the Sense HAT Emulator

Now, let's use the Raspberry Pi Sense HAT Emulator to display weather data. We will utilize the `CurrentWeather` class we just created. To see weather information displayed in the Sense HAT Emulator, do the following:

1.  Open up Thonny from **Application Menu** | **Programming** | **Thonny Python IDE**
2.  Click on the **New** icon to create a new file
3.  Type the following:

```
from sense_emu import SenseHat
from CurrentWeather import CurrentWeather

class DisplayWeather:
    current_weather = ''
    def __init__(self, current_weather):
        self.current_weather = current_weather
    def display(self):
        sense_hat_emulator = SenseHat()
        message = ("%s %sC %s wind speed %s km/h"
            %(self.current_weather.getCity(),
            self.current_weather.getTemperature(),
            self.current_weather.getWeatherConditions(),
            self.current_weather.getWindSpeed()))
        sense_hat_emulator.show_message(message)
if __name__ == "__main__":
    current_weather = CurrentWeather('Toronto')
    display_weather = DisplayWeather(current_weather)
    display_weather.display()
```

4. Save the file as `DisplayWeather.py`
5. Load the Sense HAT Emulator from **Application Menu** | **Programming** | **Sense HAT Emulator**
6. Position the Sense HAT Emulator so that you can see the display
7. Run the code

You should see a ticker of the weather information for `Toronto` on the Sense HAT Emulator display, similar to the following screenshot:

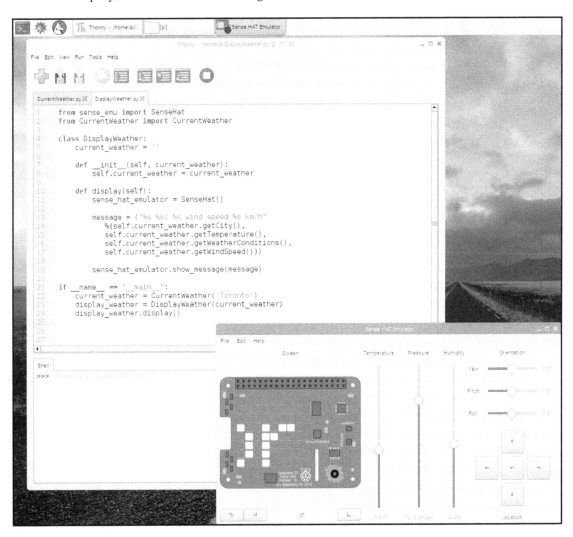

So, how did we accomplish this? The `init` and `message` methods are at the heart of this program. We initialize the `DisplayWeather` class by setting the class variable `current_weather`. Once `current_weather` is set, we extract values from it in the `display` method in order to build a message we call `message`. We then create a `SenseHat` emulator object in the `display` method as well and call it `sense_hat_emulator`. We pass in our message to the `show_message` method of the `SenseHat` emulator through the line `sense_hat_emulator.show_message(message)`:

```python
def __init__(self, current_weather):
    self.current_weather = current_weather
def display(self):
    sense_hat_emulator = SenseHat()
    message = ("%s %sC %s wind speed %s km/h"
            %(self.current_weather.getCity(),
            self.current_weather.getTemperature(),
            self.current_weather.getWeatherConditions(),
            self.current_weather.getWindSpeed()))
    sense_hat_emulator.show_message(message)
```

# Summary

We began this chapter by discussing some of the various web services that are available. We discussed the work of some of the biggest companies in information technology in the fields of artificial intelligence and IoT.

Both Amazon and Google are aiming to become the platforms that IoT devices connect with. Using its vast resources, Amazon, through its Amazon Web Services, provides significant documentation and support for its offerings. Not to be outdone, Google is also building a powerful platform for IoT. Which platform wins out remains to be seen.

IBM's foray into artificial intelligence centers on Watson, their *Jeopardy!* playing champion. Winning game shows against the best human players is of course not the ultimate goal for Watson. However, the knowledge and technology built from such pursuits will find its way into areas we can only imagine today. Watson may prove to be the so-called killer app for the IoT world.

There is probably nothing that people talk about more than the weather. In this chapter, we used the `weather-api` package to build a weather information ticker by utilizing the Raspberry Pi Sense HAT Emulator that's built into the Raspbian operating system.

In `Chapter 5`, *Controlling a Servo with Python,* we will explore other ways to communicate with the outside world by using servo motors to provide an analog display.

# Questions

1. What is IBM Watson?
2. True or false? Amazon's IoT web services allows access to other cloud-based services from Amazon.
3. True or false? Watson is a champion of the game show *Jeopardy!*
4. True or false? Google has their own global private network.
5. True or false? We need to change the names of our functions such as `getTemperature` when we introduce web service data.
6. True or false? It is a good idea to use test code in your classes in order to isolate the functionality of that class.
7. What is the purpose of the `DisplayWeather` class in our code?
8. Which method of the `SenseHat` object do we use to display weather information in the Sense HAT Emulator?

# Further reading

A Google search on the various web services that are available is a good place to start in order to expand your knowledge of web services.

# Controlling a Servo with Python 5

Analog meters and instrumentation were the only ways to display data prior to the rise of digital technologies. Once the move was made to digital, analog meters fell out of vogue. Generations that grew up learning to tell the time on an analog clock may suddenly find this skill to be out of date, as digital displays of time have become the norm.

In this chapter, we will bridge the gap between the digital and analog worlds by changing the position of a servo motor based on a digital value.

The following topics will be covered in this chapter:

- Wiring up a servo motor to the Raspberry Pi
- Controlling the servo through the command line
- Writing a Python program to control the servo

## Knowledge required to complete this chapter

The reader will need a working knowledge of the Python programming language to complete this chapter. Knowledge of using a simple breadboard to connect components is also a must.

## Project overview

In this project, we will wire up a servo motor and LED, and control it using the GPIO Zero library. We will start by designing the circuit in Fritzing, and then we will assemble it.

We will start controlling the servo using Python shell.

Finally, we will expand on this knowledge by creating a Python class that will turn the servo motor based on a percentage amount, and turn on, turn off, or flash the LED based on a number passed to the class.

This project should take about 2 hours to complete.

# Getting started

To complete this project, the following will be required:

- A Raspberry Pi Model 3 (2015 model or newer)
- A USB power supply
- A computer monitor
- A USB keyboard
- A USB mouse
- A small servo motor
- A breadboard
- A LED (any color)
- Jumper wires for the breadboard

# Wiring up a servo motor to the Raspberry Pi

This project involves wiring up a servo motor to our Raspberry Pi. Many people confuse servo motors with stepper and DC motors. Let's take a look at the differences between these types of motors.

## Stepper motors

Stepper motors are brushless DC electrical motors that move a full rotation of equal steps. The position of the motor is controlled without the use of a feedback system (open-loop system). This makes stepper motors relatively inexpensive and popular for robotics, 3-D printers, and CNC-type applications.

The following is a crude diagram of the internal workings of a stepper motor:

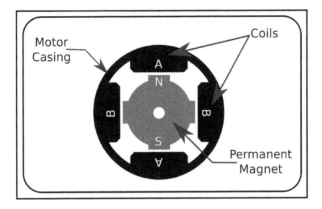

By turning on and off the coils **A** and **B** in sequence, the **Permanent Magnet** (which is attached to the shaft of the motor) is spun. Precise steps are used, allowing precise control of the motor, as the number of steps may be controlled easily.

Stepper motors tend to be heavier and bulkier than other types of small motors.

The following photo shows a typical stepper motor used in a 3-D printer:

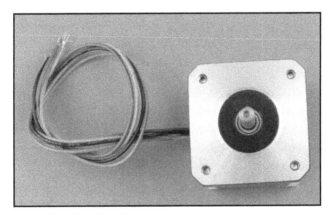

# DC motors

DC motors are similar to stepper motors, but do not divide motion into equal steps. They were the first widely used electrical motors, and are in use in electric cars, elevators, and any other application that does not require precise control of the position of the motor. DC motors may be brushed or brushless.

Brushed motors are simpler to operate, but have limitations on **revolutions per minute** (**RPM**) and usage life. Brushless motors are more complicated, and require electronics for control—for example, the **Electronic Speed Controllers** (**ESCs**) used on some drones. Brushless motors may be operated at a much higher RPM, and have a longer usage life than brushed motors.

DC motors have a much shorter response time than stepper motors, and tend to be lighter than comparable stepper motors.

The following is a photo of a typical small brushed DC motor:

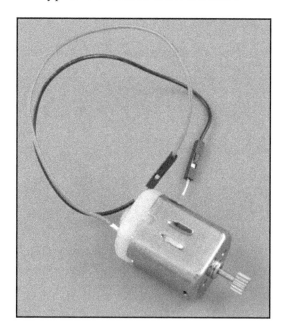

# Servo motors

Servo motors use a closed-loop feedback mechanism to provide extremely precise control of the position of the motor. They are considered a high-performance alternative to stepper motors. The range can vary depending on the servo, with some servos limited to 180-degree movement while others can move a full 360 degrees.

 Closed-loop control systems, unlike open-loop control systems, maintain an output by measuring the actual condition of the output, and comparing it to the desired outcome. Closed-loop control systems are often called feedback control systems, as it is this feedback that is used to adjust the condition.

The angle of a servo is determined by pulses passed to the control pin on the servo. Different brands of servo have different maximum and minimum values to determine the angle of the servo needle.

The following is a diagram to demonstrate the relationship between **pulse width modulation** (**PWM**) and the position of a 180-degree servo:

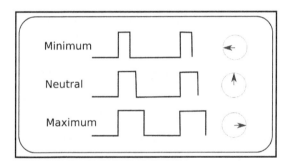

The following is a photo of the small servo motor that we will be using for our circuit. We are able to connect this servo directly to our Raspberry Pi (this may not be possible with larger servos):

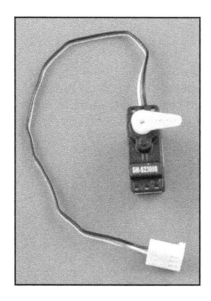

The following is a chart of servo color codes:

| Power / Positive (+) | Signal / Data | Ground (-) |
| --- | --- | --- |
| Red | Yellow | Black |
| Red | White | Black |
| Red | Orange | Black |
| Red | Orange | Brown |
| Red | Blue | Black |

# Connecting the servo motor to our Raspberry Pi

Our circuit will consist of a simple servo and LED.

The following is the Fritzing diagram of the circuit:

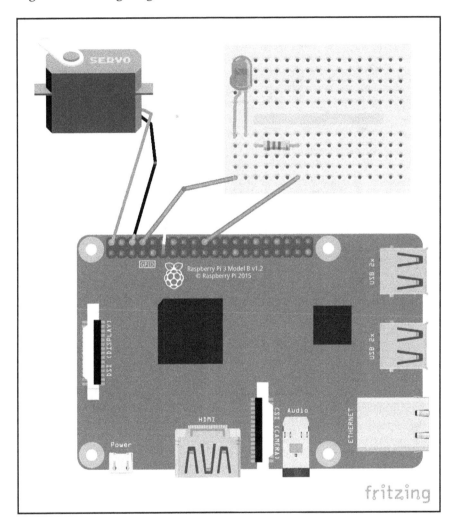

We connect:

- The positive power of the servo to the 5V DC supply, and the ground to GND
- The control signal from the servo to GPIO 17
- The positive end of the LED to GPIO 14, and the resistor to GND

Be sure to use a small servo motor, as larger ones may require more power than the Raspberry Pi is able to supply. The circuit should resemble the following:

# Control the servo through the command line

Now that our servo is connected to our Raspberry Pi, let's write some code at the command line to control it. We will use the Raspberry Pi Python library GPIO Zero to do this.

Load up Thonny and click on **Shell**:

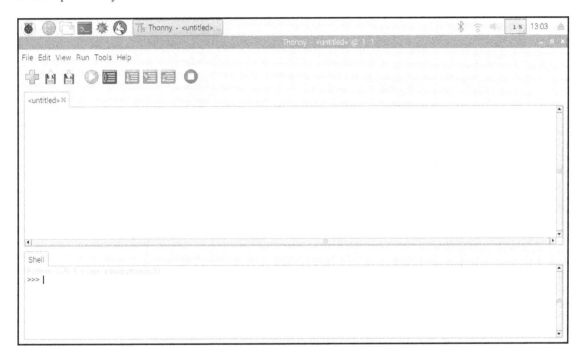

Type the following in the shell:

```
from gpiozero import Servo
```

After a short delay, the cursor should return. What we have done here is load the servo object from gpiozero into memory. We will assign pin GPIO 17 with the following statement:

```
servo = Servo(17)
```

We will now move the servo motor to the minimum (min) position. Type the following into the command line:

```
servo.min()
```

You should hear the servo motor moving, and the needle will go to its farthest position (if it is not already there).

Let's move the servo motor to the maximum ( max) position with the following command:

```
servo.max()
```

Now, move the servo to the middle ( mid) position with the following command:

```
servo.mid()
```

The servo motor should move to its middle position.

When you place your hand over the servo motor, you may feel a slight jerking motion. To temporarily disable control of the servo, type the following into the command line and press **Enter**:

```
servo.detach()
```

The jerking motion should stop, and the needle indicator attached to the servo should stay in its current position.

As we can see, it is very easy to move the servo motor to its minimum, middle, and maximum values. But what if we want to have more precise control of the servo? For those instances, we may use the value property of the servo object. A value between $-1$ (minimum) and $1$ (maximum) can be used to move the servo motor.

Type the following into the command line:

```
servo.value=-1
```

The servo should move to its minimum position. Now, type the following:

```
servo.value=1
```

The servo should now move to its maximum position. Let's use the value property to indicate weather conditions. Type the following into the command line:

```
weather_conditions = {'cloudy':-1, 'partly cloudy':-0.5, 'partly sunny':
0.5, 'sunny':1}
```

Test the code in the shell with the following:

```
weather_conditions['partly cloudy']
```

You should see the following in the shell:

```
-0.5
```

With our `servo` object and our `weather_conditions` dictionary, we may now use the servo motor to indicate the weather conditions physically. Type the following into the shell:

```
servo.value = weather_conditions['cloudy']
```

The servo motor should move to the minimum position to indicate that the weather conditions are `cloudy`. Now, let's try `sunny`:

```
servo.value = weather_conditions['sunny']
```

The servo should move to the maximum position to indicate `sunny` weather conditions.

For `partly cloudy` and `partly sunny` conditions, use the following:

```
servo.value = weather_conditions['partly cloudy']
servo.value = weather_conditions['partly sunny']
```

# Write a Python program to control the servo

Jerry Seinfeld once joked that all we need to know about the weather is: Should we bring a coat or not? For the rest of this chapter and the next, we will build an analog meter needle dashboard to indicate the wardrobe needed for the weather conditions.

We will also add an LED that will turn on to indicate that an umbrella is needed, and flash to indicate a very bad storm.

Before we can build the dashboard in `Chapter 6`, *Working with the Servo Control Code to Control an Analog Device*, we need code to control the servo and LED. We will start by creating a class to do just that.

This class will set the servo position and LED state on our circuit:

1. Open up Thonny from **Application Menu** | **Programming** | **Thonny Python IDE**
2. Click on the **New** icon to create a new file

3. Type the following:

```
from gpiozero import Servo
from gpiozero import LED

class WeatherDashboard:
    servo_pin = 17
    led_pin = 14
    def __init__(self, servo_position=0, led_status=0):
        self.servo = Servo(self.servo_pin)
        self.led = LED(self.led_pin)
        self.move_servo(servo_position)
        self.set_led_status(led_status)
    def move_servo(self, servo_position=0):
        self.servo.value=self.convert_percentage_to_integer
        (servo_position)
    def set_led_status(self, led_status=0):
        if(led_status==0):
            self.led.off()
        elif (led_status==1):
            self.led.on()
        else:
            self.led.blink()
    def convert_percentage_to_integer(self, percentage_amount):
        return (percentage_amount*0.02)-1
if __name__=="__main__":
    weather_dashboard = WeatherDashboard(50, 1)
```

4. Save the file as `WeatherDashboard.py`
5. Run the code
6. You should see the servo move to the middle position, and the LED should turn on

Experiment with other values and see if you can move the servo to 75% and have the LED blink.

Let's take a look at the code. After defining the class, we set GPIO pin values for the servo and LED with the following:

```
servo_pin = 17
led_pin = 14
```

As you saw in the circuit we built, we connected the servo and LED to GPIO 17 and GPIO 14, respectively. GPIO Zero allows us to assign GPIO values easily without boilerplate code.

In our class initialization method, we create `Servo` and `LED` objects called `servo` and `led` respectively:

```
self.servo = Servo(self.servo_pin)
self.led = LED(self.led_pin)
```

From here, we call the methods in our class that move the servo and set the LED. Let's look at the first method:

```
def move_servo(self, servo_position=0):
        self.servo.value=self.convert_percentage_to_integer
        (servo_position)
```

In this method, we simply set the value property in `servo` object. As this property only accepts values from –1 to 1, and we are passing a value from 0 to 100, we need to convert our `servo_position`. We do that with the following method:

```
def convert_percentage_to_integer(self, percentage_amount):
    return (percentage_amount*0.02)-1
```

In order to convert a percentage value to a –1 to 1 scale value, we multiply the percentage value by 0.02, and then subtract 1. It's easy to verify this math by using the percentage value of 50. The value of 50 represents the middle value in a 0 to 100 scale. Multiplying 50 by 0.02 produces the value of 1. Subtracting 1 from this value produces 0, which is the middle value in a –1 to 1 scale.

To set the status of the LED (`off`, `on`, or `blink`) we call the following method from our initialization method:

```
def set_led_status(self, led_status=0):
    if(led_status==0):
        self.led.off()
    elif (led_status==1):
        self.led.on()
    else:
        self.led.blink()
```

In `set_led_status`, we set our LED to `off` if the value passed in is 0, `on` if the value is 1, and `blink` if it is any other value.

We test out our class with the following code:

```
if __name__=="__main__":
    weather_dashboard = WeatherDashboard(50, 1)
```

In Chapter 6, *Working with the Servo Control Code to Control an Analog Device*, we will use this class to build our analog weather dashboard.

# Summary

As we can see, bridging the gap between the digital and analog worlds for data display is relatively easy using the Raspberry Pi. Its GPIO port allows for easy connection to various output devices such as motors and LEDs.

In this chapter, we connected a servo motor and LED, and controlled them using Python code. We will expand on this in Chapter 6, *Working with the Servo Control code to Control an Analog Device*, as we build an IoT weather dashboard with an analog meter display.

# Questions

1. True or false? A stepper motor is controlled using an open-loop feedback system.
2. What type of electric motor would you use if you were building an electric car?
3. True or false? Servo motors are considered a high-performance alternative to stepper motors.
4. What controls the angle of the servo motor?
5. True or false? DC motors have shorter response times than stepper motors.
6. Which Python package do we use to control our servo?
7. True or false? We are able to control a servo using the Python shell in Thonny.
8. Which command is used to move the servo to its maximum position?
9. True or false? We can only move the servo to its minimum, maximum, and middle positions.
10. How do we convert percentage values to the corresponding values that the servo object understands in our code?

# Further reading

The GPIO Zero documentation gives a complete overview of this amazing Raspberry Pi Python library. Find out more at https://gpiozero.readthedocs.io/en/stable/.

# 6

# Working with the Servo Control Code to Control an Analog Device

Continuing our journey to combine the elegance of an analog meter with the accuracy of digital data, we will take a look at what we've learned in the previous two chapters and build an IoT weather dashboard with an analog meter display.

Make sure that you have the circuit from `Chapter 5`, *Controlling a Servo with Python,* wired up before you start this chapter.

This dashboard will display wardrobe suggestions based on the outside temperature and wind speed. We will also use an LED on our dashboard to indicate whether or not we should take an umbrella with us.

The following topics will be covered in this chapter:

- Accessing weather data from the cloud
- Controlling the servo using weather data
- Enhancing our project

## Knowledge required to complete this chapter

You should have a working knowledge of the Python programming language to complete this chapter. Knowledge of using a simple breadboard that you can connect components to is also a must.

A vinyl or craft cutter may be used in this project. Knowledge of how to use a cutter would be an asset so that you can complete this project.

# Project overview

By the end of this chapter, we should have a working IoT analog weather dashboard. We will modify the code written in Chapter 4, *Subscribing to Web Services*, and Chapter 5, *Controlling a Servo with Python*, to provide data to our dashboard. A backdrop will be printed and cut out. This backdrop will give our dashboard a cartoon-like look.

We will be using the circuit from Chapter 5, *Controlling a Servo with Python*. The following is the wiring diagram from this circuit:

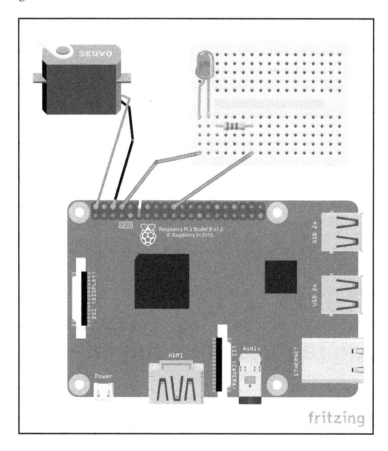

This project should take an afternoon to complete.

# Getting started

To complete this project, the following will be required:

- A Raspberry Pi Model 3 (2015 model or newer)
- A USB power supply
- A computer monitor
- A USB keyboard
- A USB mouse
- A small servo motor
- An LED (any color)
- A breadboard
- Jumper wires for the breadboard
- A color printer
- A vinyl or craft cutter (optional)

# Accessing weather data from the cloud

In `Chapter 4`, *Subscribing to Web Services*, we wrote a Python program to access weather data from Yahoo! Weather. The class, `CurrentWeather`, from that program returned the temperature, weather conditions, and wind speed for the `city` value that the class was instantiated with.

We will revisit that code and change the class name to `WeatherData`. We will also add a method to return a value from `0-100` to indicate the weather. We will take the temperature and wind speed into account when determining this number, with 0 being extreme winter-like conditions and `100` being very hot extreme summer conditions. We will use this number to control our servo. We will also check to see whether it is raining and update our LED to indicate whether or not we need an umbrella:

1. Open up Thonny from **Application Menu** | **Programming** | **Thonny Python IDE**
2. Click on the **New** icon to create a new file

3. Type the following into the file:

```
from weather import Weather, Unit

class WeatherData:
    temperature = 0
    weather_conditions = ''
    wind_speed = 0
    city = ''

    def __init__(self, city):
        self.city = city
        weather = Weather(unit = Unit.CELSIUS)
        lookup = weather.lookup_by_location(self.city)
        self.temperature = float(lookup.condition.temp)
        self.weather_conditions = lookup.condition.text
        self.wind_speed = float(lookup.wind.speed)
    def getServoValue(self):
        temp_factor = (self.temperature*100)/30
        wind_factor = (self.wind_speed*100)/20
        servo_value = temp_factor-(wind_factor/20)
        if(servo_value >= 100):
            return 100
        elif (servo_value <= 0):
            return 0
        else:
            return servo_value
    def getLEDValue(self):
        if (self.weather_conditions=='Thunderstorm'):
            return 2;
        elif(self.weather_conditions=='Raining'):
            return 1
        else:
            return 0
if __name__=="__main__":
    weather = WeatherData('Paris')
    print(weather.getServoValue())
    print(weather.getLEDValue())
```

4. Save the file as `WeatherData.py`

The heart of our code is in the `getServoValue()` and `getLEDValue()` methods:

```
def getServoValue(self):
    temp_factor = (self.temperature*100)/30
    wind_factor = (self.wind_speed*100)/20
    servo_value = temp_factor-(wind_factor/20)
```

```
if(servo_value >= 100):
    return 100
elif (servo_value <= 0):
    return 0
else:
    return servo_value
```

In the `getServoValue` method, we set the `temp_factor` and `wind_factor` variables to a percentage value based on a minimum of `0` for both of them and a maximum of `30` and `20` for the temperature and wind speeds, respectively. These are arbitrary numbers as we will consider `30` degrees Celsius to be our extreme hot temperature and 20 kph winds as our extreme wind speed. The servo value is set by subtracting the wind speed by 5 percent from the temperature (by dividing it by `20`). This, of course, is arbitrary as well. Feel free to adjust the percentage as desired.

To explain this further, consider a temperature of 10 degrees Celsius and a wind speed of 5 km/h. The temperature factor (`temp_factor`) would be 10 multiplied by 100 and then divided by 30 or 33.33. The wind speed factor (`wind_factor`) would be 5 multiplied by 100 and then divided by 20 or 25. The value we pass to our servo (`servo_value`) would be the temperature factor (33.33) minus the wind speed factor (25) after it has been divided by `20`. The value of `servo_value` is 32.08 or roughly 32 percent of the maximum servo value.

We then return the value of `servo_value` and use it to control our servo. Any value below `0` and above `100` will off our scale and will not work with our servo (as we are moving the servo between `0` and `100` percent). We use an `if` statement in the `getServoValue` method to correct such conditions.

The `getLEDValue` method simply checks the weather conditions and returns code based on whether or not it is raining. `Thunderstorm` will return a value of `2`, `Rain` and `Light Rain` will return a value of `1`, and anything else will return a value of `0`. We will use this value to blink the LED in our dashboard if there is a thunderstorm, keep it solid if it is only raining, and turn it off under all other conditions:

```
def getLEDValue(self):
    if (self.weather_conditions=='Thunderstorm'):
        return 2;
    elif(self.weather_conditions=='Rain'):
        return 1
    elif(self.weather_conditions=='Light Rain'):
        return 1
    else:
        return 0
```

At the time of writing this book, `Thunderstorm`, `Rain`, and `Light Rain` were values that were returned during a search of the weather in world cities. Please feel free to update the `if` statement to include other descriptions of extreme precipitation. As an added enhancement, you may consider using regular expressions in the `if` statement.

Run the code in Thonny. You should get a value for the servo and LED based on the weather conditions in Paris. I received the following at the time I ran the code:

```
73.075
0
```

# Controlling the servo using weather data

We are close to building our IoT weather dashboard. The final steps involve controlling our servo position based on the weather data returned from the Yahoo! Weather web service and physically building a backdrop for our servo needle.

## Correcting for servo range

As some of you may have noticed, your servo motor does not move a full 180 degrees from minimum to maximum. This is due to the minimum and maximum pulse widths of 1 ms and 2 ms set in GPIO Zero. To account for this difference, we must adjust the `min_pulse_width` and `max_pulse_width` properties accordingly when we instantiate a `Servo` object.

The following code does just that. The variable, `servoCorrection`, adds to and subtracts from the `min_pulse_width` and `max_pulse_width` values. The following code moves the servo to the minimum position and then the maximum position after 5 seconds:

1. Open up Thonny from **Application Menu** | **Programming** | **Thonny Python IDE**.
2. Click on the **New** icon to create a new file.

3. Type the following into the file:

```
from gpiozero import Servo
from time import sleep
servoPin=17

servoCorrection=0.5
maxPW=(2.0+servoCorrection)/1000
minPW=(1.0-servoCorrection)/1000

servo=Servo(servoPin, min_pulse_width=minPW,
max_pulse_width=maxPW)

servo.min()
sleep(5)
servo.max()
sleep(5)
servo.min()
sleep(5)
servo.max()
sleep(5)
servo.min()
sleep(5)
servo.max()
sleep(5)

servo.close()
```

4. Save the file as `servo_correction.py`.
5. Run the code to see if the value of `servoCorrection` fixes the issue with your servo not turning a full 180 degrees from `servo.min` to `servo.max`.
6. Adjust `servoCorrection` until your servo does move 180 degrees between `servo.min` and `servo.max`. We will use the value of `servoCorrection` in the code for our weather dashboard.

# Changing the position of the servo based on weather data

We are now ready to control the position of our servo based on weather conditions. We will modify the WeatherDashboard class we created in Chapter 5, *Controlling a servo with Python;* to do this, perform the following steps:

1. Open up Thonny from **Application Menu** | **Programming** | **Thonny Python IDE**
2. Click on the **New** icon to create a new file
3. Type the following into the file:

```python
from gpiozero import Servo
from gpiozero import LED
from time import sleep
from WeatherData import WeatherData

class WeatherDashboard:

    servo_pin = 17
    led_pin = 14
    servoCorrection=0.5
    maxPW=(2.0+servoCorrection)/1000
    minPW=(1.0-servoCorrection)/1000

    def __init__(self, servo_position=0, led_status=0):
        self.servo = Servo(self.servo_pin, min_pulse_width=
                self.minPW, max_pulse_width=self.maxPW)
        self.led = LED(self.led_pin)

        self.move_servo(servo_position)
        self.set_led_status(led_status)

    def move_servo(self, servo_position=0):
        self.servo.value = self.convert_percentage_to_integer(
                servo_position)

    def turnOffServo(self):
        sleep(5)
        self.servo.close()

    def set_led_status(self, led_status=0):
        if(led_status==0):
            self.led.off()
        elif (led_status==1):
```

```
            self.led.on()
        else:
            self.led.blink()

    def convert_percentage_to_integer(self,
percentage_amount):
        #adjust for servos that turn counter clockwise by
default
        adjusted_percentage_amount = 100 - percentage_amount
        return (adjusted_percentage_amount*0.02)-1

if __name__=="__main__":
    weather_data = WeatherData('Toronto')
    weather_dashboard = WeatherDashboard(
    weather_data.getServoValue(),
    weather_data.getLEDValue())
    weather_dashboard.turnOffServo()
```

4. Save the file as `WeatherDashboard.py`
5. Run the code and observe that the servo position changes

Let's take a look at the code.

We start out by importing the resources we need:

```
from time import sleep
from WeatherData import WeatherData
```

We add `time` to our project as we will be using it as a delay before we close our `Servo` object. `WeatherData` is added to provide the values for our servo and LED based on weather conditions.

The `servoCorrection`, `maxPW`, and `minPW` variables adjust our servo (if needed), as explained in our previous servo correction code:

```
servoCorrection=0.5
maxPW=(2.0+servoCorrection)/1000
minPW=(1.0-servoCorrection)/1000
```

The `turnOffServo` method allows us to close the connection to the servo, stopping any jerking motion that may occur:

```
def turnOffServo(self):
    sleep(5)
    self.servo.close()
```

We use the `sleep` function to delay closing the servo so that it will not be closed prior to being set to its position.

You may have also noticed a change to the `convert_percentage_to_integer` method from the code in Chapter 5, *Controlling a Servo with Python*. The motors tested for this project had a minimum position on the right. This is the opposite of what we need, so the code was changed to subtract the `percentage_amount` from 100 to reverse this behavior and give us the correct servo position (refer to Chapter 5, *Controlling a Servo with Python*, for more information on this method and use the `convert_percentage_to_integer` from this chapter if need be):

```
def convert_percentage_to_integer(self, percentage_amount):
        #adjust for servos that turn counter clockwise by default
        adjusted_percentage_amount = 100 - percentage_amount
        return (adjusted_percentage_amount*0.02)-1
```

Run the code in Thonny. You should witness the servo motor moving to a position based on the weather conditions in Toronto, Canada. The LED will either blink, stay solid, or turn off based on whether or not it is raining in Toronto at the time you run the code.

Now, let's enhance our project by building a physical backdrop for our servo and LED.

# Enhancing our project

With our code out of the way, it's now time to add a physical backdrop to our servo. With this backdrop, we bring the IoT to life for our weather data. Our dashboard will recommend which wardrobe item we should wear based on the weather.

# Printing out the main graphic

The following is the graphic we will be using for our backdrop:

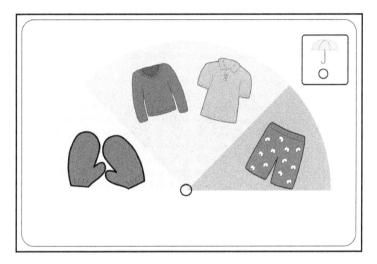

Using a color printer, print out the graphic on printable vinyl (this image file is available from our GitHub repository). Cut out the holes under the umbrella and main graphic.

To add support, cut out the back plate on hard card stock with a cutter or by hand with scissors:

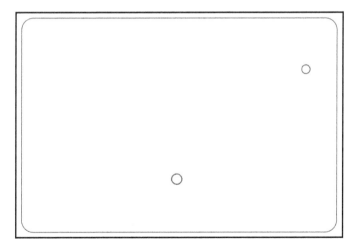

Peel the backdrop off of the printable vinyl sheet and stick it to the backplate. Use the holes to align the backdrop with the back plates:

# Adding the needle and LED

Insert the LED into the hole under the umbrella:

Insert the hub of the servo motor through the other hole. Use double-sided foam tape to secure the servo to the backplate if necessary:

Wire up the LED and servo to the breadboard using jumper wires (see the wiring diagram at the start of this chapter). The assembly should sit with a slight slant. Before we run the WeatherDashboard code with our new display, we have to install the needle to the minimum position:

1. Open up Thonny from **Application Menu** | **Programming** | **Thonny Python IDE**
2. Click on the **New** icon to create a new file
3. Type the following into the file:

```
from gpiozero import Servo
servoPin=17

servoCorrection=<<put in the correction you calculated>>
maxPW=(2.0+servoCorrection)/1000
minPW=(1.0-servoCorrection)/1000

servo=Servo(servoPin, min_pulse_width=minPW,
max_pulse_width=maxPW)

servo.min()
```

4. Save the file as servo_minimum.py
5. Run the code to have the servo position itself to the minimum value

Install the needle so that it points to the left if the servo motor turns counter-clockwise to its minimum, and to the right if the servo motor turns clockwise to its minimum (this will make more sense once you start physically working with the servo).

Run the WeatherDashboard code again. The servo should move according to the weather data, indicating a wardrobe option. If it is raining, the LED should light up. A thunderstorm will flash the LED. Otherwise, the LED will stay off.

In the following picture, the dashboard is recommending a short sleeve shirt for Toronto, Canada. An umbrella is not required for the outside weather conditions:

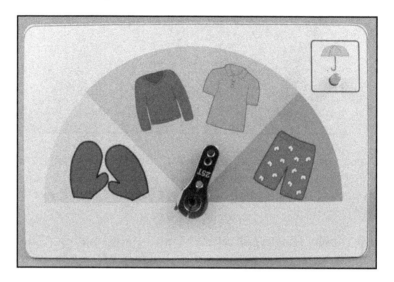

Congratulations! You've just built an IoT weather dashboard.

# Summary

In this project, we used the power of the Raspberry Pi to create an IoT analog weather dashboard. In this case, this involved an internet-controlled servo used as an analog meter. It's not too hard to imagine how we may alter our code to display data other than weather data. Picture an analog meter displaying the tank level from a distant factory, where the level data is communicated over the internet.

The intuitive nature of analog meters makes them perfect for applications where a glance of the data is all that is required. Combining analog meters with data from the internet creates a whole new world of data display.

In Chapter 7, *Setting Up a Raspberry Pi Web Server*, we will take a step away from the analog world and explore how we may use the Raspberry Pi as a web server and build a web based dashboard.

# Questions

1. True or false? A servo may be used as an IoT device.
2. True or false? Changing the minimum and maximum pulse width values on the Servo object modifies the range of the servo.
3. Why do we add a delay before calling the close() method of the Servo object?
4. True or false? We do not need a getTemperature() method in our WeatherData class.
5. True or false? A flashing LED on our dashboard indicates a clear and cloudless day.
6. What do we use a pair of shorts on our dashboard to indicate?
7. Where would you use a regular expression in our code?
8. Why do we import time in our code?
9. True or false? An IoT-enabled servo can only be used to indicate weather data.

# Further reading

In order to enhance our code, regular expressions may be used. Any documentation on Python and regular expressions is invaluable in developing strong coding skills.

# 7
# Setting Up a Raspberry Pi Web Server

We will begin our journey to create an IoT home security dashboard by learning how to use the CherryPy web server framework. Our chapter will start by introducing **CherryPy**. We will go through a few examples before we create an HTML weather dashboard using a modified version of our `CurrentWeather` class from `Chapter 4`, *Subscribing to Web Services*.

The following topics will be covered in this chapter:

- Introducing CherryPy—a minimalist Python Web framework
- Creating a simple web page using CherryPy

## Knowledge required to complete this chapter

The reader should have a working knowledge of Python in order to complete this chapter. A basic understanding of HTML, including CSS, is also required to complete the project in this chapter.

## Project overview

In this chapter, we will build an HTML weather dashboard using the CherryPy and Bootstrap frameworks. Intimate knowledge of these frameworks is not required to complete the project.

This project should take a couple of hours to complete.

# Getting started

To complete this project, the following will be required:

- A Raspberry Pi Model 3 (2015 model or newer)
- A USB power supply
- A computer monitor
- A USB keyboard
- A USB mouse

# Introducing CherryPy – a minimalist Python web framework

For our project, we will use the CherryPy Python library (be aware that it is CherryPy with a "y", not CherryPi with an "i").

## What is CherryPy?

According to their website, CherryPy is a Pythonic, object-oriented web framework. CherryPy gives developers the power to build web applications as if they were building any object-oriented Python program. In true Python style, CherryPy programs have less code and are developed in less time than other web frameworks.

## Who uses CherryPy?

Some of the companies that use CherryPy include the following:

- **Netflix**: Netflix uses CherryPy in its infrastructure through RESTful API calls. Other Python libraries used by Netflix include Bottle and SciPy.
- **Hulu**: CherryPy is used for some of Hulu's projects.
- **Indigo Domotics**: Indigo Domotics is a home automation company that uses the CherryPy framework.

# Installing CherryPy

We will use Python's `pip3` package management system to install CherryPy.

 A package management system is a program that helps install and configure applications. It can also carry out upgrades and uninstalls.

To do this, open up a Terminal window and type in the following:

```
sudo pip3 install cherrypy
```

Hit *Enter*. You should see the following in the Terminal:

```
                            pi@raspberrypi: ~                    _  □  ✗
 File  Edit  Tabs  Help
B)
    100% |██████████████████████████| 71kB 1.0MB/s
Collecting tempora>=1.8 (from portend>=2.1.1->cherrypy)
  Downloading https://files.pythonhosted.org/packages/55/f4/6909c23d920192dc9d2b
b0d0841abb561f58fb6c816cf593a35dda0a800c/tempora-1.11-py2.py3-none-any.whl
Collecting backports.functools-lru-cache (from cheroot>=6.2.4->cherrypy)
  Downloading https://files.pythonhosted.org/packages/03/8e/2424c0e65c4a066e28f5
39364deee49b6451f8fcd4f718fefa50cc3dcf48/backports.functools_lru_cache-1.5-py2.p
y3-none-any.whl
Collecting more-itertools>=2.6 (from cheroot>=6.2.4->cherrypy)
  Downloading https://files.pythonhosted.org/packages/7a/46/886917c6a4ce49dd3fff
250c01c5abac5390d57992751384fe61befc4877/more_itertools-4.1.0-py3-none-any.whl (
47kB)
    100% |██████████████████████████| 51kB 1.3MB/s
Collecting pytz (from tempora>=1.8->portend>=2.1.1->cherrypy)
  Downloading https://files.pythonhosted.org/packages/dc/83/15f7833b70d3e067ca91
467ca245bae0f6fe56ddc7451aa0dc5606b120f2/pytz-2018.4-py2.py3-none-any.whl (510kB
)
    100% |██████████████████████████| 512kB 460kB/s
Installing collected packages: six, pytz, tempora, portend, backports.functools-
lru-cache, more-itertools, cheroot, cherrypy
Successfully installed backports.functools-lru-cache-1.5 cheroot-6.2.4 cherrypy-
14.2.0 more-itertools-4.1.0 portend-2.2 pytz-2018.4 six-1.11.0 tempora-1.11
pi@raspberrypi:~ $ █
```

In Thonny, go to **Tools** | **Manage Packages**. You should see that **CherryPy** is now installed, as shown here:

# Creating a simple web page using CherryPy

To get started, let's build the most basic of programs with CherryPy. By this, I mean, of course, the ubiquitous Hello World program that we will use to say Hello Raspberry Pi!. We will work through a few examples before we build a dashboard to display weather data using a modified version of the CurrentWeather class from Chapter 4, *Subscribing to Web Services*.

# Hello Raspberry Pi!

To build the Hello Raspberry Pi! web page, do the following:

1. Open up Thonny from **Application Menu** | **Programming** | **Thonny Python IDE**.
2. Click on the **New** icon to create a new file.

3. Type the following:

```
import cherrypy

class HelloWorld():
    @cherrypy.expose
    def index(self):
        return "Hello Raspberry Pi!"
cherrypy.quickstart(HelloWorld())
```

4. Ensure that the line, `cherrypy.quickstart(HelloWorld())`, is inline with the `import` and `class` statements.

5. Save the file as `HelloRaspberryPi.py`.

6. Run the file by clicking on the green `Run current script` button.

7. You should see the CherryPy web server starting up as indicated in the shell:

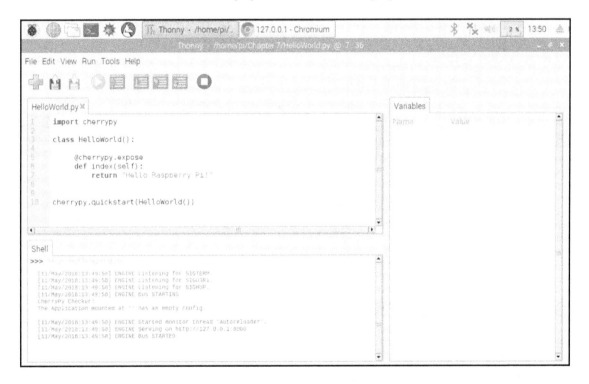

8. From the output to the shell you should be able to observe the ip address and port that CherryPy is running on, `http://127.0.0.1:8080`. You may recognize the ip address as the loopback address. CherryPy uses the port `8080`.

9. Open a web browser on your Raspberry Pi and type in the address from the previous step:

Congratulations, you have just turned your humble Raspberry Pi into a web server.

If you are like me, you probably didn't think a web server could be created with such little code. CherryPy basically focuses on one task, which is to take in an HTTP request and turn it into a Python method.

So how does it work? The decorator in our `HelloWorld` class, `@cherrypy.expose`, exposes the method index that happens to correspond to the root of the web server. When we load our web page using the loopback address (`127.0.0.1`) and port that CherryPy is running on (`8080`), the `index` method is served up as the page. In our code we simply return the string `Hello Raspberry Pi!` which is then displayed as our web page.

 The loopback address is an IP number used as the software loopback interface of a machine. This number is generally `127.0.0.1`. This address is not physically connected to a network and is used often to test the installation of a web server installed on the same machine.

# Say hello to myFriend

So what happens if we expose another method in our Python code? We can check that easily by using the decorator before a method. Let's write some code to do this:

1. Open up Thonny from **Application Menu** | **Programming** | **Thonny Python IDE**.

2. Click on the **New** icon to create a new file.

3. Type the following:

```
import cherrypy

class HelloWorld():

    @cherrypy.expose
    def index(self):
        return "Hello Raspberry Pi!"

    @cherrypy.expose
    def sayHello(self, myFriend=" my friend"):
        return "Hello " + myFriend

cherrypy.quickstart(HelloWorld())
```

4. Save the file as `SayHello.py`.
5. Stop and start the CherryPy server by clicking on the **Interrupt/Reset** button, and then the **Run current script** button.
6. Now, type the following into your browser's address bar and press *Enter*: `http://127.0.0.1:8080/sayHello`
7. You should see the following:

So what did we do differently this time? For starters, we didn't just access the root of our server. We added `/sayHello` to our URL. Usually, when we do that on a web server, we are directed to a subfolder. In this case, we are taken to the method in our `HelloWorld` class, called `sayHello()`.

If we look closely at the `sayHello()` method, we can see that it takes a parameter called `myFriend`:

```
@cherrypy.expose
def sayHello(self, myFriend=" my friend"):
        return "Hello " + myFriend
```

We can see that the `myFriend` parameter has a default value of `my Friend`. So, when we run CherryPy and navigate to the URL at `http://127.0.0.1:8080/sayHello`, the `sayHello` method is called and the `"Hello "` + `my friend` string is returned.

Now, type the following into the the address box and hit *Enter*: `http://127.0.0.1:8080/sayHello?myFriend=Raspberry%20Pi`

In this URL, we set the value of `myFriend` to `Raspberry%20Pi` (the `%20` is used instead of a space). We should get the same result as our first example.

As we can see, it is very easy to connect Python methods to an HTML output.

# What about static pages?

Static pages were at one time ubiquitous with the internet. Simple links between static pages made up what was considered a web site at the time. A lot has changed since then, however, being able to serve up a simple HTML page is still a basic requirement of a web server framework.

So, how would we would do that with CherryPy? It's pretty simple actually. We simply open a static HTML page in a method and return it. Let's have CherryPy serve up a static page by doing the following:

1. Open up Thonny from **Application Menu** | **Programming** | **Thonny Python IDE**.
2. Click on the **New** icon to create a new file.
3. Type the following:

```
<html>
    <body>
        This is a static HTML page.
    </body>
</html>
```

4. Save the file as `static.html`.
5. In Thonny click on the **New** icon to create a new file in the same directory as `static.html`.
6. Type the following:

```
import cherrypy

class StaticPage():
```

```
@cherrypy.expose
def index(self):
        return open('static.html')

cherrypy.quickstart(StaticPage())
```

7. Save the file as `StaticPage.py`.
8. If CherryPy is still running stop it by clicking on the red button.
9. Run the file `StaticPage.py` to start CherryPy.
10. You should see CherryPy starting up as indicated in the shell.
11. To view our new static web page, open up a web browser on the Raspberry Pi and type the following into the address bar: `http://127.0.0.1:8080`
12. You should see the static page displayed:

So what did we do here? We changed our `index` method so that it returned an open `static.html` file with the line return `open ('static.html')`. This opened up `static.html` in our browser as our index (or `http://127.0.0.1:8080/index`). Note that trying to type in the page name `static.html` in the url (`http://127.0.0.1:8080/static.html`) will not work. CherryPy serves up the content based on the method name. In this case the method name is index, which is the default.

# HTML weather dashboard

Now it's time to add what we learned from the previous chapters. Let's revisit the `CurrentWeather` class from `Chapter 4`, *Subscribing to Web Services*. We will rename it `WeatherData`, as this name is more appropriate for this project, and change it a little bit.

1. Open up Thonny from **Application Menu | Programming | Thonny Python IDE**
2. Click on the **New** icon to create a new file

3. Type the following:

```
from weather import Weather, Unit
import time

class WeatherData:
    temperature = 0
    weather_conditions = ''
    wind_speed = 0
    city = ''
    def __init__(self, city):
        self.city = city
        weather = Weather(unit = Unit.CELSIUS)
        lookup = weather.lookup_by_location(self.city)
        self.temperature = lookup.condition.temp
        self.weather_conditions = lookup.condition.text
        self.wind_speed = lookup.wind.speed
    def getTemperature(self):
        return self.temperature + " C"
    def getWeatherConditions(self):
        return self.weather_conditions
    def getWindSpeed(self):
        return self.wind_speed + " kph"
    def getCity(self):
        return self.city
    def getTime(self):
        return time.ctime()
if __name__ == "__main__":
    current_weather = WeatherData('London')
    print(current_weather.getTemperature())
    print(current_weather.getWeatherConditions())
    print(current_weather.getTime())
```

4. Save the file as `WeatherData.py`
5. Run the code

6. You should see the weather for London, England printed in the following shell:

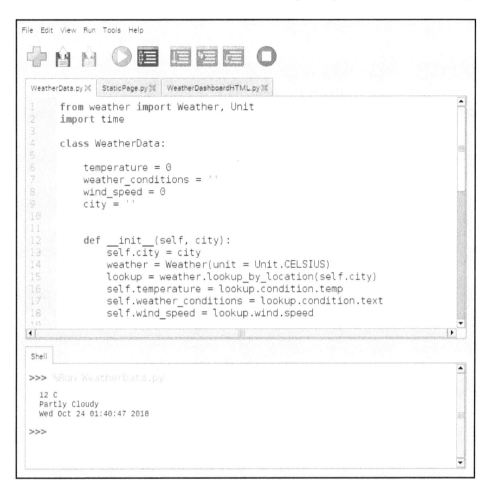

Let's take a look at the code. Basically `WeatherData.py` is exactly the same as `CurrentWeather.py` from `Chapter 4`, *Subscribing to Web Services*, but with an extra method called `getTime`:

```
def getTime(self):
    return time.ctime()
```

We use this method to return the time when the call is made to the weather web service for use in our web page.

We will now use CherryPy and the `Bootstrap` framework to create our dashboard. To do this do the following:

1. Open up Thonny from **Application Menu** | **Programming** | **Thonny Python IDE**
2. Click on the **New** icon to create a new file
3. Type the following (pay particular attention to the quotation marks):

```
import cherrypy
from WeatherData import WeatherData

class WeatherDashboardHTML:
    def __init__(self, currentWeather):
        self.currentWeather = currentWeather
    @cherrypy.expose
    def index(self):
        return """
            <!DOCTYPE html>
             <html lang="en">

             <head>
                 <title>Weather Dashboard</title>
                 <meta charset="utf-8">
                 <meta name="viewport" content="width=device-
width, initial-scale=1">
                 <link rel="stylesheet"
href="https://maxcdn.bootstrapcdn.com/bootstrap/4.1.0/css/bootstrap
.min.css">
                 <script
src="https://ajax.googleapis.com/ajax/libs/jquery/3.3.1/jquery.min.
js"></script>
                 <script
src="https://cdnjs.cloudflare.com/ajax/libs/popper.js/1.14.0/umd/po
pper.min.js"></script>
                 <script
src="https://maxcdn.bootstrapcdn.com/bootstrap/4.1.0/js/bootstrap.m
in.js"></script>
                 <style>
                     .element-box {
                         border-radius: 10px;
                         border: 2px solid #C8C8C8;
                         padding: 20px;
                     }

                     .card {
                         width: 600px;
                     }
```

```
                    .col {
                        margin: 10px;
                    }
                </style>
            </head>

            <body>
                <div class="container">
                    <br/>
                    <div class="card">
                        <div class="card-header">
                            <h3>Weather Conditions for """ +
self.currentWeather.getCity() + """
                            </h3></div>
                            <div class="card-body">
                                <div class="row">
                                    <div class="col element-box">
                                        <h5>Temperature</h5>
                                        <p>""" +
self.currentWeather.getTemperature() + """</p>
                                    </div>
                                    <div class="col element-box">
                                        <h5>Conditions</h5>
                                        <p>""" +
self.currentWeather.getWeatherConditions() + """</p>
                                    </div>
                                    <div class="col element-box">
                                        <h5>Wind Speed</h5>
                                        <p>""" +
self.currentWeather.getWindSpeed() + """</p>
                                    </div>
                                </div>
                            </div>
                            <div class="card-footer"><p>""" +
self.currentWeather.getTime() + """</p></div>
                        </div>
                    </div>
                </body>

            </html>
            """
if __name__=="__main__":
    currentWeather = WeatherData('Paris')
    cherrypy.quickstart(WeatherDashboardHTML(currentWeather))
```

4. Save the file as `WeatherDashboardHTML.py`

This may look like a whole lot of code—and it is. If we break it down, though, it's not really that complicated. Basically, we are using CherryPy to return an HTML string, which will be served up in the root of our URL through the `index` method.

Before we can do that, we instantiate the `WeatherDashboardHTML` class by passing in a `WeatherData` object. We give this `WeatherData` object the name `currentWeather`, as shown in the init (class constructor) method:

```
def __init__(self, currentWeather):
        self.currentWeather = currentWeather
```

CherryPy serves up the `index` method by printing out an HTML string that is sprinkled with parameters from our `currentWeather` object. We are using the Bootstrap component library in our HTML code. We add it by incorporating the standard Bootstrap boilerplate code:

```
<link rel="stylesheet"href="https://maxcdn.bootstrapcdn.com
        /bootstrap/4.1.0/css/bootstrap.min.css">

<script
src="https://ajax.googleapis.com/ajax/libs/jquery/3.3.1/jquery.min.js"></sc
ript>
<script
src="https://cdnjs.cloudflare.com/ajax/libs/popper.js/1.14.0/umd/popper.min
.js"></script>
<script
src="https://maxcdn.bootstrapcdn.com/bootstrap/4.1.0/js/bootstrap.min.js"><
/script>
```

We use the Bootstrap `card` component as our content container. `card` allows us to create a header, body, and footer:

```
<div class="card">
    <div class="card-header">
            .
            .
            .
```

The header section of the `card` component features the name of the city. We use the `getCity` method from our `currentWeather` object to get the name of the city:

```
<div class="card-header">
    <h3>Weather Conditions for """ + self.currentWeather.getCity() +
"""</h3>
</div>
```

In the body section of the `card` component, we create a row with three columns. Each column contains a title (`<h5>`), as well as data pulled from our `WeatherData` object, called `currentWeather`. You can see the title, `Temperature`, with the temperature value pulled from the `currentWeather` method, `getTemperature`:

```
<div class="card-body">
    <div class="row">
        <div class="col element-box">
            <h5>Temperature</h5>
            <p>""" + self.currentWeather.getTemperature() + """</p>
            .
            .
            .
```

For the footer we simply return the instantiation time of the `currentWeather` object. We will take this time as the time the weather information was checked from our program.

```
<div class="card-footer">
    <p>""" + self.currentWeather.getTime() + """</p>
</div>
```

Our style section at the top allows us to customize the look of our dashboard. We create a CSS class, called `element-box`, in order to create a silver (`#C8C8C8`) rounded corner box around our weather parameters. We also limit the width of the card (and thus the dashboard) to `600px`. Lastly, we put a margin of `10px` around the columns, so that the rounded boxes do not touch each other:

```
<style>
    .element-box {
        border-radius: 10px;
        border: 2px solid #C8C8C8;
        padding: 20px;
    }
    .card {
        width: 600px;
    }
    .col {
        margin: 10px;
    }
</style>
```

Our `main` method at the bottom instantiates a `WeatherData` class as an object, called `currentWeather`. In our example, we are using data from the city of `Paris`. Our code then passes the `currentWeather` object to the `cherrypy.quickstart()` method, as shown here:

```
if __name__=="__main__":
    currentWeather = WeatherData('Paris')
    cherrypy.quickstart(WeatherDashboardHTML(currentWeather))
```

Stop and start the CherryPy server while on the `WeatherDashboardHTML.py` file. If you do not have any errors in your code, you should see something similar to the following:

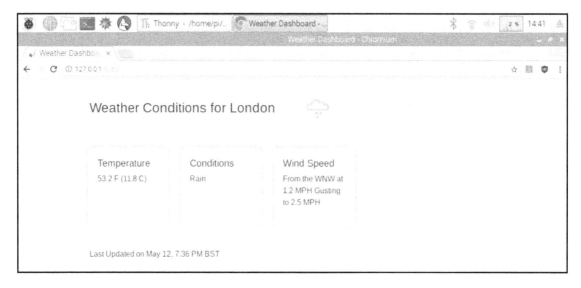

# Summary

In this chapter, we turned our Raspberry Pi into a web server using the CherryPy HTTP framework. With its minimalist architecture, CherryPy allows the developer to set up a web-enabled Python program in a very short time.

We started this chapter by installing CherryPy on our Raspberry Pi. After a few simple examples, we built an HTML weather dashboard by modifying and utilizing the web service code that we wrote in Chapter 4, *Subscribing to Web Services*.

In the coming chapters, we will use the knowledge we gained in this chapter to build an IoT home security dashboard.

# Questions

1. True or false? It's CherryPi, not CherryPy.
2. True or false? CherryPy is used by Netflix.
3. How do we tell CherryPy that we want to expose a method?
4. True or false? CherryPy requires many lines of boilerplate code.
5. Why do we rename our `CurrentWeather` class to `WeatherData`?
6. True or false? The default port used by CherryPy is `8888`.
7. Why do we add a margin to our `col` CSS class?
8. Which method from our `WeatherData` class do we use to get the image URL of the current weather conditions?
9. Which Bootstrap component do we use as our content container?
10. True or false? In our example, it is sunny and hot in London.

# Further reading

In this chapter, we only scratched the surface of the CherryPy and Bootstrap frameworks. Further reading can be found at the CherryPy website, available at `www.cherrypy.org`, and Bootstrap's site, at `https://getbootstrap.com`. This is recommended to improve the developer's knowledge of these powerful frameworks.

# 8
# Reading Raspberry Pi GPIO Sensor Data Using Python

In `Chapter 7`, *Setting Up a Raspberry Pi Web Server*, we used the GPIO Zero library to turn on servos and light up LEDs. In this chapter, we will use GPIO Zero to read inputs from the GPIO port. First, we will start with a simple button, before moving on to **Passive Infrared** (**PIR**) motion sensors and buzzers.

Having the ability to read sensory data from the GPIO will allow us to build our IoT home security dashboard. By the end of this chapter, we should become very familiar with programming the Raspberry Pi with components connected to the GPIO.

The following topics will be covered in this chapter:

- Reading the state of a button
- Reading the state from an infrared motion sensor
- Modifying `Hello LED` using an infrared sensor

## Project overview

In this chapter, we will create two different types of alarm system. We will start by learning how to read GPIO sensory data from a push-button. We will then learn how to interact with a PIR sensor and distance sensor. Lastly, we will learn how to hook up an active buzzer.

This chapter should take about 3 hours to complete.

# Getting started

To complete this project, the following will be required:

- A Raspberry Pi Model 3 (2015 model or newer)
- A USB power supply
- A computer monitor
- A USB keyboard
- A USB mouse
- A breadboard
- Jumper wires
- A PIR sensor
- A distance sensor
- A active buzzer
- An LED
- A push-button (momentary)
- A push-button (latching)
- A key switch (optional)

# Reading the state of a button

`Button`, from the `GPIO Zero` library, gives us an easy way to interact with a typical button connected to the GPIO. We will cover the following in this section:

- Using GPIO Zero with a button
- Using the Sense HAT emulator and GPIO Zero button together
- Toggling an LED with a long button press

# Using GPIO Zero with a button

Connecting a push-button is relatively easy with the GPIO. The following is the connection diagram showing the process:

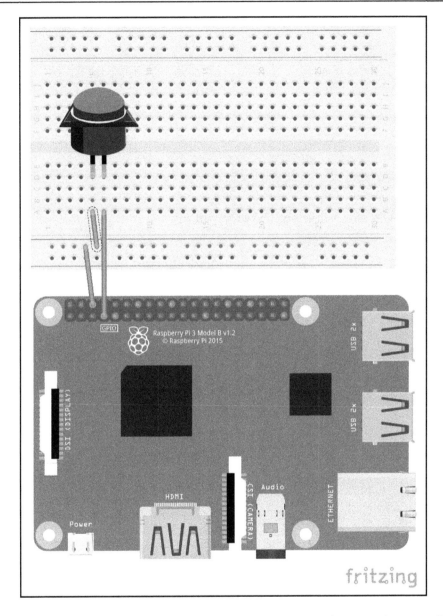

Connect the push-button so that one end is connected to ground using a jumper. Connect the other end to GPIO 4 on the Raspberry Pi.

In Thonny, create a new file and call it `button_press.py`. Then, type following into the file and run it:

```
from gpiozero import Button
from time import sleep

button = Button(4)
while True:
    if button.is_pressed:
      print("The Button on GPIO 4 has been pressed")
      sleep(1)
```

You should now see the message "The Button on GPIO 4 has been pressed" in the shell whenever you push the button. The code will run continuously until you click on the **Reset** button.

Let's take a look at the code. We start by importing `Button` from `GPIO Zero`, and `sleep` from the `time` library:

```
from gpiozero import Button
from time import sleep
```

We then create a new `button` object and assign it to GPIO pin 4 with the following code:

```
button = Button(4)
```

Our continuous loop checks to see whether the button is currently pressed, and prints out a statement to our shell if it is:

```
while True:
    if button.is_pressed:
      print("The Button on GPIO 4 has been pressed")
      sleep(1)
```

# Using the Sense HAT emulator and GPIO Zero button together

We use push-buttons every day, whether that be in selecting a floor in an elevator or starting our car. Modern technology allows us to separate the push-button from the physical device that it controls. In other words, pushing a button can set in motion many different events that really have nothing to do with the button. We can emulate this detachment with our push-button and the Sense HAT emulator.

I can just picture some of you wondering what separating a button from what it is controlling actually means. To help you visualize it, picture a latching push-button that controls a light. When the button is pressed down, the circuit is completed and electricity runs through the leads on the push-button. With the use of controllers and computers such as the Raspberry Pi, all that the push-button is required to do is change its state. The controller or computer takes that state and performs actions that are completely separated from the push-button itself.

Load the Sense HAT emulator from the **Programming** menu in Raspbian. Create a new Python file in Thonny and call it `sense-button.py`. Enter the following code into the file, and then click on the **Run** icon when done:

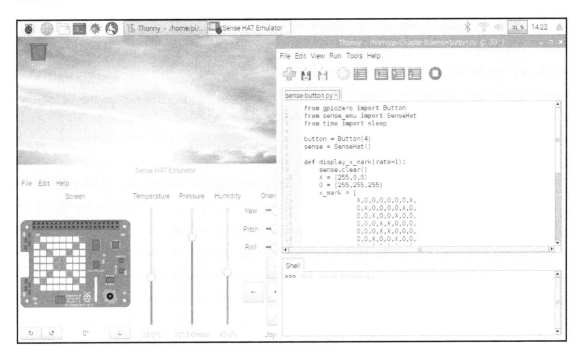

```
from gpiozero import Button
from sense_emu import SenseHat
from time import sleep

button = Button(4)
sense = SenseHat()

def display_x_mark(rate=1):
    sense.clear()
```

```
    X = (255,0,0)
    O = (255,255,255)
    x_mark = [
                X,O,O,O,O,O,O,X,
                O,X,O,O,O,O,X,O,
                O,O,X,O,O,X,O,O,
                O,O,O,X,X,O,O,O,
                O,O,O,X,X,O,O,O,
                O,O,X,O,O,X,O,O,
                O,X,O,O,O,O,X,O,
                X,O,O,O,O,O,O,X
            ]
    sense.set_pixels(x_mark)
while True:
    if button.is_pressed:
        display_x_mark()
        sleep(1)
    else:
        sense.clear()
```

If you do not have any errors in your code, you should see that the display on the Sense HAT emulator changes to a red X on a white background when you press the button:

Let's explain the preceding code a bit. We start off by importing the libraries we need for our code:

```
from gpiozero import Button
from sense_emu import SenseHat
from time import sleep
```

We then create new button and Sense HAT emulator objects. Our button is once again connected to GPIO pin 4:

```
button = Button(4)
sense = SenseHat()
```

The display_x_mark method creates an X in the display by using the SenseHat method set_pixels:

```
def display_x_mark(rate=1):
    sense.clear()
    X = (255,0,0)
    O = (255,255,255)
    x_mark = [
                X,O,O,O,O,O,O,X,
                O,X,O,O,O,O,X,O,
                O,O,X,O,O,X,O,O,
                O,O,O,X,X,O,O,O,
```

```
            O,O,O,X,X,O,O,O,
            O,O,X,O,O,X,O,O,
            O,X,O,O,O,O,X,O,
            X,O,O,O,O,O,O,X
    ]
    sense.set_pixels(x_mark)
```

The X and O variables are used to hold color codes, with (255,0,0) being red, and (255,255,255) as white. The variable x_mark creates an 8 x 8 pattern that matches the resolution of the Sense HAT emulator screen. x_mark is passed into the set_pixels method of the SenseHAT object.

Our continuous loop checks the is_pressed status of the button and calls the display_x_mark method if the status returns true. This method then prints a red X against a white background.

The display is cleared with sense.clear() when the button is not in the pressed state:

```
    while True:
        if button.is_pressed:
            display_x_mark()
            sleep(1)
        else:
            sense.clear()
```

# Toggling an LED with a long button press

With the GPIO Zero library, we can not only detect when a button has been pressed, but can also detect how long it has been pressed for. We will use the hold_time property and the when_held method to determine whether the button has been pressed for a certain duration. If this duration time has been exceeded, then we will turn an LED on and off.

The following is the circuit diagram for our program. Keep the push-button wired to GPIO pin 4. Use GPIO pin 17 for the LED, as shown here:

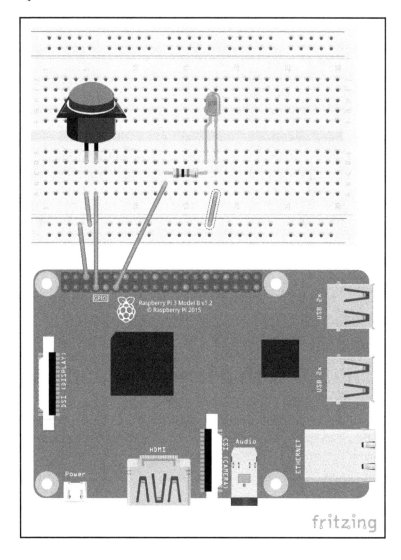

Create a new file in Thonny and call it `buttonheld-led.py`. Type in the following and click on **Run**:

```
from gpiozero import LED
from gpiozero import Button

led = LED(17)
button = Button(4)
button.hold_time=5

while True:
    button.when_held = lambda: led.toggle()
```

Hold down the push-button for 5 seconds. You should see the LED toggle on. Now hold it again for another 5 seconds. The LED should toggle off.

We've covered the first four lines of the code in previous examples. Let's look at where the hold time for the button is set:

```
button.hold_time=5
```

This line sets the hold time for the button at 5 seconds. The `when_held` method is called in our continuous loop:

```
button.when_held = lambda: led.toggle()
```

Using lambda, we are able to create an anonymous function so that we may call `toggle()` on the `LED` object, `led`. This toggles the LED both on and off.

# Reading the state from an infrared motion sensor

Alarm systems using motion sensors are a ubiquitous part of our society. With our Raspberry Pi, they are incredibly easy to build. We will cover the following in this section:

- What is a PIR sensor?
- Using the `GPIO buzzer` class
- Building a basic alarm system

# What is a PIR sensor?

PIR sensors, a type of motion sensor, are used to detect motion. Applications for PIR sensors are pretty much based on detecting motion for security systems. PIR stands for passive infrared, and PIR sensors contain a crystal that detects low-level radiation. PIR sensors are actually constructed in two halves, as it is the difference between the halves that detects motion. The following is a photo of an inexpensive PIR sensor:

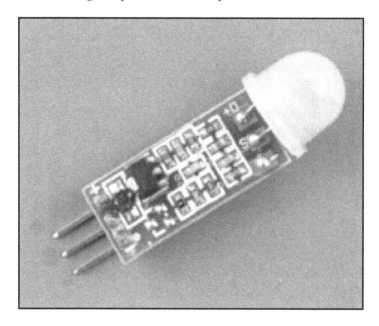

 In the preceding photo, we can see the positive (+), negative (-), and signal (**S**) pins. This particular PIR sensor sits well on a breadboard.

The following is the wiring diagram of our PIR circuit. The positive pin connects to the 5 V DC output on the Raspberry Pi. The negative pin connects to ground (GND), and the signal connects to GPIO pin 4:

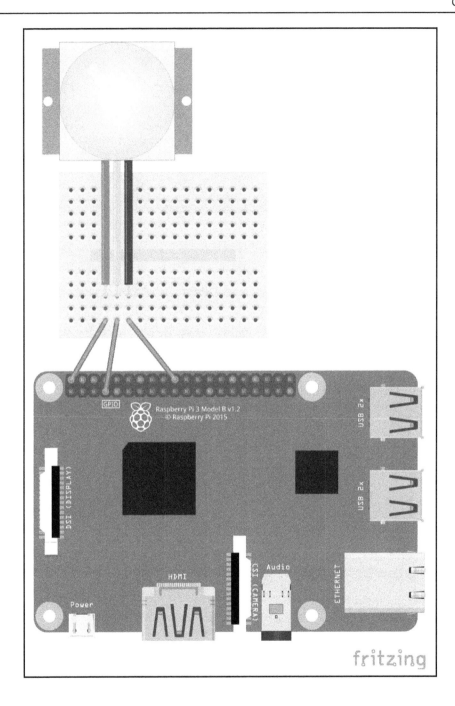

Create a new Python file in Thonny and call it `motion-sensor.py`. Type in the following code and run it:

```
from gpiozero import MotionSensor
from time import sleep

motion_sensor = MotionSensor(4)

while True:
    if motion_sensor.motion_detected:
        print('Detected Motion!')
        sleep(2)
    else:
        print('No Motion Detected!')
        sleep(2)
```

You should see a message reading `Detected Motion!` when you get close to the PIR sensor. Try staying still and see whether you can get the message `No Motion Detected!` to display in the shell.

Our code begins by importing the `MotionSensor` class from the `GPIO Zero` library:

```
from gpiozero import MotionSensor
```

After importing the `sleep` class, we create a new `MotionSensor` object, called `motion_sensor`, with the number 4 appended in order to make our program look for the signal on GPIO pin 4:

```
motion_sensor = MotionSensor(4)
```

In our continuous loop, we check the `motion_sensor` for motion with this line:

```
if motion_sensor.motion_detected:
```

From here on in the code, we define the messages to print to the shell.

# Using the GPIO Zero buzzer class

Generally, there are two types of electronic buzzers: active and passive. An active buzzer has an internal oscillator and will make a sound when a direct current, or DC, is applied to it. A passive buzzer requires an alternating current, or AC, in order for it to make a sound. Passive buzzers are basically small electromagnetic speakers. The easiest way to tell the difference is to apply a DC supply and listen for a sound. For the purposes of our code, we will be using an active buzzer, as shown in the following photo:

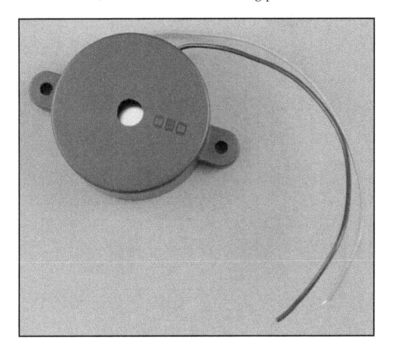

There is a `buzzer` class in the `GPIO Zero` library. We will use this class to generate a piercing alarm sound with our active buzzer. Configure the circuit as shown in the following diagram. The positive wire on the active buzzer connects to GPIO pin 17:

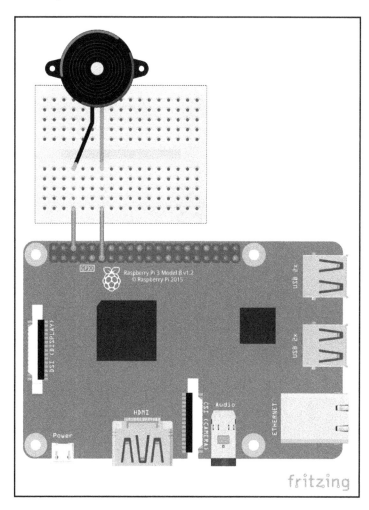

Create a new Python file in Thonny and call it `buzzer-test1.py`. Type in the following code and run it:

```
from gpiozero import Buzzer
from time import sleep

buzzer = Buzzer(17)
```

```
while True:
    buzzer.on()
    sleep(2)
    buzzer.off()
    sleep(2)
```

Depending on the active buzzer you chose, you should hear a piercing sound for two seconds followed by 2 seconds of silence. The following line turns on the buzzer:

```
buzzer.on()
```

Likewise, this line in the preceding code turns off the buzzer:

```
buzzer.off()
```

The code may be simplified by using the `toggle` method on the `buzzer` object. Create a new Python file in Thonny. Call it `buzzer-test2.py`. Type in the following and run it:

```
from gpiozero import Buzzer
from time import sleep

buzzer = Buzzer(17)

while True:
    buzzer.toggle()
    sleep(2)
```

You should get the same results. A third way to do the same thing would be to use the `beep` method from the `buzzer` object. Create a new Python file in Thonny. Call it `buzzer-test3.py`. Type in the following and run it:

```
from gpiozero import Buzzer

buzzer = Buzzer(17)

while True:
    buzzer.beep(2,2,10,False)
```

The `buzzer` should turn on for 2 seconds, and then off for 2 seconds, and repeat this for a total of 10 times. The `beep` method takes the following four parameters:

- `on_time`: This is the number of seconds the sound is on. The default is 1 second.
- `off_time`: This is the number of seconds the sound is off. The default is 1 second.
- n: This is the number of times the process will run. The default is None, which means forever.

- `background`: This determines whether or not to start a background thread to run the process. A `True` value runs the process in a background thread and returns right away. When set to `False`, return does not happen until the process is finished (please note that when n is `None`, the method never returns).

# Building a basic alarm system

Now let's build a basic alarm system around the buzzer. Hook up the PIR sensor to GPIO pin 4, and a latching push-button to GPIO pin 8. The following is the circuit diagram for our system:

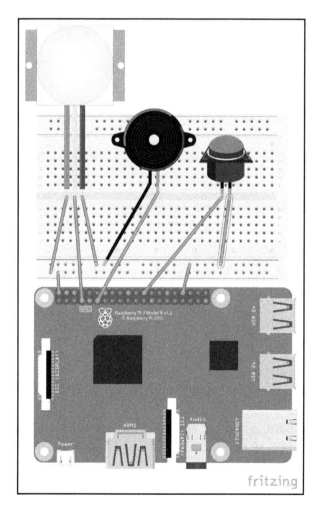

Create a new file in Thonny and call it `basic-alarm-system.py`. Type in the following and click on **Run**:

```python
from gpiozero import MotionSensor
from gpiozero import Buzzer
from gpiozero import Button
from time import sleep

buzzer = Buzzer(17)
motion_sensor = MotionSensor(4)
switch = Button(8)

while True:
    if switch.is_pressed:
        if motion_sensor.motion_detected:
            buzzer.beep(0.5,0.5, None, True)
            print('Intruder Alert')
            sleep(1)
        else:
            buzzer.off()
            print('Quiet')
            sleep(1)
    else:
        buzzer.off()
        sleep(1)
```

What we have done here is create an alarm system with our components. We are using a latching push-button to turn the alarm system on and off. We could easily replace the latching push-button with a key switch. The following picture shows this change:

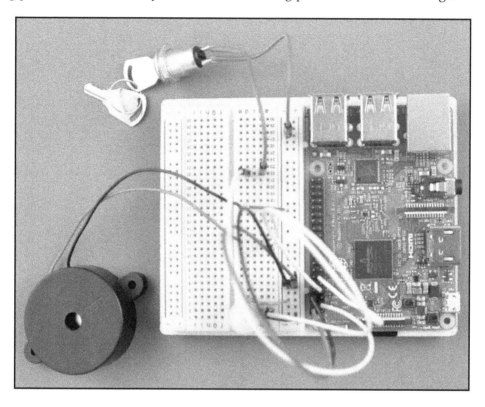

This circuit can easily be transferred to a project box for use as an alarm system.

# Modifying Hello LED using infrared sensor

We will continue our exploration of sensors by modifying our original Hello LED code. In this project, we will combine a distance sensor with our PIR sensor, and flash an LED based on the values of these sensors. This circuit will not only tell us that someone is approaching, but will also give us an indication of how close they are.

We will cover the following in this section:

- Configuring a distance sensor
- Taking Hello LED to another level

# Configuring a distance sensor

We will start by configuring the distance sensor and running some code. The following is a circuit diagram of our distance sensor circuit:

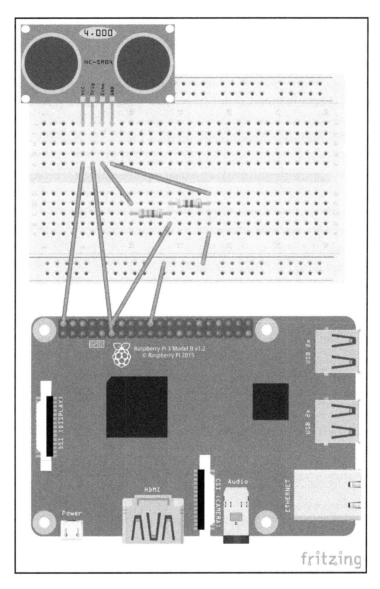

The following are the connections to be made:

- VCC from the motion sensor connects to the 5 V DC output from the Raspberry Pi
- GPIO pin 17 connects to Trig on the distance sensor
- Echo on the distance sensor connects to a 330 Ohm resistor
- GND on the distance sensor connects to GND on the Raspberry Pi and a 470 Ohm resistor
- The other end of the 330 Ohm resistor, from the echo pin on the distance sensor, connects to the 470 Ohm resistor (the two resistors create a voltage divider circuit)
- GPIO pin 18 from the Raspberry Pi connects to the intersection of the resistors

Of note in this circuit is the voltage divider that is created by the two resistors. We use this divider to connect GPIO pin 18.

Create a new Python file in Thonny and call it `distance-sensor-test.py`. Type in the following code and run it:

```
from gpiozero import DistanceSensor
from time import sleep

distance_sensor = DistanceSensor(echo=18, trigger=17)
while True:
    print('Distance: ', distance_sensor.distance*100)
    sleep(1)
```

You should see an output similar to following screenshot. As you place your hand, or any other object, in front of the distance sensor, the value printed to the **Shell** should change, as shown here:

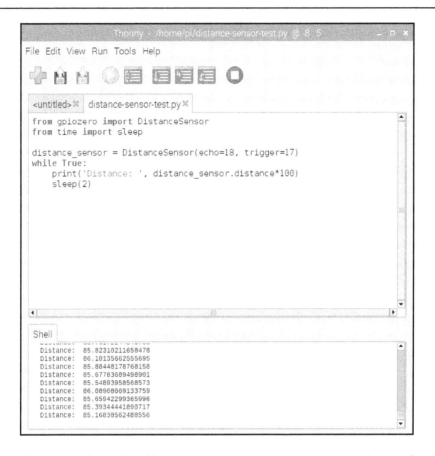

Be sure to have the distance sensor on a secure, non-moving surface, such as a breadboard.

# Taking Hello LED to another level

Our original `Hello LED!` system was a simple circuit, which involved making an LED, connected to the GPIO port, blink on and off. We have covered so much more since creating that circuit. We will take what we've learned and create a new `Hello LED` circuit. With this circuit, we will create an alarm system where the distance from the alarm is indicated by the blinking frequency of the LED.

The following is the circuit diagram for our new `Hello LED` system:

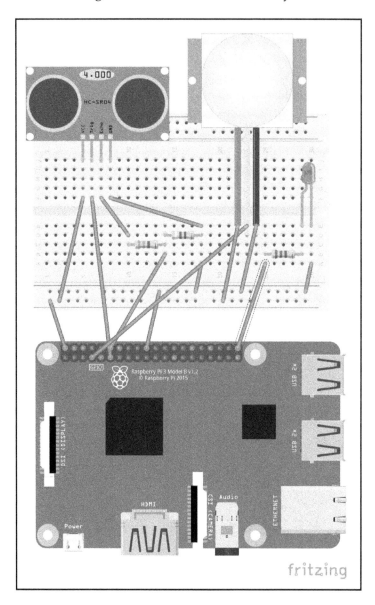

This may look a little complex, with wires going every which way; however, it is quite a simple circuit. The distance sensor part is the same as it was previously. For the other components, connect as follows:

- The PIR sensor's positive pin connects to 5V DC on the breadboard
- The PIR sensor's negative pin connects to GND on the breadboard
- The PIR sensor's signal pin connects to GPIO pin 4
- The LED's positive pin connects to GPIO pin 21 through a 220 Ohm resistor
- The LED's negative pin connects to GND on the breadboard

Create a new Python file in Thonny and call it `hello-led.py`. Type in the following code and run it:

```
from gpiozero import DistanceSensor
from gpiozero import MotionSensor
from gpiozero import LED
from time import sleep

distance_sensor = DistanceSensor(echo=18, trigger=17)
motion_sensor = MotionSensor(4)
led = LED(21)

while True:
    if(motion_sensor.motion_detected):
        blink_time=distance_sensor.distance
        led.blink(blink_time,blink_time,None,True)
    sleep(2)
```

The LED should start blinking as soon as motion is detected. The frequency of the LED's blinking will speed up as you place your hand closer and closer to the distance sensor.

# Summary

We should now be quite familiar with interacting with sensors and our Raspberry Pi. This chapter should be considered an exercise in creating sensory circuits using our Raspberry Pi with ease.

We will use this knowledge in `Chapter 9`, *Building a Home Security Dashboard*, where we will create an IoT home security dashboard.

# Questions

1. What is the difference between an active buzzer and a passive buzzer?
2. True or false? We check the `button.is_pressed` parameter to confirm whether or not our push-button has been pressed.
3. True or false? We require a voltage divider circuit in order to connect our PIR sensor.
4. What are the three different methods we can use to have our active buzzer beep on and off?
5. True or false? Push-buttons must connect directly to a circuit in order to be useful.
6. Which `DistanceSensor` parameter do we use to check the distance of an object from the distance sensor?
7. Which method from the Sense HAT emulator do we use to print pixels to the screen?
8. How would we set up our `MotionSensor` to read from GPIO pin 4?
9. True or false? Basic alarm systems are far too complicated for our Raspberry Pi to create.
10. True or false? The Sense HAT emulator may be used to interact with outside sensors connected to the GPIO.

# Further reading

Consult the GPIO Zero documentation `https://gpiozero.readthedocs.io/en/stable/` for further information on using this library.

# Building a Home Security
# Dashboard

# 9

In `Chapter 7`, *Setting Up a Raspberry Pi Web Server*, we were introduced to the web framework CherryPy. Using CherryPy, we are able to turn our Raspberry Pi into a web server. In `Chapter 8`, *Reading Raspberry Pi GPIO Sensor Data Using Python*, we learned how to read sensory data from the GPIO.

In this chapter, we will take the lessons that we learned from the previous two and create a home security dashboard.

The following topics will be covered in this chapter:

- Creating our dashboard using CherryPy
- Displaying sensory data on our dashboard

# Knowledge required to complete this chapter

The reader will need a working knowledge of the Python programming language to complete this chapter. A basic understanding of HTML, including CSS, is also required.

# Project overview

We will build two different home security dashboards in this chapter. The first one will involve the use of a temperature and humidity sensor, and the next one will involve an active buzzer.

This project should take a couple of hours to complete.

# Getting started

To complete this project, the following will be required:

- A Raspberry Pi Model 3 (2015 model or newer)
- A USB power supply
- A computer monitor
- A USB keyboard
- A USB mouse
- A breadboard
- A DHT11 temperature sensor
- A latching push-button, switch, or key switch
- A PIR sensor
- An active buzzer
- A Raspberry Pi camera module

# Creating our dashboard using CherryPy

To create our home security dashboard, we will modify the code we wrote in Chapter 7, *Setting Up a Raspberry Pi Web Server*. These modifications include adding sensory data from the GPIO—something we became very good at by the end of Chapter 8, *Reading Raspberry Pi GPIO Sensor Data Using Python*.

Two of the inputs, the temperature and humidity sensor and the Pi camera, will require additional steps so that we can integrate them into our dashboard.

# Using the DHT11 to find temperature and humidity

The DHT11 temperature and humidity sensor is a low-cost hobbyist-grade sensor, capable of providing basic measurements. The DHT11 comes in two different versions, the four-pin model and the three-pin model.

We will be using the three-pin model for our project (see the following picture):

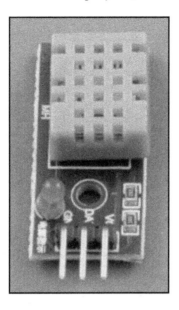

The library we will be using to read DHT11 data, the Adafruit DHT library, does not come pre-installed on Raspbian (as of the time of writing). To install it, we will clone the library's GitHub project and build it from the source.

Open up a Terminal window, and type the following command to use git and download the source code (at the time of writing, git came pre-installed with Raspbian):

```
git clone https://github.com/adafruit/Adafruit_Python_DHT.git
```

You should see the progress of the code downloading. Now, change directories by using the following command:

```
cd Adafruit_Python_DHT
```

You will be in the source code directory.

Build the project with the following command:

```
sudo python3 setup.py install
```

You should see the progress displayed in the Terminal:

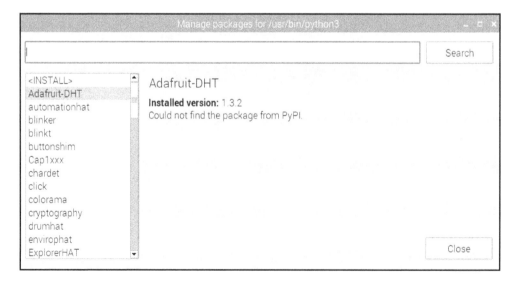

If you do not receive any errors, the `Adafruit DHT` library should now be installed on your Raspberry Pi. To verify this, open up Thonny and check the packages:

Now, let's wire up the circuit. Connect the DHT11 sensor to the Raspberry Pi as follows:

- GND from DHT11 to GND on the Raspberry Pi
- VCC on DHT11 to 5V DC on the Raspberry Pi
- Signal on the DHT11 to GPIO pin 19

See the following Fritzing diagram for more information:

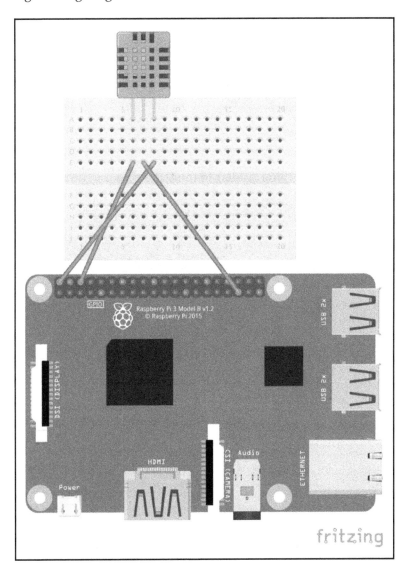

Once the DHT11 is wired up, it is time to write some code:

1. Open up Thonny from **Application Menu** | **Programming** | **Thonny Python IDE**
2. Click on **New** to create a new file
3. Type the following into the file:

```
import Adafruit_DHT

dht_sensor = Adafruit_DHT.DHT11
pin = 19
humidity, temperature = Adafruit_DHT.read_retry(dht_sensor, pin)

print(humidity)
print(temperature)
```

4. Save the file as `dht-test.py`
5. Run the code
6. You should see something similar to the following:

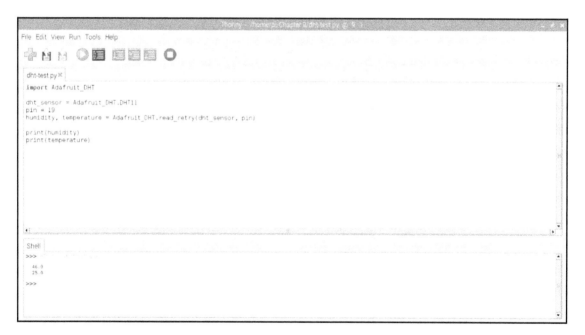

Let's take a look at the code. We will start by importing the `Adafruit_DHT` library. We then create a new `DHT11` object, and call it `dht_sensor`. The `humidity` and `temperature` are set from the `read_retry` method on the `Adafruit_DHT` class.

We then print out the values of `humidity` and `temperature` to the shell.

# Using the Pi camera to take a photo

In `Chapter 3`, *Using the GPIO to Connect to the Outside World,* we tried out the special Raspberry Pi camera module and wrote code to turn on a camera preview. It's time to put the camera to use.

Install a Raspberry Pi camera module onto the Raspberry Pi through the CSI camera port (be sure to enable the camera in the Raspberry Pi Configuration screen, if it's not already enabled). Let's write some code:

1. Open up Thonny from **Application Menu | Programming | Thonny Python IDE**
2. Click on **New** to create a new file
3. Type the following into the file:

```
from picamera import PiCamera
from time import sleep

pi_cam = PiCamera()

pi_cam.start_preview()
sleep(5)
pi_cam.capture('/home/pi/myimage.png')
pi_cam.stop
```

4. Save the file as `pi-camera-test.py`
5. Run the code

This program imports `PiCamera` and sleeps before creating a new `PiCamera` object called `pi_cam`. The `start_preview` method shows us what the camera sees in a full screen.

The capture method creates a new image file called `myimage.png`, and stores it in the default directory `/home/pi`.

We have 5 seconds to position our camera before a photo is taken.

The following is a picture of my work area, taken with the Raspberry Pi camera:

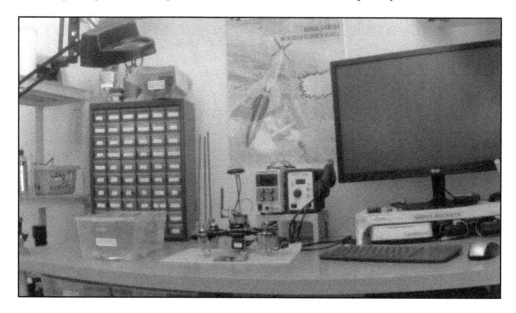

# Creating our dashboard using CherryPy

In Chapter 7, *Setting Up a Raspberry Pi Web Server*, we created a weather dashboard using the Bootstrap framework with the WeatherDashboardHTML.py file. We will revisit that code and modify it for our home security dashboard.

To create our home security dashboard, do the following:

1. Open up Thonny from **Application Menu** | **Programming** | **Thonny Python IDE**
2. Click on **New** to create a new file
3. Type the following into the file:

```
import cherrypy
from SecurityData import SecurityData

class SecurityDashboard:
    def __init__(self, securityData):
        self.securityData = securityData
    @cherrypy.expose
    def index(self):
        return """
```

```html
<!DOCTYPE html>
<html lang="en">

<head>
    <title>Home Security Dashboard</title>
    <meta charset="utf-8">
    <meta name="viewport"
        content="width=device-width,
        initial-scale=1">

    <meta http-equiv="refresh" content="30">

    <link rel="stylesheet"
        href="https://maxcdn.bootstrapcdn.com
        /bootstrap/4.1.0/css/bootstrap.min.css">

    <link rel="stylesheet" href="led.css">

    <script src="https://ajax.googleapis.com
        /ajax/libs/jquery/3.3.1/jquery.min.js">
    </script>

    <script src="https://cdnjs.cloudflare.com
        /ajax/libs/popper.js/1.14.0
        /umd/popper.min.js">
    </script>

    <script src="https://maxcdn.bootstrapcdn.com
        /bootstrap/4.1.0/js/bootstrap.min.js">
    </script>

    <style>
        .element-box {
            border-radius: 10px;
            border: 2px solid #C8C8C8;
            padding: 20px;
        }

        .card {
            width: 600px;
        }

        .col {
            margin: 10px;
        }
    </style>
</head>
```

```
<body>
    <div class="container">
        <br/>
        <div class="card">
            <div class="card-header">
                <h3>Home Security Dashboard</h3>
            </div>
            <div class="card-body">
                <div class="row">
                    <div class="col element-box">
                        <h6>Armed</h6>
                        <div class = """ +
                            self.securityData
                            .getArmedStatus() +
                        """>
                        </div>
                    </div>
                    <div class="col element-box">
                        <h6>Temp / Humidity</h6>
                        <p>""" + self.securityData
                            .getRoomConditions()
                        + """</p>
                    </div>
                    <div class="col element-box">
                        <h6>Last Check:</h6>
                        <p>""" + self
                            .securityData.getTime()
                        + """</p>
                    </div>
                </div>
            </div>
            <div class="card-footer"
                    align="center">

                <img src=""" + self.securityData
                    .getSecurityImage() + """/>
                <p>""" + self.securityData
                    .getDetectedMessage() + """</p>
            </div>
        </div>
    </div>
</body>

</html>
"""
if __name__=="__main__":
    securityData = SecurityData()
    conf = {
```

```
                    '/led.css':{
                        'tools.staticfile.on': True,
                        'tools.staticfile.filename': '/home/pi/styles/led.css'
                        },
                    '/intruder.png':{
                        'tools.staticfile.on': True,
                        'tools.staticfile.filename':
                            '/home/pi/images/intruder.png'
                        },
                    '/all-clear.png':{
                        'tools.staticfile.on': True,
                        'tools.staticfile.filename': '/home/pi/images
                            /all-clear.png'
                        },
                    '/not-armed.png':{
                        'tools.staticfile.on': True,
                        'tools.staticfile.filename': '/home/pi
                            /images/not-armed.png'
                        }
                }
            cherrypy.quickstart(SecurityDashboard(securityData),'/',conf)
```

4. Save the file as `security-dashboard.py`

Do not run the code yet, as we still have to create the `SecurityData` class.

As you can see, we've made a few changes to `WeatherDashboardHTML.py` in order to create `security-dashboard.py`. Before we run the code, let's point out a few of the changes.

The most obvious change is the use of the `SecurityData` class. As you can imagine, this class will be used to obtain data for our dashboard:

```
from SecurityData import SecurityData
```

We use the following line to automatically refresh our page every 30 seconds (we did not automatically refresh our weather dashboard, as weather data does not change often):

```
<meta http-equiv="refresh" content="30">
```

For our home security dashboard, we use a bit of CSS magic to represent a blinking LED. This is accomplished by the adding the `led.css` file:

```
<link rel="stylesheet" href="led.css">
```

For the data fields, we will access methods from our `SecurityData` object. We will go into more detail on these methods in the upcoming section. For our main section, we will create a dictionary called `conf`:

```
if __name__=="__main__":
    securityData = SecurityData()
    conf = {
        '/led.css':{
            'tools.staticfile.on': True,
            'tools.staticfile.filename': '/home/pi/styles/led.css'
            },
        '/intruder.png':{
            'tools.staticfile.on': True,
            'tools.staticfile.filename':
                '/home/pi/images/intruder.png'
            },
        '/all-clear.png':{
            'tools.staticfile.on': True,
            'tools.staticfile.filename': '/home/pi/images
                /all-clear.png'
            },
        '/not-armed.png':{
            'tools.staticfile.on': True,
            'tools.staticfile.filename': '/home/pi
                /images/not-armed.png'
            }
        }
    cherrypy.quickstart(SecurityDashboard(securityData),'/',conf)
```

We use the `conf` dictionary to pass configuration data to the `cherrypy` `quickstart` method. This configuration data allows us to use the static files `led.css`, `intruder.png`, `all-clear.png`, and `not-armed.png` with our CherryPy server.

The CSS file `led.css` was mentioned previously. The other three files are self-described images that are used in our dashboard.

 In order to use static files or directories with CherryPy, you must create and then pass in configuration information. An absolute path (as opposed to a relative path) must be part of the configuration information.

The configuration information states that the CSS and image files are located in the directories named `styles` and `images`, respectively. These directories are both located in the `/home/pi` directory.

The following is a screenshot of the files in the `images` directory (be sure to place your files in the correct directories):

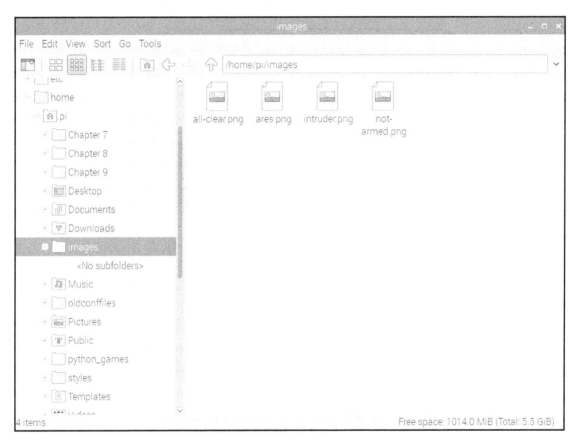

# Displaying sensory data on our dashboard

To provide our dashboard data, we will create a new Python file called `SecurityData.py` where we will store the `SecurityData` class. Before we do that, let's build our circuit.

# Home security dashboard with a temperature sensor

We will build our first version of the home security dashboard with a DHT11 temperature and humidity sensor, a PIR sensor, and a latching button (or key switch). The following is the Fritzing diagram for our home security dashboard:

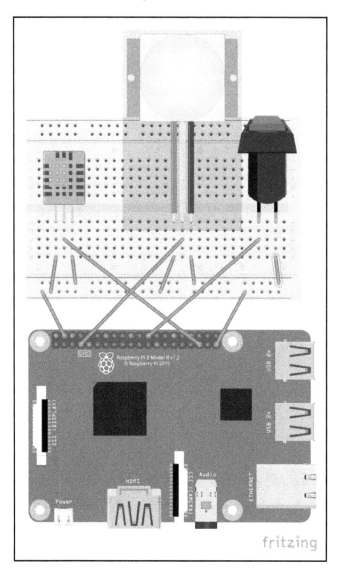

The circuit connects as follows:

- GND from DHT11 to GND
- VCC on DHT11 to 5V DC
- Signal on the DHT11 to GPIO pin 19
- GND from PIR sensor to GND
- VCC on PIR sensor to 5V DC
- Signal on PIR sensor to GPIO pin4
- One end of the latching button to GPIO pin 8
- The other end of the latching button to GND
- Pi camera module to CSI port (not shown)

Following is a photo of our circuit. One thing to note is the separate breadboard for our DHT11 sensor (easier to fit on a micro breadboard), as well as the key switch in place of a latching button:

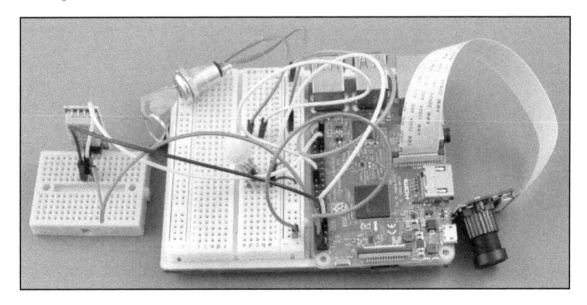

Now it's time to write the code:

1. Open up Thonny from **Application Menu | Programming | Thonny Python IDE**
2. Click on **New** to create a new file

3. Type the following into the file:

```
from gpiozero import MotionSensor
from gpiozero import Button
from datetime import datetime
from picamera import PiCamera
import Adafruit_DHT

class SecurityData:
    humidity=''
    temperature=''
    detected_message=''



    dht_pin = 19
    dht_sensor = Adafruit_DHT.DHT11
    switch = Button(8)
    motion_sensor = MotionSensor(4)
    pi_cam = PiCamera()
    def getRoomConditions(self):
        humidity, temperature = Adafruit_DHT
            .read_retry(self.dht_sensor, self.dht_pin)

        return str(temperature) + 'C / ' + str(humidity) + '%'
    def getDetectedMessage(self):
        return self.detected_message
    def getArmedStatus(self):
        if self.switch.is_pressed:
            return "on"
        else:
            return "off"

    def getSecurityImage(self):
        if not(self.switch.is_pressed):
            self.detected_message = ''
            return "/not-armed.png"
        elif self.motion_sensor.motion_detected:
            self.pi_cam.resolution = (500, 375)
            self.pi_cam.capture("/home/pi/images/intruder.png")
            self.detected_message = "Detected at: " +
                self.getTime()
            return "/intruder.png"

        else:
            self.detected_message = ''
            return "/all-clear.png"
    def getTime(self):
```

```
                        return datetime.now().strftime('%Y-%m-%d %H:%M:%S')
        if __name__ == "__main__":
            while True:
                security_data = SecurityData()
                print(security_data.getRoomConditions())
                print(security_data.getArmedStatus())
                print(security_data.getTime())
```

4. Save the file as `SecurityData.py`
5. Run the code

You should get an output to the shell indicating the `temperature` and `humidity` level in the room, an `on` or `off` indicating the position of the switch, and the current time. Try turning the switch on and off to see if the value changes in the output.

Before we run the dashboard code (`security-dashboard.py`), let's review the `SecurityData` class. As we can see, the first part of the code is standard boilerplate code that we have already become familiar with. The `getRoomConditions` and `getDetectedMessage` methods are either self-explanatory or something we have already covered.

Our `getArmedStatus` method does a little trick to keep our code simple and compact:

```
def getArmedStatus(self):
    if self.switch.is_pressed:
        return "on"
    else:
        return "off"
```

We can see that `getArmedStatus` returns either `on` or `off`, not `True` or `False` as most methods with a binary return do. We do this for the armed section of our dashboard code.

Here is the HTML-generated code from the `index` method of the `SecurityDashboard` class:

```
<div class="col element-box">
    <h6>Armed</h6>
    <div class = """ + self.securityData.getArmedStatus() + """>
    </div>
</div>
```

As we can see, the `getArmedStatus` method is called during the construction of the a div tag in place of the CSS class name. The words `on` and `off` refer to CSS classes in our `led.css` file. When `on` is returned, we get a blinking red LED-type graphic. When `off` is returned, we get a black dot.

Thus, the position of the latching switch (or key switch) determines whether or not the div tag has a CSS class name of on or a CSS class name of off through the getArmedStatus method of the SecurityData class.

Our code gets really interesting with the getSecurityImage method:

```
def getSecurityImage(self):
        if not(self.switch.is_pressed):
            self.detected_message = ''
            return "/not-armed.png"
        elif self.motion_sensor.motion_detected:
            self.pi_cam.resolution = (500, 375)
            self.pi_cam.capture("/home/pi/images/intruder.png")
            self.detected_message = "Detected at: " +
                self.getTime()
            return "/intruder.png"

        else:
            self.detected_message = ''
            return "/all-clear.png"
```

Our first conditional statement checks to see whether the circuit is armed (switch is in the on position). If it's not armed, then all that we need to do is set the detected message to nothing, and return a reference to the not-armed.png file (/not-armed.png was defined in the configuration information that we set up in the security-dashboard.py file).

If we take a look at the code in the SecurityDashboard class (security-dashboard.py file), we can see that the getSecurityImage method is called near the bottom of the generated HTML code:

```
<div class="card-footer" align="center">
    <img src=""" + self.securityData.getSecurityImage() + """/>
    <p>""" + self.securityData.getDetectedMessage() + """</p>
</div>
```

If the switch in our circuit is not on, we will get the following in our dashboard footer with no description after it (blank detected_message value):

The second conditional statement in our code is reached when the switch is on and motion has been detected. In this case, we set the resolution of our Pi camera and then take a photo.

 We probably could have set the resolution of the Pi camera during the instantiation of the class, and this would probably have made more sense. However, putting this line here makes it easier to adjust the resolution prior to completing the code, as the line exists in the method we are focusing on.

We call the file `intruder.png` and store it in the location where the configuration code in the `security-dashboard.py` file can find it.

We also create a `detected_message` value based on the current time. This message will provide a timestamp to the image we acquire from the Pi camera.

The final `else:` statement is where we return `/all-clear.png`. By the time our code has reached this point, we know that the switch is on and there hasn't been any motion detected. The image we will see at the footer of our dashboard will be the following:

As with the NOT ARMED message, there won't be a description after ALL CLEAR. We will only see this graphic when the switch is on and the PIR sensor did not pick up any motion (`motion_detected` is false).

Now, let's run the dashboard code. If you haven't done so already, stop the `SecurityData` program by clicking on the red button. Click on the tab for the `security-dashboard.py` file, and click **Run**. Wait a few seconds in order to let CherryPy get running.

Open up a web browser, and navigate to the following address:

```
http://127.0.0.1:8080
```

With the switch in the `off` position, you should see the following dashboard screen:

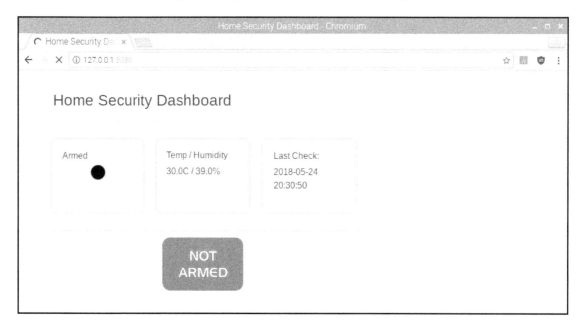

As we can see, the LED under the **Armed** section is black, and we get a NOT ARMED message in the footer. We can also see that `temperature` and `humidity` are displayed, even though the system is not armed.

The **Last Check** box shows us when the code last checked the status of the switch. If you wait 30 seconds, you should see the page refresh with the same information.

Now, turn on the switch, and stand back so that the PIR sensor does not detect you. You should see a screen similar to the following:

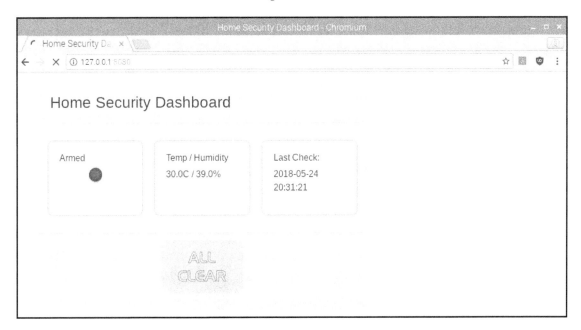

You will notice that the LED in the **Armed** section now turns to a flashing red, the `temperature` and `humidity` readings are either the same or slightly different, the **Last Check** has been updated to the current time, and the `ALL CLEAR` message appears in the footer.

Let's see if we can capture an intruder. Point the Pi camera to a doorway, and wait for the PIR sensor to trigger:

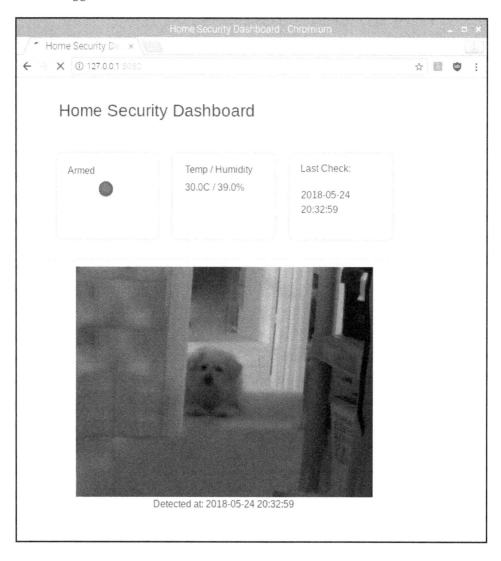

It appears that we have caught our intruder!

# Home security dashboard with quick response

You may have noticed that it takes a really long time for our page to refresh. This is due to the 30-second refresh time, of course, as well as the long time it takes for the DHT11 to read a value.

Let's change our code to make it quicker, and give it a buzzer to scare away an intruders.

Replace the DHT11 with a buzzer connected to GPIO pin 17 (we shouldn't need a Fritzing diagram for this simple change).

We will start by creating the `SecurityDataQuick` data class:

1. Open up Thonny from **Application Menu | Programming | Thonny Python IDE**
2. Click on **New** to create a new file
3. Type the following into the file:

```python
from gpiozero import MotionSensor
from gpiozero import Button
from datetime import datetime
from picamera import PiCamera
from gpiozero import Buzzer
from time import sleep

class SecurityData:
    alarm_status=''
    detected_message=''
    switch = Button(8)
    motion_sensor = MotionSensor(4)
    pi_cam = PiCamera()
    buzzer = Buzzer(17)
    def sound_alarm(self):
        self.buzzer.beep(0.5,0.5, 5, True)
        sleep(1)
    def getAlarmStatus(self):
        if not(self.switch.is_pressed):
            self.alarm_status = 'not-armed'
            return "Not Armed"
        elif self.motion_sensor.motion_detected:
            self.alarm_status = 'motion-detected'
            self.sound_alarm()
            return "Motion Detected"

        else:
            self.alarm_status = 'all-clear'
```

```
                    return "All Clear"
        def getDetectedMessage(self):
            return self.detected_message
        def getArmedStatus(self):
            if self.switch.is_pressed:
                return "on"
            else:
                return "off"

        def getSecurityImage(self):
            if self.alarm_status=='not-armed':
                self.detected_message = ''
                return "/not-armed.png"
            elif self.alarm_status=='motion-detected':
                self.pi_cam.resolution = (500, 375)
                self.pi_cam.capture("/home/pi/images/intruder.png")

                self.detected_message = "Detected at: " +
                    self.getTime()

                return "/intruder.png"

            else:
                self.detected_message = ''
                return "/all-clear.png"
        def getTime(self):
            return datetime.now().strftime('%Y-%m-%d %H:%M:%S')
if __name__ == "__main__":
        while True:
            security_data = SecurityData()
            print(security_data.getArmedStatus())
            print(security_data.getTime())
```

4. Save the file as `SecurityDataQuick.py`

5. Run the code

In our shell, we should see the values of the switch and current time. Stop the program by clicking on the red button.

As we can see, there have been a few changes. One change we did not make was changing the class name. Keeping it as `SecurityData` means fewer changes for our dashboard code later on.

We added the library for the `GPIO Zero` buzzer, and have removed any code relating to the DHT11 sensor. We have also created a new method called `sound_buzzer`, which we will call in the event that an intruder is detected.

A new variable called `alarm_status` has been added, with a corresponding `getAlarmStatus` method. We have moved the core logic of our class to this method (away from `getSecurityImage`), as it is here where we check on the status of our switch and PIR sensor. The variable, `alarm_status`, is used elsewhere to determine if a photo is to be taken. We also sound the alarm in this method if an intruder is detected.

As a result of adding the new method, we change `getSecurityImage`. By using `alarm_status` in the `getSecurityImage` method, we do not need to check the status of the sensors. We may now use `getSecurityImage` for its intended use—taking a photo if an intruder has been detected.

It's now time to change the dashboard code:

1. Open up Thonny from **Application Menu | Programming | Thonny Python IDE**
2. Click on **New** to create a new file
3. Type the following into the file:

```python
import cherrypy
from SecurityDataQuick import SecurityData

class SecurityDashboard:

    def __init__(self, securityData):
        self.securityData = securityData

    @cherrypy.expose
    def index(self):
        return """
            <!DOCTYPE html>
            <html lang="en">

            <head>
                <title>Home Security Dashboard</title>
                <meta charset="utf-8">

                <meta name="viewport" content="width=device-
            width, initial-scale=1">

                <meta http-equiv="refresh" content="2">

                <link rel="stylesheet"
            href="https://maxcdn.bootstrapcdn.com
                /bootstrap/4.1.0/css/bootstrap.min.css">
```

```
                    <link rel="stylesheet" href="led.css">

                    <script src="https://ajax.googleapis.com
            /ajax/libs/jquery/3.3.1/jquery.min.js">
                    </script>

                    <script src="https://cdnjs.cloudflare.com
            /ajax/libs/popper.js/1.14.0
            /umd/popper.min.js">
                    </script>

                    <script src="https://maxcdn.bootstrapcdn.com
            /bootstrap/4.1.0/js/bootstrap.min.js">
                    </script>

                    <style>
                        .element-box {
                            border-radius: 10px;
                            border: 2px solid #C8C8C8;
                            padding: 20px;
                        }

                        .card {
                            width: 600px;
                        }

                        .col {
                            margin: 10px;
                        }
                    </style>
            </head>

            <body>
                <div class="container">
                    <br />
                    <div class="card">
                        <div class="card-header">
                            <h3>Home Security Dashboard</h3>
                        </div>
                        <div class="card-body">
                            <div class="row">
                                <div class="col element-box">
                                    <h4>Armed</h4>

                                    <div class=""" + self
            .securityData
            .getArmedStatus()
            + """>
```

```
                                </div>
                            </div>

                            <div class="col element-box">
                                <h4>Status</h4>
                                <p>""" + self.securityData
                                    .getAlarmStatus()
                                    + """</p>
                            </div>

                            <div class="col element-box">
                                <h4>Last Check:</h4>

                                <p>""" + self.securityData
                                    .getTime() + """
                                </p>
                            </div>
                        </div>
                    </div>
                    <div class="card-footer" align="center">
                        <img src=""" + self.securityData
        .getSecurityImage() + """ />
                        <p>""" + self.securityData
                            .getDetectedMessage() + """</p>
                    </div>
                </div>
            </div>
        </body>

        </html>
        """

    if __name__=="__main__":
        securityData = SecurityData()
        conf = {
            '/led.css':{
            'tools.staticfile.on': True,
            'tools.staticfile.filename': '/home/pi/styles/led.css'
            },
            '/intruder.png':{
            'tools.staticfile.on': True,
            'tools.staticfile.filename': '/home/pi
            /images/intruder.png'
            },
            '/all-clear.png':{
            'tools.staticfile.on': True,
            'tools.staticfile.filename': '/home/pi
            /images/all-clear.png'
```

```
            },
            '/not-armed.png':{
            'tools.staticfile.on': True,
            'tools.staticfile.filename': '/home/pi
            /images/not-armed.png'
            }
        }
    cherrypy.quickstart(SecurityDashboard(securityData),'/',conf)
```

4. Save the file as `SecurityDataQuick.py`
5. Run the code
6. Navigate back to your web browser and refresh the dashboard page

Our dashboard should now match the following screenshots:

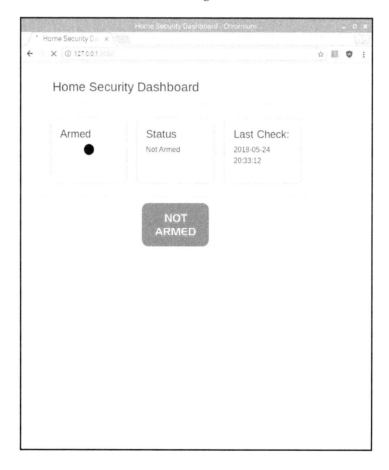

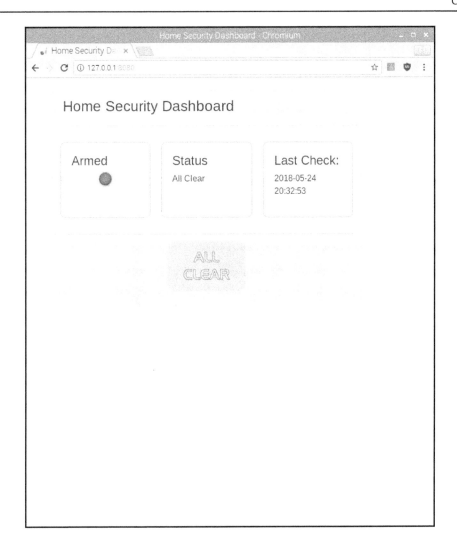

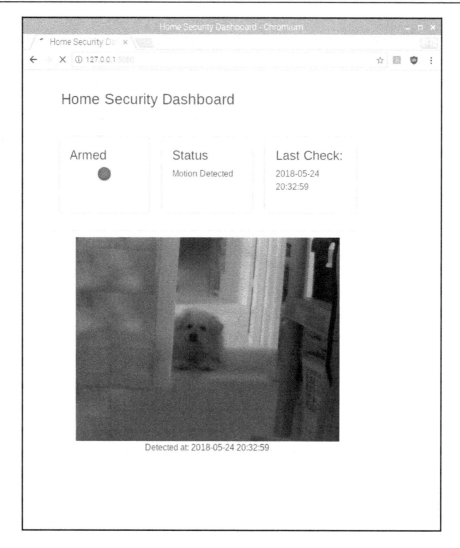

Our dashboard should refresh every two seconds instead of 30, and a buzzer should sound when motion is detected in armed mode.

Let's take a look at the code. The changes to our dashboard are pretty self-explanatory. Of note, however, is the change to the middle box on our dashboard:

```
<div class="col element-box">
    <h4>Status</h4>
    <p>""" + self.securityData.getAlarmStatus() + """</p>
</div>
```

We replaced room `temperature` and `humidity` with the status of the switch and PIR sensor through the `getAlarmStatus` method. With this change, we are able to use the `getAlarmStatus` method as our `initialization` method where we set the status of the `SecurityData` class variable `alarm_status`.

 If we really wanted to be sticklers about it, we could change our code so that we initialize the `SecurityData` class with the values of the switch and PIR sensor. As it stands, `SecurityData` is more of a utility type class where certain methods must be called before others. We'll let it slide for now.

# Summary

As we can see, building a security application with the Raspberry Pi is pretty easy. Although we our viewing our dashboard and hosting our sensors on the same Raspberry Pi, it is not too difficult to set up the Raspberry Pi to serve up the dashboard to other computers in your network (or even the internet). In `Chapter 10`, *Publishing to Web Services*, we will take our interaction with
sensory data a step further and publish it to the internet.

# Questions

1. True or false? The DHT11 sensor is an expensive and highly accurate sensor for temperature and humidity.
2. True or false? The DHT11 sensor can detect UV rays from the sun.
3. True or false? Code needed to run the DHT11 comes pre-installed with Raspbian.
4. How do you set the resolution of the Pi camera module?
5. How do you set up CherryPy so that it can access local static files?
6. How do you set up an automatic refresh for a web page?
7. True or false? Through the use of CSS, we are able to simulate a flashing LED.
8. What is the purpose of the `SecurityData` class?
9. Who or what did we find as our intruder?
10. If we wanted to be sticklers, how would we change our `SecurityData` class?

# Further reading

The refresh method used in our code is effective, but a little clunky. Our dashboards may be improved through the use of AJAX code, where the fields are updated but not the page. Please consult the CherryPy documentation for further information.

# 10
# Publishing to Web Services

At the heart of the IoT are web services that allow interaction with physical devices. In this chapter, we will explore the use of web services for the purposes of displaying sensory data from our Raspberry Pi. We will also look into Twilio, a text messaging service, and how we can use this service to send ourselves a text message from our Raspberry Pi.

The following topics will be covered in this chapter:

- Publishing sensory data to cloud-based services
- Setting up an account for text message transmission

## Project overview

In this chapter, we will write code to display our sensory data to an IoT dashboard. As well as this, we will also explore Twilio, a text messaging service. We will then put these two concepts together to enhance the home security dashboard that we built in `Chapter 9`, *Building a Home Security Dashboard*.

## Getting started

To complete this project, the following will be required:

- A Raspberry Pi Model 3 (2015 model or newer)
- A USB power supply
- A computer monitor
- A USB keyboard
- A USB mouse

- A breadboard
- Jumper wires
- A DHT-11 temperature sensor
- A PIR sensor
- A push-button (latching)
- A key switch (optional)

# Publishing sensory data to cloud-based services

In this section, we will publish sensory data to an online dashboard using the MQTT protocol. This will involve setting up an account with the ThingsBoard website and making use of the demo environment.

## Install the MQTT library

We will use the MQTT protocol in order to communicate with the dashboard in ThingsBoard. To set up the library on the Raspberry Pi, do the following:

1. Open a Terminal appliance from the main tool bar
2. Type **sudo pip3 install pho-mqtt**
3. You should see the library install

## Set up an account and create a device

To start, navigate to the ThingsBoard website at www.thingsboard.io:

1. Click on the **TRY IT NOW** button at the top of the screen. Scroll down and click on the **LIVE DEMO** button under the **Thing Board Community Edition** section:

2. You will be presented with a sign-up window. Enter the appropriate information to set up an account. Once your account has been successfully set up, you will see a dialog showing the following:

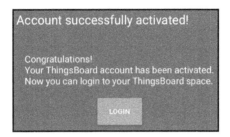

3. Click on **LOGIN** to get into the app. After this, you should see a menu at the left-hand side of the screen:

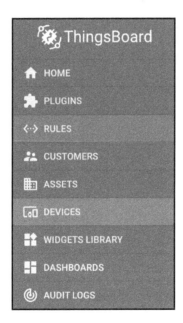

4. Click on **DEVICES**. Look for a round orange graphic with a plus sign at the bottom right-hand side of the screen, as follows:

5. Click on this orange circle to add a new device. Type Room Conditions for the **Name\*** and select **default** for the **Device type\*** in the **Add Device** dialog. Do not select **Is gateway**. Click on **ADD**:

6. You should see a new box under your **Devices**, named **Room Conditions**:

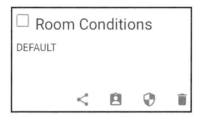

7. Click on this box and a menu should slide from the right. Click on the **COPY ACCESS TOKEN** button to copy this token to your clipboard:

What we have done here is set up a ThingsBoard account and a new device inside ThingsBoard. We will use this device to retrieve sensory information from our Raspberry Pi and make a dashboard of these values.

# Reading sensory data and publishing to ThingsBoard

It's now time to create our circuit and code. Install the DHT-11 sensor using GPIO pin 19 (refer to Chapter 9, *Building a Home Security Dashboard*, if you are unsure of how to connect the DHT-11 sensor to the Raspberry Pi):

1. Open up Thonny and create a new file called dht11-mqtt.py. Type the following into the file and run it. Be sure to paste in the access token from your clipboard:

```
from time import sleep
import Adafruit_DHT
import paho.mqtt.client as mqtt
import json

host = 'demo.thingsboard.io'
access_token = '<<access token>>'
dht_sensor = Adafruit_DHT.DHT11
pin = 19

sensor_data = {'temperature': 0, 'humidity': 0}
```

```
client = mqtt.Client()
client.username_pw_set(access_token)

while True:
    humidity, temperature = Adafruit_DHT
        .read_retry(dht_sensor, pin)

    print(u"Temperature: {:g}\u00b0C, Humidity
        {:g}%".format(temperature, humidity))

    sensor_data['temperature'] = temperature
    sensor_data['humidity'] = humidity
    client.connect(host, 1883, 20)
    client.publish('v1/devices/me/telemetry',
        json.dumps(sensor_data), 1)
    client.disconnect()
    sleep(10)
```

2. You should see an output in the shell similar to the following screenshot:

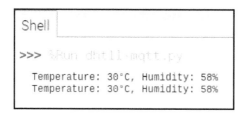

3. There should be a new line every 10 seconds. As you can see, it's pretty hot and humid in the room.

Let's take a closer look at the preceding code:

1. Our import statements give us access to the modules needed for our code:

```
from time import sleep
import Adafruit_DHT
import paho.mqtt.client as mqtt
import json
```

We are already familiar with sleep, Adafruit_DHT, and json. The Paho MQTT library gives us access to the client object, which we will use to publish our sensory data to the dashboard.

2. The next two lines in the code are used to set variables for the URL of the demo server and the access token we retrieved from our device previously. We require both of these values in order to connect to the MQTT server and publish our sensory data:

```
host = 'demo.thingsboard.io'
access_token = '<<access token>>'
```

3. We define the dht_sensor variable as a DHT11 object from the Adafruit library. And we use pin 19 for the sensor:

```
dht_sensor = Adafruit_DHT.DHT11
pin = 19
```

4. We then define a dictionary object to store the sensory data that will be published to the MQTT server:

```
sensor_data = {'temperature': 0, 'humidity': 0}
```

5. We then create a client object of the mqtt Client type. The username and password is set with the access_token defined previously in the code:

```
client = mqtt.Client()
client.username_pw_set(access_token)
```

6. The continuous while loop contains the code that reads the sensory data, and then publishes it to the MQTT server. The humidity and temperature are set by reading from the read_retry method, and we set the corresponding sensor_data dictionary values as follows:

```
while True:
    humidity, temperature = Adafruit_DHT
                        .read_retry(dht_sensor, pin)

    print(u"Temperature: {:g}\u00b0C, Humidity
            {:g}%".format(temperature, humidity))

    sensor_data['temperature'] = temperature
    sensor_data['humidity'] = humidity
```

7. The following `client` code is the code responsible for publishing our sensory data to the MQTT server. We connect using the `connect` method of the `client` object passing in the host value, the port (default port), and a keepalive time of `20` seconds. Unlike many MQTT examples, we do not create a loop and look for a callback, as we are only interested in publishing the sensory value, and not subscribing to the topic. In this case, the topic we are publishing to is `v1/devices/me/telemetry`, as per the ThingsBoard documentation example code. We then disconnect from `client`:

```
client.connect(host, 1883, 20)
client.publish('v1/devices/me/telemetry',
          json.dumps(sensor_data), 1)
client.disconnect()
sleep(10)
```

We will now create a dashboard in ThingsBoard to display the sensory values sent from our code.

# Creating a dashboard in ThingsBoard

The following are the steps to add the humidity value to a dashboard:

1. Navigate back to ThingsBoard and click on **Devices**, and then **ROOM CONDITIONS**. The side menu should slide from the right:

2. Click on the **LATEST TELEMETRY** tab.

3. You should see values for **humidity** and **temperature**, and the time when these values were last updated. Select **humidity** by clicking on the check box to the left. Now, click on **SHOW ON WIDGET**:

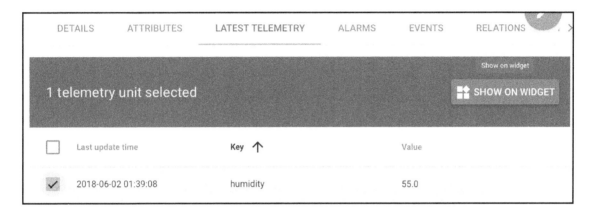

4. Select the **Current bundle** to **Analogue gauges** and cycle through the gauges until you get to the **humidity** dial widget. Click on the **ADD TO DASHBOARD** button:

5. Select **Create new dashboard** and type in `Room Conditions` as the name:

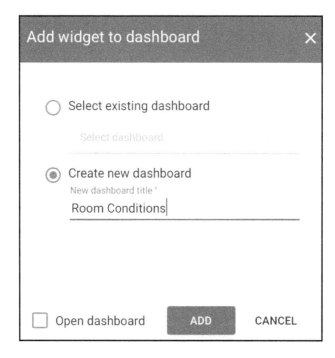

6. Do not select the **Open dashboard** checkbox. Click on the **ADD** button.

7. Repeat the previous steps for the temperature value. Select a temperature widget, and add your widget to the **Room Conditions** dashboard. This time, select **Open dashboard** before clicking on **ADD**:

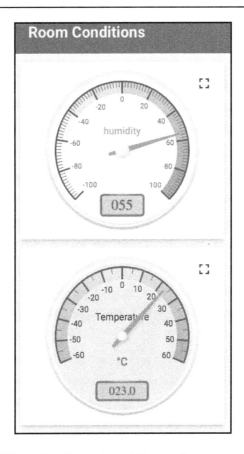

You should now see a dashboard with the humidity and temperature values shown in analogue dials.

# Sharing your dashboard with a friend

If you would like to make this dashboard public, so that others may see it, you need to do the following:

1. Navigate to the dashboards screen by clicking on **DASHBOARDS**:

2. Click on the **Make dashboard public** option:

3. You will see the dialog reading **Dashboard is now public**, as shown in the following screenshot. You may copy and paste the URL, or share it via social media:

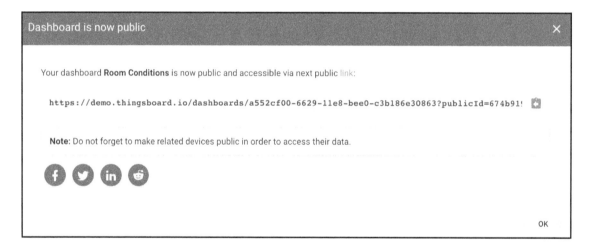

# Setting up an account for text message transmission

In this section, we will connect to a text message transmission service and send a text message from our Raspberry Pi to our phone. We will use this information, and what we've learned so far about publishing sensory information, to create an enhancement to our security dashboard in Chapter 9, *Building a Home Security Dashboard*.

# Setting up a Twilio account

Twilio is a service that gives software developers the ability to create and receive text and phone calls programmatically through the use of its web service APIs. Let's start by setting up a Twilio account:

1. In a web browser, navigate to www.twilio.com
2. Click on the red sign up at the top-right corner of the page
3. Enter the appropriate personal information and a password, and then select **SMS**, **Arrival Alerts**, and **Python** for the fields below the password:

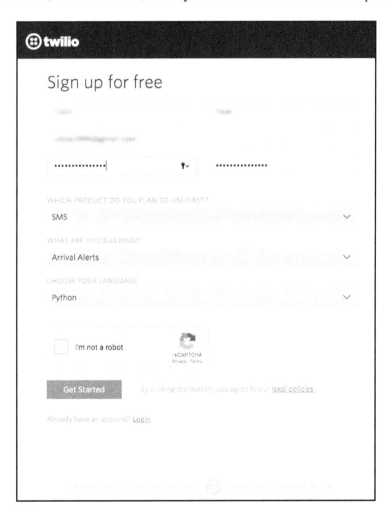

4. Provide a phone number to receive an authorization code via SMS, as follows:

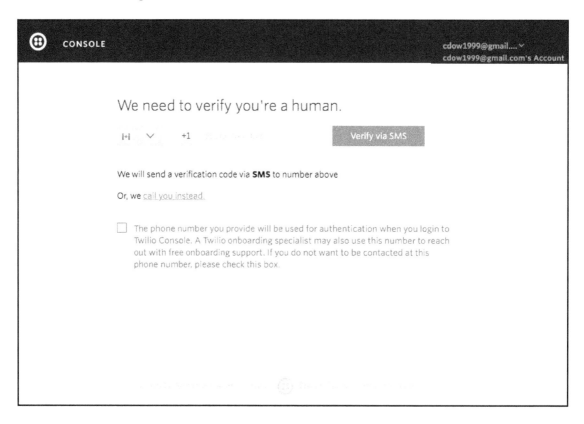

5. Enter the authorization code you receive, as shown here:

6. The next step is to name the project that you will be working on. We will name it `Doorbell`. Enter the name and click **Continue**:

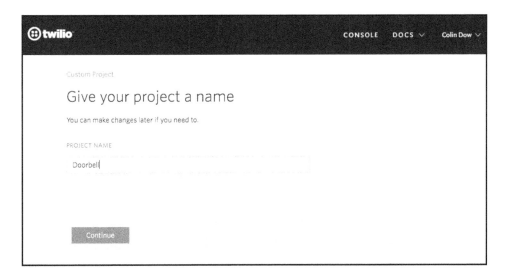

7. We need a phone number for our account in order to be able to interact with it. Click on **Get a Number**:

8. A number will be presented to you. If this number works for you, click on **Choose this number**:

9. You are now set up and ready to use Twilio:

Twilio is a paid service. You will be given an initial amount to work with. Please check the costs of using this service before creating your apps.

# Installing Twilio on our Raspberry Pi

To access Twilio from Python, we need to install the `twilio` library. Open up a Terminal and type in the following:

```
pip3 install twilio
```

You should see the progress of Twilio being installed in the Terminal.

# Sending a text through Twilio

Before sending a text, we need to get credentials. In your Twilio account, click on **Settings | General**, and scroll down to **API Credentials**:

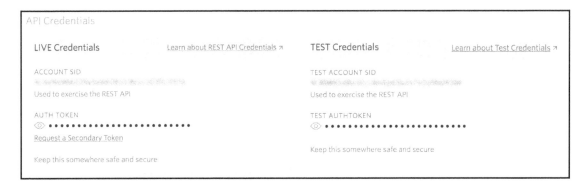

We will use both the **LIVE Credentials** and **TEST Credentials** values. Open up Thonny and create a new file called `twilio-test.py`. Type the following code into the file and run it. Be sure to paste in the **LIVE Credentials** (please note that your account will be charged for sending a text):

```
from twilio.rest import Client

account_sid = '<<your account_sid>>'
auth_token = '<<your auth_token>>'
client = Client(account_sid, auth_token)

message = client.messages.create(
                        body='Twilio says hello!',
                        from_='<<your Twilio number>>',
                        to='<<your cell phone number>>'
                )
print(message.sid)
```

You should get a text on your cell phone, with the message `Twilio says hello!`.

# Creating a new home security dashboard

In `Chapter 9`, *Building a Home Security Dashboard*, we created a home security dashboard using CherryPy. The power behind the IoT is the ability to build an application with devices, located anywhere in the world, that are connected to each other. We will take this idea to our home security dashboard. If not already assembled, build the home security dashboard with the temperature sensor from `Chapter 9`, *Building a Home Security Dashboard*:

1. We will start our code by encapsulating our sensory data in a `class` container. Open up Thonny and create a new file called `SensoryData.py`:

```
from gpiozero import MotionSensor
import Adafruit_DHT

class SensoryData:
    humidity=''
    temperature=''
    detected_motion=''
    dht_pin = 19
    dht_sensor = Adafruit_DHT.DHT11
    motion_sensor = MotionSensor(4)
    def __init__(self):
        self.humidity, self.temperature = Adafruit_DHT
                            .read_retry(self.dht_sensor,
```

```
                                            self.dht_pin)

            self.motion_detected =
        self.motion_sensor.motion_detected
            def getTemperature(self):
                return self.temperature
            def getHumidity(self):
                return self.humidity
            def getMotionDetected(self):
                return self.motion_detected

    if __name__ == "__main__":
        while True:
            sensory_data = SensoryData()
            print(sensory_data.getTemperature())
            print(sensory_data.getHumidity())
            print(sensory_data.getMotionDetected())
```

2. Run the program to test our sensors. There isn't anything here we haven't covered already. We are basically just testing out our circuit and sensors. You should see the sensory data print out in the shell.

3. Now, let's create our sensory dashboard. Open up Thonny and create a new file called `SensoryDashboard.py`. The code is as follows:

```
import paho.mqtt.client as mqtt
import json
from SensoryData import SensoryData
from time import sleep

class SensoryDashboard:
    host = 'demo.thingsboard.io'
    access_token = '<<your access_token>>'
    client = mqtt.Client()
    client.username_pw_set(access_token)
    sensory_data = ''
    def __init__(self, sensoryData):
        self.sensoryData = sensoryData
    def publishSensoryData(self):
        sensor_data = {'temperature': 0, 'humidity': 0,
                        'Motion Detected':False}

        sensor_data['temperature'] =  self.sensoryData
                                        .getTemperature()

        sensor_data['humidity'] =
    self.sensoryData.getHumidity()
```

```
                    sensor_data['Motion Detected'] = self.sensoryData
                                              .getMotionDetected()
                    self.client.connect(self.host, 1883, 20)
                    self.client.publish('v1/devices/me/telemetry',
                                        json.dumps(sensor_data), 1)
                    self.client.disconnect()
                    return sensor_data['Motion Detected']
        if __name__=="__main__":
            while True:
                    sensoryData = SensoryData()
                    sensory_dashboard = SensoryDashboard(sensoryData)

                    print("Motion Detected: " +
                            str(sensory_dashboard.publishSensoryData()))

                    sleep(10)
```

What we've done here is encapsulate the dht-mqtt.py file, from the previous code, in a class container. We instantiate our object with a SensoryData object in order to obtain data from our sensors. The publishSensoryData() method sends the sensory data to our MQTT dashboard. Notice how it returns the state of the motion sensor? We use this return value in our main loop to print out the value of the motion sensor. However, this return value will be more useful in our future code.

Let's add the motion sensor to our ThingsBoard dashboard:

1. Open up ThingsBoard in a browser
2. Click on the **Devices** menu
3. Click on the **Room Conditions** device
4. Select **LATEST TELEMETRY**
5. Select the **Motion Detected** value
6. Click on **SHOW ON WIDGET**
7. Under **Cards**, find the widget made up of a big orange square, as shown here:

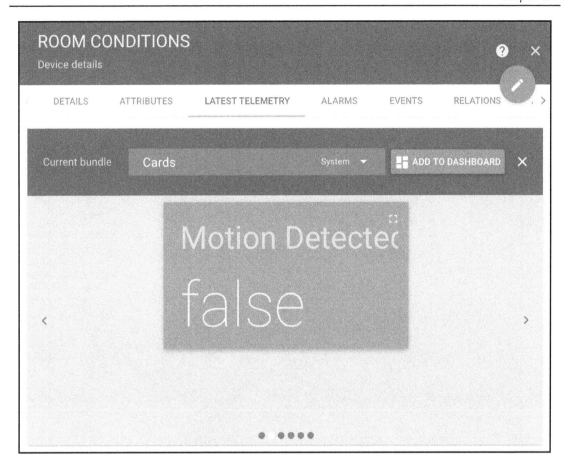

8. Click on **ADD TO DASHBOARD**
9. Select the existing **Room Conditions** dashboard
10. Check off **Open Dashboard**
11. Click **Add**

You should see the new widget added to the **Room Conditions** dashboard. By clicking on the orange pencil icon at the bottom-right of the page, you are able to move and resize the widgets. Edit the widgets so they look like the following screenshot:

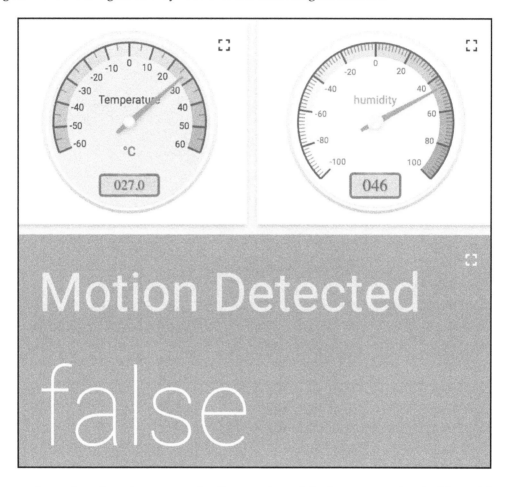

What we have done here is recreate the first version of the home security dashboard from Chapter 9, *Building a Home Security Dashboard*, with a more distributed architecture. No longer are we relying on our Raspberry Pi to serve up the sensory information via a CherryPy web page. We are able to reduce the role of our Raspberry Pi to a source of sensory information. As you can imagine, it is quite easy to use multiple Raspberry Pis with the same dashboard.

Test out this new dashboard by moving near the PIR sensor. See if you can get the **Motion Detected** widget to change to `true`.

To make our new home security dashboard even more distributed, let's add the ability to send a text message whenever the PIR motion sensor is activated. Open up Thonny and create a new file called `SecurityDashboardDist.py`. The following is the code to insert into the file:

```
from twilio.rest import Client
from SensoryData import SensoryData
from SensoryDashboard import SensoryDashboard
from gpiozero import Button
from time import time, sleep

class SecurityDashboardDist:
    account_sid = ''
    auth_token = ''
    time_sent = 0
    test_env = True
    switch = Button(8)
    def __init__(self, test_env = True):
        self.test_env = self.setEnvironment(test_env)
    def setEnvironment(self, test_env):
        if test_env:
            self.account_sid = '<<your Twilio test account_sid>>'
            self.auth_token = '<<your Twilio test auth_token>>'
            return True
        else:
            self.account_sid = '<<your Twilio live account_sid>>'
            self.auth_token = '<<your Twilio live auth_token>>'
            return False
    def update_dashboard(self, sensoryDashboard):
        self.sensoryDashboard = sensoryDashboard

        motion_detected = self
                        .sensoryDashboard
                        .publishSensoryData()
        if motion_detected:
            return self.send_alert()
        else:
            return 'Alarm not triggered'
    def send_alert(self):
        if self.switch.is_pressed:
            return self.sendTextMessage()
        else:
            return "Alarm triggered but Not Armed"
    def sendTextMessage(self):
```

```
            message_interval = round(time() - self.time_sent)
            if message_interval > 600:
                twilio_client = Client(self.account_sid,
                                       self.auth_token)
                if self.test_env:
                    message = twilio_client.messages.create(
                            body='Intruder Alert',
                            from_= '+15005550006',
                            to='<<your cell number>>'
                        )
                else:
                    message = twilio_client.messages.create(
                            body='Intruder Alert',
                            from_= '<<your Twilio number>>',
                            to='<<your cell number>>'
                        )
                self.time_sent=round(time())

                return 'Alarm triggered and text message sent - '
                        + message.sid
            else:
                return 'Alarm triggered and text
                        message sent less than 10 minutes ago'
    if __name__=="__main__":
        security_dashboard = SecurityDashboardDist()
        while True:
            sensory_data = SensoryData()
            sensory_dashboard = SensoryDashboard(sensory_data)
            print(security_dashboard.update_dashboard(
                    sensory_dashboard))
            sleep(5)
```

Utilizing the first version of the home security dashboard circuit from Chapter 9, *Building a Home Security Dashboard*, this code uses the key switch in order to arm the call to send out a text message if the motion sensor detects motion. With the key switch in the off position, you will get a message, reading `Alarm triggered but Not Armed`, whenever the motion sensor detects motion.

If not already turned on, turn on the key switch to arm the circuit. Activate the motion sensor by moving around. You should get a notification that a text message was sent. The SID of the message should show as well. You may have noticed that you didn't actually get a text message. This is due to the fact that the code defaults to the Twilio test environment. Before we turn on the live environment, let's go over the code.

We start out by importing the libraries we need for our code:

```
from twilio.rest import Client
from SensoryData import SensoryData
from SensoryDashboard import SensoryDashboard
from gpiozero import Button
from time import time, sleep
```

There's not too much here that we haven't seen before; however, take note of the
`SensoryData` and `SensoryDashboard` imports. As we have encapsulated the code to read
sensory data, we can now just look at it as a black box. We know we need sensory data for
our security dashboard, but we don't care how we get this data and where it will be
displayed. `SensoryData` gives us access to the sensory data we need, and
`SensoryDashboard` sends it off to a dashboard somewhere. We don't have to concern
ourselves with these details in our `SecurityDashboardDist.py` code.

We create a class called `SecurityDashboardDist` for our distributed security dashboard.
It is important to distinguish our classes by their names, and to pick names that describe
what the `class` is:

```
class SecurityDashboardDist:
```

After declaring some class variables that are accessible throughout the class, we then come
to our class initialization method:

```
account_sid = ''
auth_token = ''
time_sent = 0
test_env = True
switch = Button(8)
def __init__(self, test_env = True):
    self.test_env = self.setEnvironment(test_env)
```

In the `initialization` method, we set our class scoped `test_env` variable (for the `test`
environment). The default is `True`, meaning we have to conscientiously override the
default in order to run the dashboard live. We use the `setEnvironment()` method to set
`test_env`:

```
def setEnvironment(self, test_env):
    if test_env:
        self.account_sid = '<<your Twilio test account_sid>>'
        self.auth_token = '<<your Twilio test auth_token>>'
        return True
    else:
        self.account_sid = '<<your Twilio live account_sid>>'
```

```
        self.auth_token = '<<your Twilio live auth_token>>'
        return False
```

The `setEnvironment()` method sets up the class scoped `account_id` and `auth_token` values to either the test environment, or the live environment, depending on the value of `test_env`. We are basically just passing back the state of `test_env` with the `setEnvironment()` method, while setting up the variables we need to enable a test or live text message environment.

The `update_dashboard()` method makes the call to the sensors and sensory dashboard through the use of the `SensoryDashboard` object that we pass into the method. This here is the beauty of the object-oriented approach we have taken, as we do not need to concern ourselves with how the sensors are read or how the dashboard is updated. We only need to pass in a `SensoryDashboard` object to get this done:

```
def update_dashboard(self, sensoryDashboard):
        self.sensoryDashboard = sensoryDashboard

        motion_detected = self
                        .sensoryDashboard
                        .publishSensoryData()
        if motion_detected:
            return self.send_alert()
        else:
            return 'Alarm not triggered'
```

The `update_dashboard` method is also responsible for determining whether or not a text message will be sent, by checking on the status of the motion sensor. Do you remember how we returned the state of the motion sensor when we called the `publishSensoryData()` method on our `SensoryDashboard` class? This is where it comes in really handy. We can use this return value to determine whether or not we should send an alert. We don't have to check on the state of the motion sensor in our class at all, as it is easily available from the `SensoryDashboard` class.

The `send_alert()` method checks on the state of the switch in order to determine whether a text message should be sent:

```
def send_alert(self):
        if self.switch.is_pressed:
            return self.sendTextMessage()
        else:
            return "Alarm triggered but Not Armed"
```

You may be wondering why we are checking on the state of a sensor (a switch, in this case) here, as opposed to checking it from the SensoryDashboard class. The answer? We are building a home security dashboard by encapsulating a sensory data dashboard. There is no need for a switch in the SensorDashboard class, as it is not concerned with turning on and off the reading and transmitting of sensory data from the GPIO to the MQTT dashboard. The switch is the domain of a security system; in this case, the SecurityDashboardDist class.

The heart of the SecurityDasboardDist class is the sendTextMessage() method, outlined here:

```
def sendTextMessage(self):
        message_interval = round(time() - self.time_sent)
        if message_interval > 600:
            twilio_client = Client(self.account_sid,
                                      self.auth_token)
            if self.test_env:
                message = twilio_client.messages.create(
                        body='Intruder Alert',
                        from_= '+15005550006',
                        to='<<your cell number>>'
                    )
            else:
                message = twilio_client.messages.create(
                        body='Intruder Alert',
                        from_= '<<your Twilio number>>',
                        to='<<your cell number>>'
                    )
            self.time_sent=round(time())

            return 'Alarm triggered and text message sent - '
                    + message.sid
        else:
            return 'Alarm triggered and text
                message sent less than 10 minutes ago'
```

We use the message_interval method variable to set the duration of time between texts. We do not want to send a text message every time the motion sensor has detected motion. In our case, the minimum time left between texts is 600 seconds, or 10 minutes.

If this is the first time, or if it has been more than 10 minutes since the time that a text message was last sent, then the code sends the text message in either the test environment, or simply live. Take note of how the `15005550006` phone number is used for the test environment. Your Twilio number is required for the live environment, and your own phone number for the `to` field. For both the test and live environments, the `Alarm triggered and text message sent` message is returned, followed by the SID of the message. The difference is that you will not actually receive a text message (although there is a call to Twilio from the code).

If it has been less than 10 minutes since the last time a text message was sent, then the message will read `Alarm triggered and text message sent less than 10 minutes ago`.

In our main function, we create a `SecurityDashboardDist` object and call it `security_dashboard`. By not passing in anything, we allow the dashboard to be set up for the test environment by default:

```
if __name__=="__main__":
    security_dashboard = SecurityDashboardDist()
    while True:
        sensory_data = SensoryData()
        sensory_dashboard = SensoryDashboard(sensory_data)
        print(security_dashboard.update_dashboard(
                sensory_dashboard))
        sleep(5)
```

The continuous loop that follows creates a `SensoryData` and `SensoryDashboard` object every 5 seconds. The `SensoryData` object (`sensory_data`) is used to instantiate a `SensoryDashboard` object (`sensory_dashboard`), as it is the former that gives us the current sensory data, and the latter that creates the sensory dashboard.

By naming our classes according to what they are, and our methods by what they do, the code becomes pretty self-explanatory.

We then pass this `SensoryDashboard` object (`sensory_dashboard`) to the `update_dashboard` method of the `SecurityDashboard` (`security_dashboard`). As the `update_dashboard` method returns a string, we are able to use it to print to our shell, and thus, see the status of our dashboard printed every 5 seconds. We keep the instantiation of the `SecurityDashboardDist` object out of the loop, as we only need to set the environment once.

Now that we understand the code, it's time to run it in the live Twilio environment. Please note that the only part of the code that changes when we switch to live is the actual sending of text messages. To turn our dashboard into a live text-sending machine, simply change the first line of the main method to the following:

```
security_dashboard = SecurityDashboardDist(True)
```

# Summary

After completing this chapter, we should be very familiar with publishing sensory data to an IoT dashboard. We should also be familiar with sending text messages from our Raspberry Pi using the Twilio web service.

We will take a look at Bluetooth libraries in Chapter 11, *Creating a Doorbell Button Using Bluetooth*, before putting that information and the information we acquired in this chapter together to make an IoT doorbell.

# Questions

1. What is the name of the service we used to send text messages from our Raspberry Pi?
2. True or false? We use a PIR sensor to read temperature and humidity values.
3. How do you create a dashboard in ThingsBoard?
4. True or false? We built our enhanced security dashboard by using a sensory dashboard.
5. What is the name of the library we use to read temperature and humidity sensory data?
6. True or false? The library that we require to send text messages comes pre-installed with Raspbian.
7. When naming classes in our code, what do we try to do?
8. True or false? In order to change our environment from test to live, do we have to rewrite the entire code in our enhanced home security dashboard.
9. True or false? The account_sid number for our Twilio account is the same for the live environment as it is for the test environment.
10. Where do we create a SecurityDashboardDist object in our SecurityDashboardDist.py code?

# Further reading

To further your understanding of the technologies behind Twilio and ThingsBoard, please refer to the following links:

- The Twilio documentation:
  `https://www.twilio.com/docs/quickstart`
- The documentation for ThingsBoard:
  `https://thingsboard.io/docs/`

# 11
# Creating a Doorbell Button Using Bluetooth

In this chapter, we will turn our focus to Bluetooth. Bluetooth is a wireless technology used in the exchange of data over short distances. It operates in the 2.4 to 2.485 GHz frequency band, and generally has a range of up to 10 meters.

We will be utilizing the Blue Dot app on Android for the projects in this chapter, in which we will build a simple Bluetooth doorbell, before building a more advanced one that accepts secret swiping gestures.

The following topics will be covered in this chapter:

- Introducing Blue Dot
- What is an RGB LED?
- Reading our button state using Bluetooth and Python

## Project overview

In this chapter, we will build a Bluetooth-enabled doorbell using our Raspberry Pi and an Android phone or tablet. We will use an app on our Android phone or tablet, called Blue Dot, which is designed to work with Raspberry Pi projects.

We will start off by looking at RGB LEDs, wherein we will write a small program to cycle through these three colors. We will then create an alarm using a RGB LED and an active buzzer. We will test out the alarm with Python code.

We will write Python code to read button information from Blue Dot. We will then incorporate the code from both the alarm and Blue Dot to create a Bluetooth doorbell system.

The projects in this chapter should take a morning or afternoon to complete.

# Getting started

The following is required to complete this project:

- Raspberry Pi Model 3 (2015 model or newer)
- USB power supply
- Computer monitor
- USB keyboard
- USB mouse
- Breadboard
- Jumper wires
- 330 Ohm resistors (3 of them)
- RGB LED
- Active buzzer
- Android phone or tablet

# Introducing Blue Dot

Blue Dot is an Android app available in the Google Play Store. It works as a Bluetooth remote for the Raspberry Pi. When loaded into your Android phone or tablet, it is basically a big blue dot that you press to send a signal to the Raspberry Pi. The following is a picture of the Blue Dot app loaded onto a tablet:

It may be used as a Bluetooth joystick of sorts, as positional, slider, and rotational data may be sent from the app to your Raspberry Pi, depending on how you interact with the dot on the screen. We will add some of this functionality to our doorbell application by creating custom rings based on how the Blue Dot is pressed. To install Blue Dot on your Android phone or tablet, visit the Google Play Store and search for **Blue Dot**.

# Installing the bluedot library on the Raspberry Pi

To install the `bluedot` library on the Raspberry Pi, do the following:

1. Open up a Terminal app
2. Type the following into the Terminal:

```
sudo pip3 install bluedot
```

3. Press *Enter* to install the library

# Pairing Blue Dot with your Raspberry Pi

In order to make use of the Blue Dot app, you must pair it to your Raspberry Pi. To do that, follow these steps:

1. From the top-right corner of the Raspbian desktop client, click on the Bluetooth symbol:

2. If Bluetooth is not on, click on the Bluetooth icon and select Turn on Bluetooth
3. Select the **Make Discoverable** option from the Bluetooth drop-down menu
4. On your Android phone or tablet, go to the Bluetooth settings (this may be in different places depending on the particular OS on the phone or tablet)
5. You should be able to see the Raspberry Pi in the **Available Devices** list
6. Click on it to pair your device to the Raspberry Pi
7. You should get a message on the Raspberry Pi, reading something like `Device 'Galaxy Tab E' has requested a pairing. Do you accept the request?`
8. Click **OK** to accept

9. You may get a `connection failed` message. I was able to ignore this message and still have the Blue Dot app work with my Raspberry Pi, so don't worry too much

10. Load the Blue Dot app onto your Android phone or tablet

11. You should see a list with the Raspberry Pi as an item

12. Click on the Raspberry Pi item to connect the Blue Dot application to the Raspberry Pi

To test our connection, do the following:

1. Open up Thonny by following **Application Menu** | **Programming** | **Thonny Python IDE**

2. Click on the **New** icon to create a new file

3. Type the following into the file:

```
from bluedot import BlueDot
bd = BlueDot()
bd.wait_for_press()
print("Thank you for pressing the Blue Dot!")
```

4. Save the file as `bluest-test.py` and run it

5. You should get a message in the Thonny shell, reading **Server started**, followed by the Bluetooth address of the Raspberry Pi

6. You should then get a message reading `Waiting for connection`

7. If your Blue Dot app disconnected from the Raspberry Pi, connect it again by selecting the Raspberry Pi item in the list

8. Once the Blue Dot app is connected to the Raspberry Pi, you will get the message `Client connected`, followed by the Bluetooth address of your phone or tablet

9. Press the big **Blue Dot**

10. The Thonny shell should now print the following message: `Thank you for pressing the Blue Dot!`

# Wiring up our circuit

We will create a doorbell circuit using an active buzzer and an RGB LED. Since we have not discussed RGB LEDs before, we will take a quick look at this amazing little electronic component. We then write a simple test program, using our Raspberry Pi, that will light up the RGB LED and sound the active buzzer.

# What is an RGB LED?

An RGB LED is really just three LEDs in one unit: a red one, a green one, and a blue one. Almost any color may be achieved by applying electric current at varying power levels across the selection of input pins. The following is a diagram of such an LED:

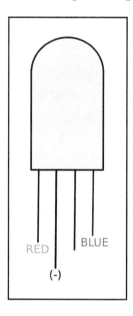

As you can see there are red, green, and blue pins, plus a negative pin (-) . When an RGB LED has a negative pin (-), it is said to have a common cathode. Some RGB LEDs have a common positive pin (+), and, as such, are referred to as having a common anode. For our circuit, we will use an RGB LED with a common cathode. Both the common cathode and common anode have the longest pins of the RGB LED, and are identified by this characteristic.

# Testing our RGB LED

We will now build a circuit with which we can test our RGB LED. The following is a wiring diagram of our circuit:

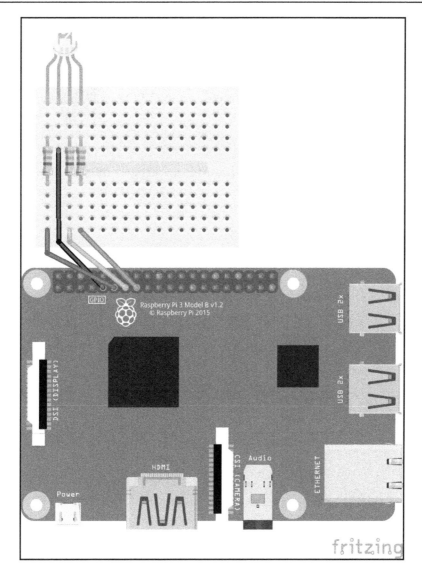

To build the circuit as shown in the diagram, do the following:

1. Using a breadboard, insert the RGB LED into the breadboard, such that the common cathode is inserted into the second slot from the left

2. Connect a 330 Ohm resistor to the red, green, and blue pins across the central gap on the breadboard

3. Connect a female-to-male jumper wire from GPIO pin 17 to the first slot on the left of the breadboard
4. Connect a female-to-male jumper wire from GPIO GND to the cathode pin of the RGB LED (the second from the left)
5. Connect a female-to-male jumper wire from GPIO pin 27 to the third slot on the left of the breadboard
6. Connect a female-to-male jumper wire from GPIO pin 22 to the fourth slot on the left of the breadboard
7. Open up Thonny from **Application Menu** | **Programming** | **Thonny Python IDE**
8. Click on the **New** icon to create a new file
9. Type the following into the file:

```
from gpiozero import RGBLED
from time import sleep

led = RGBLED(red=17, green=27, blue=22)

while True:
    led.color=(1,0,0)
    sleep(2)
    led.color=(0,1,0)
    sleep(2)
    led.color=(0,0,1)
    sleep(2)
    led.off()
    sleep(2)
```

10. Save the file as `RGB-LED-test.py` and run it

You should see the RGB LED light up in red for 2 seconds. The RGB LED should then light up green for 2 seconds, before turning blue for 2 seconds. It will then turn off for 2 seconds, before starting the sequence again.

In the code, we start off by importing `RGBLED` from the GPIO Zero library. We then set up a variable, called `led`, by assigning it the pin numbers for the red, green, and blue colors of the RGB LED. From there, we simply turn on each color using the `led.color` property. It's easy to see that assigning a value of `1`, `0`, `0` to the `led.color` property turns on the red LED and turns off the green and blue LEDs. The `led.off` method turns off the RGB LED.

Try experimenting with different values for `led.color`. You may even put in a value that is less than `1` to vary the intensity of the color (the range is any value between `0` and `1`). If you look closely, you may be able to see the different LEDs lighting up inside the RGB LED.

# Completing our doorbell circuit

Now let's add an active buzzer to our circuit to complete the construction of our doorbell system. The following is the diagram for our doorbell circuit:

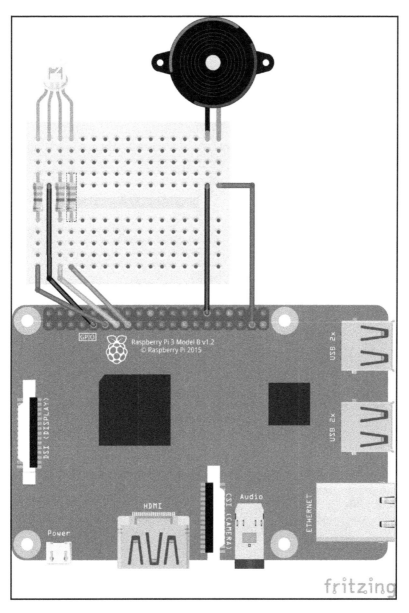

To build the circuit, follow these steps:

1. Using our existing circuit, insert an active buzzer into the opposite end of the breadboard
2. Connect a female-to-male jumper wire from GPIO pin 26 to the positive pin of the active buzzer
3. Connect a female-to-male jumper wire from GPIO GND to the negative pin of the active buzzer
4. Open up Thonny from **Application Menu | Programming | Thonny Python IDE**
5. Click on the **New** icon to create a new file
6. Type the following into the file:

```python
from gpiozero import RGBLED
from gpiozero import Buzzer
from time import sleep

class DoorbellAlarm:
    led = RGBLED(red=17, green=22, blue=27)
    buzzer = Buzzer(26)
    num_of_times = 0
    def __init__(self, num_of_times):
        self.num_of_times = num_of_times
    def play_sequence(self):
        num = 0
        while num < self.num_of_times:
            self.buzzer.on()
            self.light_show()
            sleep(0.5)
            self.buzzer.off()
            sleep(0.5)
            num += 1
    def light_show(self):
        self.led.color=(1,0,0)
        sleep(0.1)
        self.led.color=(0,1,0)
        sleep(0.1)
        self.led.color=(0,0,1)
        sleep(0.1)
        self.led.off()

if __name__=="__main__":

    doorbell_alarm = DoorbellAlarm(5)
    doorbell_alarm.play_sequence()
```

7. Save the file as `DoorbellAlarm.py` and run it

8. You should hear the buzzer go off five times, as well as see the RGB LED go through its light sequence the same number of times

Let's take a look at the code:

1. We start off by importing the libraries that we need, as follows:

```
from gpiozero import RGBLED
from gpiozero import Buzzer
from time import sleep
```

2. After that, we create our class with the `DoorbellAlarm` classname, before setting initial values:

```
led = RGBLED(red=17, green=22, blue=27)
buzzer = Buzzer(26)
num_of_times = 0
```

3. The class initialization sets the number of times that the alarm sequence will play, using the `num_of_times` class variable:

```
def __init__(self, num_of_times):
    self.num_of_times = num_of_times
```

4. The `light_show` method simply flashes each color in the RGB LED in sequence for $0.1$ seconds:

```
def light_show(self):
    self.led.color=(1,0,0)
    sleep(0.1)
    self.led.color=(0,1,0)
    sleep(0.1)
    self.led.color=(0,0,1)
    sleep(0.1)
    self.led.off()
```

5. The `play_sequence` method turns the buzzer on and off for the number of times set when the `DoorbellAlarm` class is initialized. It also runs through the RGB LED `light_show` function every time the buzzer is sounded:

```
def play_sequence(self):
    num = 0
    while num < self.num_of_times:
        self.buzzer.on()
        self.light_show()
```

```
                  sleep(0.5)
                  self.buzzer.off()
                  sleep(0.5)
                  num += 1
```

6. We test out our code by instantiating the `DoorbellAlarm` class with a value of 5, and assigning it to the `doorbell_alarm` variable. We then play the sequence by calling the `play_sequence` method:

```
if __name__=="__main__":

    doorbell_alarm = DoorbellAlarm(5)
    doorbell_alarm.play_sequence()
```

# Reading our button state using Bluetooth and Python

As mentioned previously, we are able to interact with the Blue Dot app in more ways than just a simple button press. The Blue Dot app can interpret where on the button a user presses, as well as detect double presses and swipes. In the following code, we will read from the Blue Dot app using Python.

## Reading button information using Python

Do the following :

1. Open up Thonny from **Application Menu** | **Programming** | **Thonny Python IDE**
2. Click on the **New** icon to create a new file
3. Type the following into the file:

```
from bluedot import BlueDot
from signal import pause

class BlueDotButton:
    def swiped(swipe):
        if swipe.up:
            print("Blue Dot Swiped Up")
        elif swipe.down:
            print("Blue Dot Swiped Down")
        elif swipe.left:
```

```
                print("Blue Dot Swiped Left")
            elif swipe.right:
                print("Blue Dot Swiped Right")
        def pressed(pos):
            if pos.top:
                print("Blue Dot Pressed from Top")
            elif pos.bottom:
                print("Blue Dot Pressed from Bottom")
            elif pos.left:
                print("Blue Dot Pressed from Left")
            elif pos.right:
                print("Blue Dot Pressed from Right")
            elif pos.middle:
                print("Blue Dot Pressed from Middle")
        def double_pressed():
            print("Blue Dot Double Pressed")
        blue_dot = BlueDot()
        blue_dot.when_swiped = swiped
        blue_dot.when_pressed = pressed
        blue_dot.when_double_pressed = double_pressed
    if __name__=="__main__":

        blue_dot_button = BlueDotButton()
        pause()
```

4. Save the file as `BlueDotButton.py` and run it

You may have to connect the Blue Dot app to your Raspberry Pi each time you run this program (simply select it from the list in the Blue Dot app). Try pressing the Blue Dot in the middle, on the top, on the left, and so on. You should see messages in the shell that tell you where you've pressed. Now try swiping and double-pressing. The messages in the shell should indicate these gestures as well.

So, what have we done here? Let's take a look at the code:

1. We start off by importing the libraries that we need:

```
from bluedot import BlueDot
from signal import pause
```

We obviously need `BlueDot`, and we also need `pause`. We use `pause` to pause the program and wait for a signal from the Blue Dot app. Since we are using the `when_pressed`, `when_swiped`, and `when_double_swiped` events, we need to pause and wait (as opposed to other methods, such as `wait_for_press`). I believe using `when`-instead of `wait`-type events makes the code a little cleaner.

2. At the heart of our program is the instantiation of a `BlueDot` object and its related call back definitions:

```
blue_dot = BlueDot()
blue_dot.when_swiped = swiped
blue_dot.when_pressed = pressed
blue_dot.when_double_pressed = double_pressed
```

Please note that these callback definitions have to be put after the methods they are referring to, or you will get an error.

3. The methods themselves are pretty straightforward. The following is the `swiped` method:

```
def swiped(swipe):
    if swipe.up:
        print("Blue Dot Swiped Up")
    elif swipe.down:
        print("Blue Dot Swiped Down")
    elif swipe.left:
        print("Blue Dot Swiped Left")
    elif swipe.right:
        print("Blue Dot Swiped Right")
```

4. We define this method with a variable called `swipe` inside the method signature. Note that we do not have to use `self` inside the method signature, as we are not using class variables inside our methods.

# Creating a Bluetooth doorbell

Now that we know how to read button information from Blue Dot, we can build a Bluetooth doorbell button. We will rewrite our `DoorbellAlarm` class, and use a simple button press from Blue Dot to activate the alarm, as follows:

1. Open up Thonny from **Application Menu** | **Programming** | **Thonny Python IDE**
2. Click on the **New** icon to create a new file
3. Type the following into the file:

```
from gpiozero import RGBLED
from gpiozero import Buzzer
from time import sleep

class DoorbellAlarmAdvanced:
```

```
led = RGBLED(red=17, green=22, blue=27)
buzzer = Buzzer(26)
num_of_times = 0
delay = 0

def __init__(self, num_of_times, delay):
    self.num_of_times = num_of_times
    self.delay = delay


def play_sequence(self):
    num = 0
    while num < self.num_of_times:
        self.buzzer.on()
        self.light_show()
        sleep(self.delay)
        self.buzzer.off()
        sleep(self.delay)
        num += 1


def light_show(self):
    self.led.color=(1,0,0)
    sleep(0.1)
    self.led.color=(0,1,0)
    sleep(0.1)
    self.led.color=(0,0,1)
    sleep(0.1)
    self.led.off()


if __name__=="__main__":

    doorbell_alarm = DoorbellAlarmAdvanced(5,1)
    doorbell_alarm.play_sequence()
```

4. Save the file as `DoorbellAlarmAdvanced.py`

Our new class, `DoorbellAlarmAdvanced`, is a modified version of the `DoorbellAlarm` class. What we have done is basically add a new class property that we call `delay`. This class property will be used to change the delay time between buzzer rings. As you can see in the code, the two methods modified for the change are `__init__` and `play_sequence`.

Now that we have the changes in place for our alarm, let's create a simple doorbell program as follows:

1. Open up Thonny from **Application Menu | Programming | Thonny Python IDE**
2. Click on the **New** icon to create a new file
3. Type the following into the file:

```
from bluedot import BlueDot
from signal import pause
from DoorbellAlarmAdvanced import DoorbellAlarmAdvanced

class SimpleDoorbell:

  def pressed():
  doorbell_alarm = DoorbellAlarmAdvanced(5, 1)
  doorbell_alarm.play_sequence()


  blue_dot = BlueDot()
  blue_dot.when_pressed = pressed



if __name__=="__main__":

  doorbell_alarm = SimpleDoorbell()
  pause()
```

4. Save the file as `SimpleDoorbell.py` and run it
5. Connect the Blue Dot app to the Raspberry Pi, if it is not already connected
6. Push the big blue dot

You should hear five rings, each lasting one second, from the buzzer in one-second intervals. You will also see that the RGB LED went through a short light show. As you can see, the code is pretty straightforward. We import our new `DoorbellAlarmAdvanced` class, and then call the `play_sequence` method after we initialize the class with the `doorbell_alarm` variable in the `pressed` method.

The changes we made in creating the `DoorbellAlarmAdvanced` class are utilized in our code to allow us to set the delay time between rings.

# Creating a secret Bluetooth doorbell

Wouldn't it be nice to know who is at the door before we answer it? We can take advantage of the swiping capabilities of the Blue Dot app. To create a secret Bluetooth doorbell (the secret being the way in which we interact with the doorbell, not a secret location for the doorbell), do the following:

1. Open up Thonny from **Application Menu** | **Programming** | **Thonny Python IDE**

2. Click on the **New** icon to create a new file

3. Type the following into the file:

```python
from bluedot import BlueDot
from signal import pause
from DoorbellAlarmAdvanced import DoorbellAlarmAdvanced

class SecretDoorbell:
    def swiped(swipe):
        if swipe.up:
            doorbell_alarm = DoorbellAlarmAdvanced(5, 0.5)
            doorbell_alarm.play_sequence()
        elif swipe.down:
            doorbell_alarm = DoorbellAlarmAdvanced(3, 2)
            doorbell_alarm.play_sequence()
        elif swipe.left:
            doorbell_alarm = DoorbellAlarmAdvanced(1, 5)
            doorbell_alarm.play_sequence()
        elif swipe.right:
            doorbell_alarm = DoorbellAlarmAdvanced(1, 0.5)
            doorbell_alarm.play_sequence()
    blue_dot = BlueDot()
    blue_dot.when_swiped = swiped
if __name__=="__main__":

    doorbell = SecretDoorbell()
    pause()
```

4. Save the file as `SecretDoorbell.py` and run it

5. Connect the Blue Dot app to the Raspberry Pi, if it is not already connected

6. Swipe in the up direction on the Blue Dot

You should hear five short rings, as well as seeing the RGB LED light show. Try swiping in the down, left, and right directions. You should get a different ring sequence each time.

So, what did we do here? Basically, we attached a callback to the `when_swiped` event, and through `if` statements, we created new `DoorbellAlarmAdvanced` objects with varying initial values.

With this project we can now know who is at the door, as we can assign various swipe gestures to our different friends.

# Summary

In this chapter, we created a Bluetooth doorbell application using the Raspberry Pi and the Blue Dot Android app. We started out by learning a little bit about RGB LEDs, before incorporating one in an alarm circuit with an active buzzer.

With the Blue Dot app, we learned how to connect a Bluetooth button to our Raspberry Pi. We also learned how to use some of the Blue Dot gestures, and created a doorbell application with various ring durations.

In `Chapter 12`, *Enhancing Our IoT Doorbell*, we will extend the functionality of our doorbell, and have a text message sent whenever someone presses the button.

# Questions

1. How does an RGB LED differ from a regular LED?
2. True or false? The Blue Dot app is found in the Google Play store.
3. What is a common anode?
4. True or false? The three colors inside the RGB LED are red, green, and yellow.
5. How do you pair the Blue Dot application with the Raspberry Pi?
6. True or false? Bluetooth is a communication technology built for extremely long distances.
7. What is the difference between `DoorbellAlarm` and `DoorbellAlarmAdvanced`?
8. True or false? The GPIO Zero library contains a class named `RGBLED`.
9. True or false? The Blue Dot app may be used to record swipe gestures.
10. What is the difference between the `SimpleDoorbell` and `SecretDoorbell` classes?

# Further reading

To find out more about the Blue Dot Android app, visit the documentation page at `https:/ /bluedot.readthedocs.io.`

# 12
# Enhancing Our IoT Doorbell

In Chapter 10, *Publishing to Web Services*, we explored web services. We then introduced Bluetooth in Chapter 11, *Creating a Doorbell Button Using Bluetooth*, and built a Bluetooth doorbell using the Android app Blue Dot and our Raspberry Pi.

In this chapter, we will enhance our Bluetooth doorbell by adding the ability to send messages when someone is at the door. We will take what we've learned, and apply it to add text message functionality using the Twilio account we set up in Chapter 10, *Publishing to Web Services*.

The following topics will be be covered in this chapter:

- Sending a text message when someone is at the door
- Creating a secret doorbell application with text messaging

# Project overview

For the two projects in this chapter, we will use the circuit from Chapter 11, *Creating a Doorbell Button Using Bluetooth*. We will also make use of the Blue Dot app for Android devices as described in Chapter 11, *Creating a Doorbell Button Using Bluetooth*. The following is a diagram of the application we will create in this chapter:

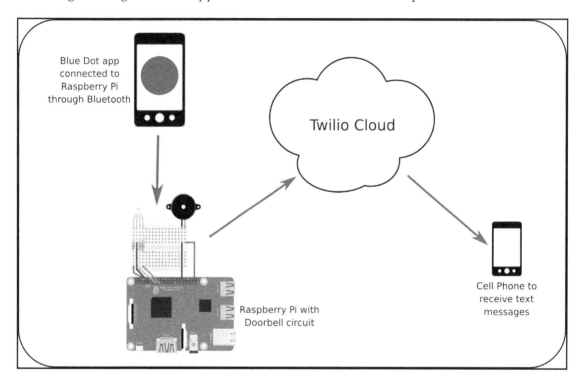

We will create two versions of this application. The first version of our application will be a simple Bluetooth doorbell, where pressing the blue dot fires off the buzzer and RGB LED light show. After the alarm has been triggered, a text message will be sent using Twilio Cloud Services.

An altered version of the application will use swiping gestures on the Blue Dot app to indicate particular visitors. Each of the four potential visitors will have their own unique swiping gesture with the blue dot. After the custom buzzer ring and RGB LED light show, a text message will be sent informing the recipient of who is at the door. The Twilio Cloud will be used for this as well.

Both projects should take a morning or afternoon to complete.

# Getting started

The following is required to complete this project:

- Raspberry Pi Model 3 (2015 model or newer)
- USB power supply
- Computer monitor
- USB keyboard
- USB mouse
- Breadboard
- Jumper wires
- 330 Ohm resistors (3 of them)
- RGB LED
- Active buzzer
- Android device (phone/tablet)

# Sending a text message when someone is at the door

In `Chapter 10`, *Publishing to Web Services*, we created text messages using a technology called Twilio. In that instance, we used Twilio to send text messages when an intruder was detected. In `Chapter 11`, *Creating a Doorbell Button Using Bluetooth*, we created a Bluetooth doorbell using the Blue Dot app on an Android phone or tablet. The doorbell sounded a buzzer and gave a little light show on an RGB LED.

For this project, we will combine Twilio with the Bluetooth doorbell, and have a text message sent when someone pushes the Blue Dot doorbell (refer to `Chapter 10`, *Publishing to Web Services*, and `Chapter 11`, *Creating a Doorbell Button Using Bluetooth*, to familiarize yourself with these technologies).

# Creating a simple doorbell application with text messaging

To create our simple doorbell application do the following:

1. Open up Thonny from **Application Menu** | **Programming** | **Thonny Python IDE**
2. Click on the **New** icon to create a new file
3. Type the following:

```python
from twilio.rest import Client
from gpiozero import RGBLED
from gpiozero import Buzzer
from bluedot import BlueDot
from signal import pause
from time import sleep

class Doorbell:
    account_sid = ''
    auth_token = ''
    from_phonenumber=''
    test_env = True
    led = RGBLED(red=17, green=22, blue=27)
    buzzer = Buzzer(26)
    num_of_rings = 0
    ring_delay = 0
    msg = ''
    def __init__(self,
                    num_of_rings = 1,
                    ring_delay = 1,
                    message = 'ring',
                    test_env = True):
        self.num_of_rings = num_of_rings
        self.ring_delay = ring_delay
        self.message = message
        self.test_env = self.setEnvironment(test_env)
    def setEnvironment(self, test_env):
        if test_env:
            self.account_sid = '<<test account_sid>>'
            self.auth_token = '<<test auth_token>>'
            return True
        else:
            self.account_sid = '<<live account_sid>>'
            self.auth_token = '<<live auth_token>>'
            return False
    def doorbell_sequence(self):
```

```
                num = 0
                while num < self.num_of_rings:
                    self.buzzer.on()
                    self.light_show()
                    sleep(self.ring_delay)
                    self.buzzer.off()
                    sleep(self.ring_delay)
                    num += 1
                return self.sendTextMessage()
            def sendTextMessage(self):
                twilio_client = Client(self.account_sid,
        self.auth_token)
                if self.test_env:
                    message = twilio_client.messages.create(
                            body=self.message,
                            from_= '+15005550006',
                            to='<<your phone number>>'
                    )
                else:
                    message = twilio_client.messages.create(
                            body=self.message,
                            from_= '<<your twilio number>>',
                            to='<<your phone number>>'
                    )
                return 'Doorbell text message sent - ' + message.sid
            def light_show(self):
                self.led.color=(1,0,0)
                sleep(0.5)
                self.led.color=(0,1,0)
                sleep(0.5)
                self.led.color=(0,0,1)
                sleep(0.5)
                self.led.off()
        def pressed():
            doorbell = Doorbell(2, 0.5, 'There is someone at the door')
            print(doorbell.doorbell_sequence())

    blue_dot = BlueDot()
    blue_dot.when_pressed = pressed
    if __name__=="__main__":
        pause()
```

4. Save the file as `Doorbell.py` and run it
5. Open up the Blue Dot app on your Android device
6. Connect to the Raspberry Pi
7. Push the big blue dot

You should hear the ring and see the light sequence cycle twice, with a short delay between rings. You should get something similar to the following printed in the shell:

```
Server started B8:27:EB:12:77:4F
Waiting for connection
Client connected F4:0E:22:EB:31:CA
Doorbell text message sent - SM5cf1125acad44016840a6b76f99b3624
```

The first three lines indicate that the Blue Dot app has connected to our Raspberry Pi through our Python program. The last line indicates that a text message was sent. As we are using the test environment, an actual text message was not sent, but the Twilio service was called.

Let's take a look at the code. We start by defining our class and giving it the name `Doorbell`. This is a good name for our class, as we have written our code such that everything to do with a doorbell is contained in `Doorbell.py` file. This file holds both the `Doorbell` class, used to alert a user, as well as the Blue Dot code, used to trigger the doorbell. The Blue Dot code actually sits outside of the `Doorbell` class definition, as we view it as part of the Blue Dot app, not the doorbell itself. We certainly could have designed our code such that the `Doorbell` class contains code to trigger the alarm; however, this separation of the alarm from the alarm trigger makes it easier to reuse the `Doorbell` class as an alerting mechanism in the future.

Choosing class names can be tricky. However, it is very important to choose the correct class name, as it will make it easier to build your application with class names that fit the purpose they are intended for. Class names are usually nouns, and the methods inside the classes are verbs. Generally, it is better to have a class represent one thing or idea. For example, we named our class `Doorbell`, as we have designed it to encapsulate what a doorbell does: alert the user that someone is at the door. Taking that idea into account, it makes sense that the `Doorbell` class would contain code to light up an LED, sound a buzzer, and send a text message, as those three actions fall under the idea of alerting a user.

After we define our class, we create class variables that are used in our class as follows:

```
class Doorbell:
    account_sid = ''
    auth_token = ''
    from_phonenumber=''
    test_env = True
    led = RGBLED(red=17, green=22, blue=27)
    buzzer = Buzzer(26)
    num_of_rings = 0
```

```
ring_delay = 0
msg = ''
```

The init and setEnvironment methods set the variables we use in our class.
The test_env variable determines whether we use the Twilio test or live environments in
our code. The test environment is used by default:

```
def __init__(self,
             num_of_rings = 1,
             ring_delay = 1,
             message = 'ring',
             test_env = True):
    self.num_of_rings = num_of_rings
    self.ring_delay = ring_delay
    self.message = message
    self.test_env = self.setEnvironment(test_env)

 def setEnvironment(self, test_env):
     if test_env:
         self.account_sid = '<<test account sid>>'
         self.auth_token = '<<test auth token>>'
         return True
     else:
         self.account_sid = '<<live account sid>>'
         self.auth_token = '<<auth_token>>'
         return False
```

The doorbell_sequence, sendTextMessage, and light_show methods are similar to
methods we've covered previously in this book. It is through these three methods that we
alert a user that someone is at the door. Of note here is the return value sent from the
sendTextMessage method: return 'Doorbell text message sent - ' +
message.sid. By having this in the code, we are able to use
the sendTextMessage method to provide a printed confirmation in our shell that a text
message has been sent.

As mentioned previously, the Blue Dot portion of our code sits outside of the class
definition:

```
def pressed():
    doorbell = Doorbell(2, 0.5, 'There is someone at the door')
    print(doorbell.doorbell_sequence())

blue_dot = BlueDot()
blue_dot.when_pressed = pressed
```

The previous code is something we've seen before. We define the `pressed` method, where we instantiate a new `doorbell` object, and then call the `doorbell_sequence` method of `doorbell`. The `blue_dot` variable is a `BlueDot` object, where we are only concerned with the `when_pressed` event.

Of note here is the line containing the `doorbell = Doorbell(2, 0.5, 'There is someone at the door')` statement. In this line, we instantiate a `Doorbell` object, which we call `doorbell`, with `num_of_rings` equal to 2; `ring_delay` (or duration) equal to 0.5; and a message equal to `There is someone at the door`. We do not pass in a `test_env` environment value. Thus, the default setting of `True` is used to set our `doorbell` object to use the Twilio test environment, where no text message is sent. To change it so that a text message will be sent, change the statement to this:

```
doorbell = Doorbell(2, 0.5, 'There is someone at the door', False)
```

Make sure that you set up the Twilio account parameters accordingly. You should get a text message on your cell phone telling you that someone is at the door. The following is the message I received on my iPhone:

# Creating a secret doorbell application with text messaging

Now that we have the ability to send a text message whenever someone pushes the big blue button on our Android device, let's make it a bit more complicated. We will modify the `SecretDoorbell` class we created in `Chapter 11`, *Creating a Doorbell Button Using Bluetooth*, and give it the ability to send text messages telling us who is at the door. Like we did previously, we will put all our code into one file to keep it compact:

1. Open up Thonny from **Application Menu** | **Programming** | **Thonny Python IDE**
2. Click on the **New** icon to create a new file
3. Type the following:

```python
from twilio.rest import Client
from gpiozero import RGBLED
from gpiozero import Buzzer
from bluedot import BlueDot
from signal import pause
from time import sleep

class Doorbell:
    account_sid = ''
    auth_token = ''
    from_phonenumber=''
    test_env = True
    led = RGBLED(red=17, green=22, blue=27)
    buzzer = Buzzer(26)
    num_of_rings = 0
    ring_delay = 0
    msg = ''
    def __init__(self,
                    num_of_rings = 1,
                    ring_delay = 1,
                    message = 'ring',
                    test_env = True):
        self.num_of_rings = num_of_rings
        self.ring_delay = ring_delay
        self.message = message
        self.test_env = self.setEnvironment(test_env)
    def setEnvironment(self, test_env):
        if test_env:
            self.account_sid = '<<test account_sid>>'
            self.auth_token = '<<test auth_token>>'
            return True
```

```
        else:
            self.account_sid = '<<live account_sid>>'
            self.auth_token = '<<live auth_token>>'
            return False
    def doorbell_sequence(self):
        num = 0
        while num < self.num_of_rings:
            self.buzzer.on()
            self.light_show()
            sleep(self.ring_delay)
            self.buzzer.off()
            sleep(self.ring_delay)
            num += 1
        return self.sendTextMessage()
    def sendTextMessage(self):
        twilio_client = Client(self.account_sid,
self.auth_token)
        if self.test_env:
            message = twilio_client.messages.create(
                    body=self.message,
                    from_= '+15005550006',
                    to='<<your phone number>>'
            )
        else:
            message = twilio_client.messages.create(
                    body=self.message,
                    from_= '<<your twilio number>>',
                    to='<<your phone number>>'
            )
        return 'Doorbell text message sent - ' + message.sid
    def light_show(self):
        self.led.color=(1,0,0)
        sleep(0.5)
        self.led.color=(0,1,0)
        sleep(0.5)
        self.led.color=(0,0,1)
        sleep(0.5)
        self.led.off()

class SecretDoorbell(Doorbell):
    names=[['Bob', 4, 0.5],
           ['Josephine', 1, 3],
           ['Ares', 6, 0.2],
           ['Constance', 2, 1]]
    message = ' is at the door!'
    def __init__(self, person_num, test_env = True):
        Doorbell.__init__(self,
                          self.names[person_num][1],
```

```
                            self.names[person_num][2],
                            self.names[person_num][0] +
        self.message,
                            test_env)
    def swiped(swipe):
        if swipe.up:
            doorbell = SecretDoorbell(0)
            print(doorbell.doorbell_sequence())
        elif swipe.down:
            doorbell = SecretDoorbell(1)
            print(doorbell.doorbell_sequence())
        elif swipe.left:
            doorbell = SecretDoorbell(2)
            print(doorbell.doorbell_sequence())
        elif swipe.right:
            doorbell = SecretDoorbell(3)
            print(doorbell.doorbell_sequence())
    blue_dot = BlueDot()
    blue_dot.when_swiped = swiped
    if __name__=="__main__":
        pause()
```

4. Save the file as `SecretDoorbell.py` and run it
5. Open up the Blue Dot app on your Android device
6. Connect to the Raspberry Pi
7. Swipe the blue dot downwards from the top position
8. You should hear the buzzer sound once for about three seconds, and see the RGB LED perform its light show once. Something similar to the following will be displayed at the bottom of the shell:

```
Server started B8:27:EB:12:77:4F
Waiting for connection
Client connected F4:0E:22:EB:31:CA
Doorbell text message sent - SM62680586b32a42bdacaff4200e0fed78
```

9. As in the previous project, we will get a message indicating that a text message was sent, but we will not actually receive a text message, due to being in the Twilio test environment

Before we get our application to send us a text message that will tell us who is at the door based on how they swiped, let's take a look at the code.

Our `SecretDoorbell.py` file is exactly the same as our `Doorbell.py` file, with the exception of the following code:

```
class SecretDoorbell(Doorbell):
    names=[['Bob', 4, 0.5],
           ['Josephine', 1, 3],
           ['Ares', 6, 0.2],
           ['Constance', 2, 1]]
    message = ' is at the door!'
    def __init__(self, person_num, test_env = True):
        Doorbell.__init__(self,
                          self.names[person_num][1],
                          self.names[person_num][2],
                          self.names[person_num][0] +
self.message,
                          test_env)
    def swiped(swipe):
        if swipe.up:
            doorbell = SecretDoorbell(0)
            print(doorbell.doorbell_sequence())
        elif swipe.down:
            doorbell = SecretDoorbell(1)
            print(doorbell.doorbell_sequence())
        elif swipe.left:
            doorbell = SecretDoorbell(2)
            print(doorbell.doorbell_sequence())
        elif swipe.right:
            doorbell = SecretDoorbell(3)
            print(doorbell.doorbell_sequence())
    blue_dot = BlueDot()
    blue_dot.when_swiped = swiped
```

The class, `SecretDoorbell`, is created as a subclass of `Doorbell`, thereby inheriting the methods from `Doorbell`. The `names` array that we created stores the names and ring properties associated with the names in the array. So, for example, the first element has the name of `Bob`, a `num_of_rings` value of `4`, and a `ring_delay` (duration) value of `0.5`. When this record is used in a live Twilio environment, you should hear the buzzer and see the RGB LED light show cycle four times, with a short delay between the the rings. The `init` method of `SecretDoorbell` collects `person_num` (or, basically, position information in the names array) and uses it to instantiate the `Doorbell` parent class. The `test_env` value is defaulted to `True`, meaning we can only turn on the live Twilio environment by specifically overriding this value. This keeps us from accidentally using up our Twilio account balance before we are ready to actually deploy the application.

The Blue Dot code in our file sits outside of the `SecretDoorbell` class definition. We did the same in the previous project, as it allows us to keep the doorbell functionality separate from the doorbell trigger (the Blue Dot app on our Android device).

In our Blue Dot code, we instantiate a `BlueDot` object that we call `blue_dot`, before assigning the `when_swiped` event to `swiped`. In `swiped`, we instantiate a `SecretDoorbell` object with the value of `0` for the `swipe.up` gesture, `1` for `swipe.down`, `2` for `swipe.left`, and `3` for `swipe.right`. These values correspond to the array positions in the names array of the `SecretDoorbell` class. We do not pass in a value for `test_env` when we instantiate a `SecretDoorbell` object for any of the gestures, thus a text message is not sent. Just as in the previous project, we print to the shell the successful result of running the `doorbell_sequence` method.

To have a text message sent, we only have to override the default `test_env` value with the `False` value. We do this when we instantiate a `SecretDoorbell` object for our swipe gestures in the `swiped` method. Our code is designed in such a way that we can have a text message sent for one or many gestures. Modify the following `elif` statement in `swiped`:

```
elif swipe.down:
    doorbell = SecretDoorbell(1, False)
    print(doorbell.doorbell_sequence())
```

What we have done here, is turn on the live Twilio environment for the `swipe.down` gesture by overriding the `test_env` variable. The `1` value, which we instantiate our `SecretDoorbell` object with, corresponds to the second element in the `names` array in `SecretDoorbell`.

Thus, when you run the app and swipe from top to bottom on the blue dot, you should receive a text message from Twilio saying that Josephine is at the door, as follows:

# Summary

In this chapter, we learned how to add text messaging to our doorbell application. This creates a doorbell fit for the age of the Internet of Things. It's easy to see how the concept of the IoT Bluetooth doorbell could be expanded—imagine turning on the porch lights when someone pushes the doorbell.

We can also see how the Blue Dot app could be utilized in other ways as well. We could program a certain swiping sequence with our Blue Dot app, perhaps to unlock the door. Imagine not having to carry around keys!

This is the last chapter before we introduce our robot car. In the following chapters, we will take the concepts we have learned so far and apply them to a robot that we control through the internet.

# Questions

1. How does the Blue Dot app connect to our Raspberry Pi?
2. True or false? Running a message through the Twilio test environment creates a text message that is sent to your phone.
3. What is the name of the service we use to send text messages?
4. True or false? We create our `SecretDoorbell` class as a subclass of the `Doorbell` class.
5. What are the four Blue Dot gestures we use in our second application?
6. True or false? Naming a class in a way that describes what it does makes coding easier.
7. What is the difference between `Doorbell` and `SecretDoorbell`?
8. True or false? Josephine's ring pattern involves one long buzzer sound.
9. True or false? You need to use an Android phone in order to receive text messages from our applications.
10. How should Constance swipe the blue dot, so we know that it's her at the door?

# Further reading

We touched a little on the Twilio service. However, there is still more to learn—visit `https://www.twilio.com/docs/tutorials` for more information.

# 13
# Introducing the Raspberry Pi Robot Car

I would like to introduce you to T.A.R.A.S, the robot car. T.A.R.A.S is actually a backronym; I took the name from a business mentor of mine who helped me get started. After scratching my head trying to come up with something, I finally figured out how to turn my friend Taras into T.A.R.A.S, this Amazing Raspberry-Pi Automated Security agent. As you can probably tell from the name, T.A.R.A.S will monitor things for us and act as an automated security guard.

T.A.R.A.S will use Raspberry Pi for a brain and motor driver boards to control both the movement of its camera gimbal and wheels. T.A.R.A.S will also have sensory inputs as well as LED and buzzer outputs. T.A.R.A.S will be an aggregation of the skills we have acquired throughout this book.

We will spend this chapter building T.A.R.A.S and writing code to control it.

The following topics will be covered in this chapter:

- The parts of the robot car
- Building the robot car

# The parts of the robot car

I designed T.A.R.A.S to be as simple to put together as possible. T.A.R.A.S consists of a laser cut hardboard chassis, 3D printed wheel, and camera mount parts (there is an option to use laser cut wheel mounts, too). In order for you to build T.A.R.A.S, I have provided SVG files for the chassis and STL files for the 3D printed parts. All other parts may be purchased online. The following is a photo of T.A.R.A.S. before assembly:

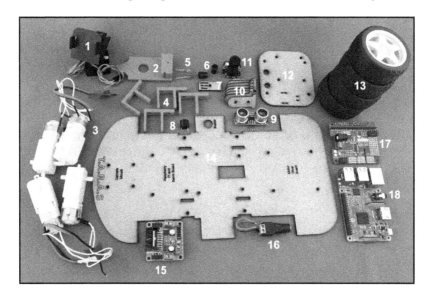

1. Servo camera mount (shown assembled)—search www.aliexpress.com for a camera platform anti-vibration camera mount
2. 3D printed bracket (camera brace)
3. DC motors for wheels (shown with motor wires and extension wires attached)—search www.aliexpress.com for a smart car robot plastic tire wheel
4. Wheel mounts (3D printed)
5. LEDs
6. LED holders—search www.aliexpress.com for a lamp LED holder black clip
7. Camera mount brace (laser cut)
8. Active buzzer—search www.aliexpress.com for a 5V active buzzer
9. Distance sensor (HC-SR04)—search www.aliexpress.com for an HC-SR04
10. Alternative wheel mounts (laser cut)

11. Raspberry Pi camera (long lens version, shown without cable)—search `www.aliexpress.com`

12. Motor driver plate (laser cut)

13. Wheels—search `www.aliexpress.com` for a smart car robot plastic tire wheel

14. Robot car chassis (laser cut)

15. Motor driver board—search `www.aliexpress.com` for an L298N motor driver board module

16. DC barrel jack (shown with wires attached)—`www.aliexpress.com`

17. Adafruit 16-Channel PWM/Servo HAT—`https://www.adafruit.com/product/2327`

18. Raspberry Pi

19. 40-pin single-row male pin header connector strip (not shown)—`www.aliexpress.com`

20. Various loose wires and breadboard jumper wires (not shown)—it's a good idea to buy many different wires and breadboard jumper wires; you can search `www.aliexpress.com` for breadboard jumper wires

21. Heat shrink (not shown)

22. 7.4V rechargeable battery with DC jack (not shown)—search `www.aliexpress.com` for a 7.4V 18650 Li-ion lithium ion rechargeable battery pack (be sure to pick one that fits with the DC barrel jack in 16)

23. Alternatively to part 22, you may use an AA sized power battery storage case box instead of parts 16 and 22—`www.aliexpress.com`

24. Mini breadboard (not shown)—search `www.aliexpress.com` for an SYB-170 mini solderless prototype experiment test breadboard

25. Various standoffs (not shown)—it should be able to have a standoff height of at least 40 mm; it's a good idea to have as many standoffs as you can as they always seem to come in handy, and you can search `www.aliexpress.com` for standoffs in electronics

26. 330 and 470 Ohm resistors (not shown)—it's a good idea to buy many resistors as they do indeed come in handy; search `www.aliexpress.com` for a resistor pack

27. Portable USB power pack (not shown)—this type is used to charge cell phones on the go; we will use this power pack to power the Raspberry Pi

# Building the robot car

The following are the steps to build T.A.R.A.S, our robot car. Your version of T.A.R.A.S may be built close to the one used in this book or you may make modifications as desired. For one thing, I am using a Raspberry Pi camera module with a longer lens (night-vision models have longer lenses). I am also using the Adafruit 16-Channel PWM/Servo HAT to drive the servos for the camera mount. You may choose to use another board or forgo the servos altogether and mount the camera in a fixed position.

One of my favorite robot backronyms is Vincent from the 1980s Disney movie *The Black Hole*. Vincent, or more accurately, V.I.N.CENT, stands for Vital Information Necessary Centralized. If you know the movie, you will know that V.I.N.CENT is quite clever and very polite. V.I.N.CENT is also a bit of a know-it-all and can be a little irritating at times.

I have included two different ways to mount the wheel motors: using a 3D printed wheel mount or using a laser cut wheel mount. I prefer the 3D printed brace as it allows for the screws to be countersunk, thereby providing more space between the chassis and the wheel.

If you are 3D printing the wheel mounts and camera brace yourself, you may use whichever solid filament type you desire. Personally, I used PETG as I like the way it bends without breaking. PLA is fine as well. Be sure to 3D print the wheel mounts on their sides so that they print wide and not high. This will result in a print that may be a little messy around the holes (for PETG, at least), but it will be a much stronger part. I managed to print a single wheel mount in 30 minutes and the camera brace in about 90 minutes.

Building the robot car should take an afternoon of your time.

# Step 1 – Adafruit 16-Channel PWM/Servo HAT for Raspberry Pi

If you haven't heard of it, there is this amazing company in New York City that caters to electronics hobbyists around the world called Adafruit. Adafruit creates many **HATs** (**Hardware Added on Top**) for Raspberry Pi, including the one we will use for our robot, the Adafruit 16-Channel PWM/Servo HAT.

With this HAT, the repetitive time pulses needed to control servos are offloaded from Raspberry Pi and onto the HAT. With this HAT, you may control up to 16 servos.

The following is a photo of the HAT and the headers that come with it:

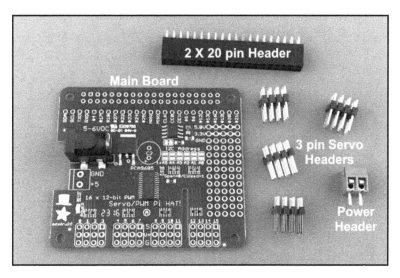

For our purposes, we need to solder headers onto the board:

1. As we are only using two servos, solder two of the **3 pin servo headers** to the board.

2. Solder the **2 X 20 pin header**. A good way to hold the board and pins in place while soldering is to use some Play-Doh! (make sure you don't go too close to the Play-Doh! with the hot soldering iron while soldering):

3. As we will be using wires from our motor board to power the servo board, solder the power header onto the board.

4. We need to access GPIO pins from Raspberry Pi, so another pin row must be added. Break off 25 pins from a 40-pin pin header connector. Solder the pins onto the board:

# Step 2 – Wiring up the motors

We need to wire up the motors so that two always spin at the same time and in the same direction:

1. Cut eight equal pieces of wire and strip a little insulation off both ends of all pieces:

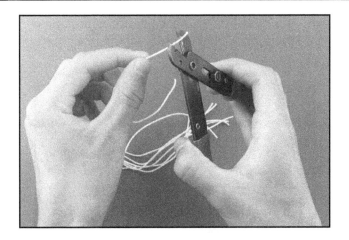

2. Solder an end to each terminal on the motors:

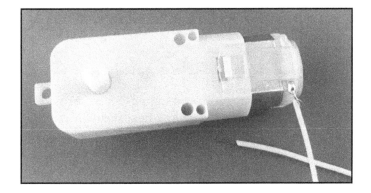

3. Apply heat shrink to the terminal to insulate it:

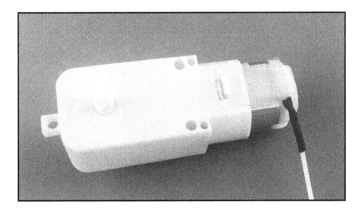

4. Group and connect the wires from each motor so that the wire on the top of one motor connects to the wire on the bottom of the other motor (see photo for clarity):

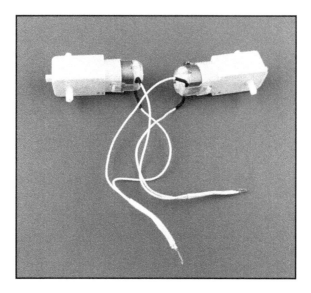

5. For extra strength and protection, you may use heat shrink to keep the wires together (in the previous photo, a yellow heat shrink is used).

6. Extension wires may be added to the ends (I have chosen to do this for my build as the wire length was a little short). The blue labeling tape added to the ends will help out later one when wiring the motors up to the motor driver board:

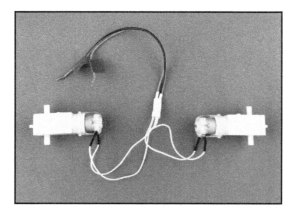

# Step 3 – Assembling the servo camera mount

With our servo camera mount, T.A.R.A.S has the ability to move its head side to side and up and down. This will come in handy for our project in `Chapter 14`, *Controlling the Robot Car Using Python*. When you pour the pieces of the servo camera mount onto the table, it may seem a little daunting as to how you are going to assemble it into something useful.

The following is a photo of the parts of the servo camera mount,. Rather than try to name the parts, I'll just put letters down and refer to the letters for assembly:

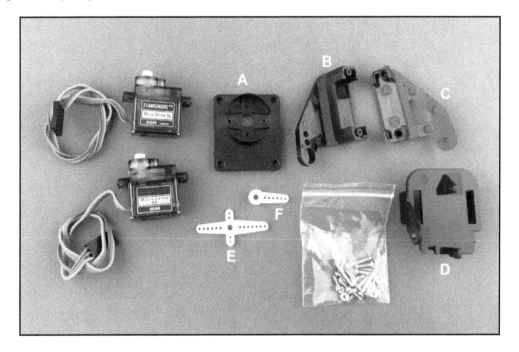

To assemble the servo camera mount do the following:

1. Place part **E** inside of part **A** so that the protruding cylinder from part **E** is facing up:

2. Flip over and screw part **E** to part **A** by using the smallest screws in the pack:

3. Screw a servo into part **D** using small screws (see the following photo):

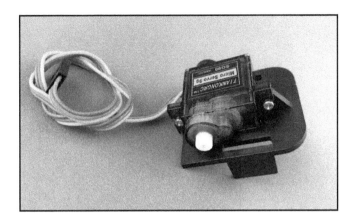

4. Place part **B** over the servo and insert part **F** into the groove made for it. Screw part **F** into place. The servo should be able to move freely up and down while attached to parts **B** and **F**:

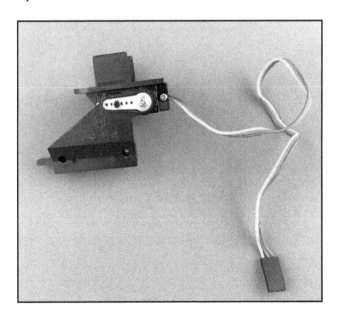

5. Flip the assembled part over and insert the other servo into part **B**:

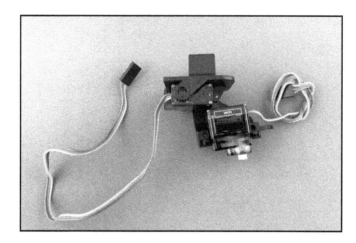

6. Place part **C** over the servo. You may have to bend part **D** a bit to get part **C** to fit:

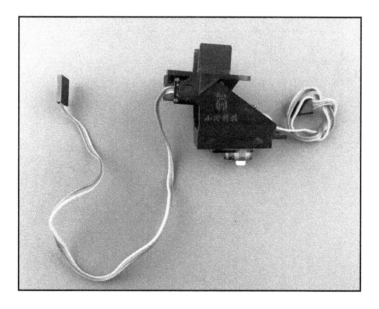

7. Flip the assembled part over and screw parts **B** and **C** together:

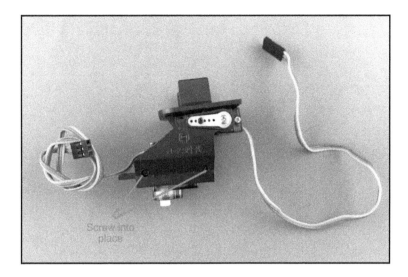

8. Insert the assembled part into part **E**:

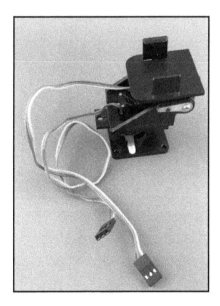

9. Screw part **A** to the bottom of the assembled part:

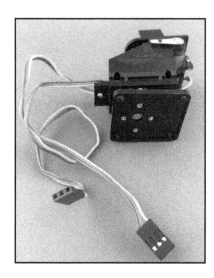

# Step 4 – Attaching the head

Let's face it. A robot just isn't a robot unless it has a face of some sort (with apologies to R2D2). In this step, we will attach the parts to build the head and face of T.A.R.A.S.

According to Rodney Brooks, founder of Rethink Robotics, robots do not have faces just to make them friendly. Faces on robots are used as visual cues for humans to pick up on. For example, if a robot moves its head in a certain direction, we can safely assume that the robot is analyzing something in that direction. When we move the head of T.A.R.A.S, we are giving cues to those around us that T.A.R.A.S is looking that way.

The following is a photo of the parts needed to complete the head:

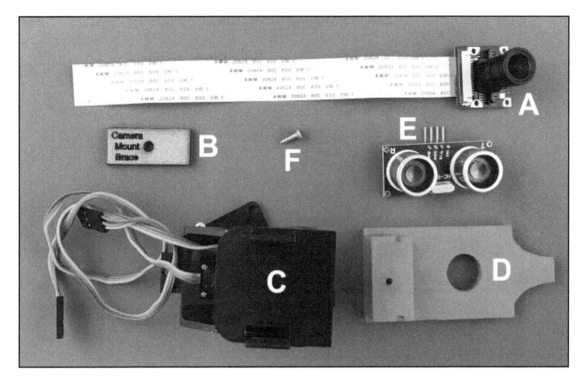

We will now assemble the head of T.A.R.A.S. The following is a list of the parts:

- **A**: Raspberry Pi camera module
- **B**: Camera mount brace
- **C**: Assembled camera mount with servos
- **D**: 3D printed bracket
- **E**: Distance sensor
- **F**: Screw

To assemble the head, do the following:

1. Apply small pieces of double-sided foam tape to the Raspberry Pi camera module and distance sensor:

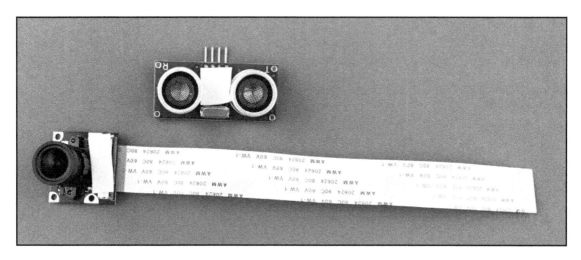

2. Stick the Raspberry Pi camera module and distance sensor in place in the appropriate places on the 3D printed bracket (see the following photo for clarification):

3. Slide the assembly into place on the assembled camera mount and screw it into place (see the following photo for clarification):

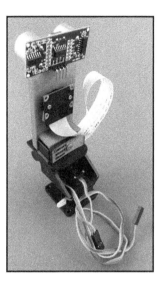

4. Add female-to-female jumpers to the distance sensor's pins. Here, I have used a four-pin connector to 4 individual pins. You may use separate jumpers instead:

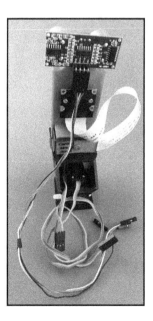

5. Turn the assembled piece around and apply the sticker for teeth:

# Step 5 – Assembling the DC motor plate

The DC motor plate is at the back of T.A.R.A.S and houses the DC motor driver that moves the wheels. The DC Barrel Jack and tail light LEDs also sit on the DC motor plate. We will start this step by creating the tail light LEDs.

The following photo shows the parts that are needed to make the tail light LEDs:

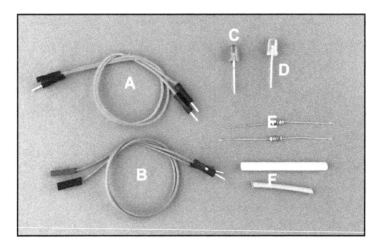

The following is a list of the parts:

- **A**: Red jumper wires (one end must be female)
- **B**: Brown jumper wires (one end must be female)
- **C**: Red LED
- **D**: Green LED
- **E**: 330 Ohm resistors
- **F**: Heat shrink

The following are the steps to create the LED tail lights:

1. Solder a 330 Ohm resistor to the anode (longer leg) of the LED.
2. Apply heat shrink to the connection to provide strength and insulation.
3. Strip one end of a red jumper wire (make sure that the other end is female) and solder it to the end of the resistor. This is the positive end of the assembly:

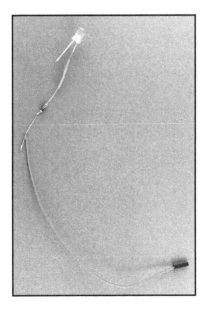

4. Apply heat shrink over the entire resistor:

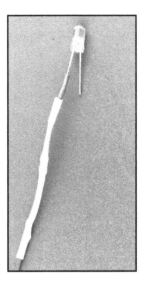

5. Solder a brown wire to the cathode and apply heat shrink (in this photo, we show a red LED with an extended brown wire). This is the negative end of the assembly:

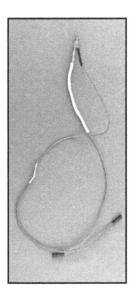

6. Now that we have completed the assembly of the two tail lights, let's put the DC motor board together. The following is a photo of the pieces we need to put the DC motor board together:

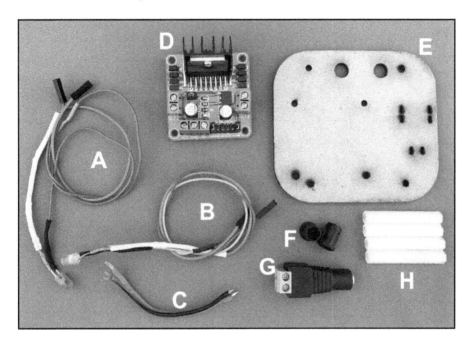

The following is a list of the parts:

- **A**: Red tail light
- **B**: Green tail light
- **C**: Short power wire
- **D**: Motor driver board
- **E**: DC motor plate (laser cut)
- **F**: LED holders
- **G**: DC barrel jack
- **H**: 40 mm standoffs
- Eight M3X10 bolts (not shown)
- Four M3 nuts (not shown)
- Zip ties (not shown)

Let's start putting it together:

1.  Screw the 40 mm standoffs (**H**) to **E** using four 10 mm M3 bolts. Refer to the following photo for the proper orientation:

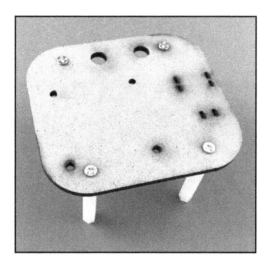

2.  Screw the motor driver board (**D**) to **E** using four 10 mm M3 bolts and nuts. Refer to the following photo for the proper orientation:

Here is the side view:

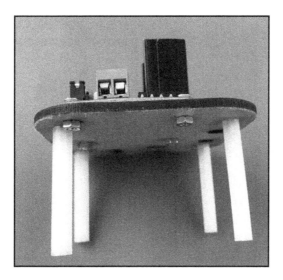

3. Attach wire **C** to the DC barrel jack (**G**) ports. Make sure that the red wire goes to positive and that the black goes to negative. Attach the other end of wire **C** into the motor driver board (**D**). Make sure that the red wire goes to VCC and that the black wire goes to GND. Secure the DC barrel jack (**G**) to the DC motor plate (**E**) with zip ties. See the following photo for clarification:

Here is the wiring diagram:

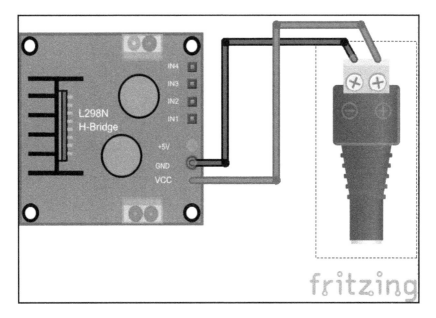

4.  Alternatively, you may use an AA battery four-pack for power. Be sure to follow the same wiring with the red wire connected to VCC and the black wire connected to GND:

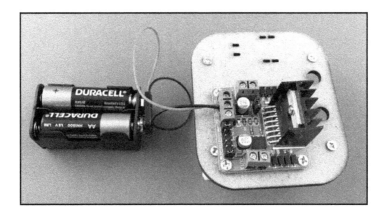

5. Thread the tail light (**B**) through the LED holes and through an LED holder (**F**):

6. Push the LED holder (**F**) into place. If the hole is too tight, use a small file to make the hole a little bigger (the LED holder should fit in tight). Repeat for the red tail light:

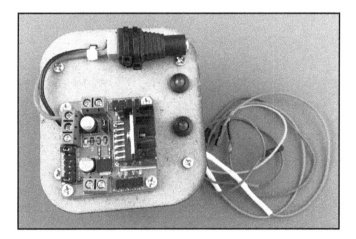

# Step 6 – Attaching the motors and wheels

In this step, we will begin attaching parts to the chassis. We will start by securing the wheel mounts, followed by the motors. The wheel mounts we will use in this step are the 3D printed ones.

The parts needed for this step are shown in the following photo:

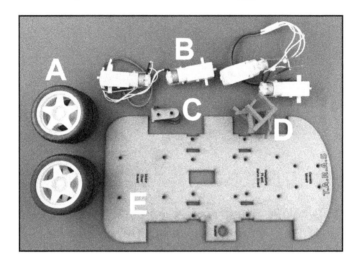

The following is a list of the parts:

- **A**: Wheels
- **B**: Motors
- **C**: Alternative wheel mounts (laser cut)
- **D**: Wheel mounts (3D printed)
- **E**: Robot car chassis (laser cut)
- Eight M3 10 mm bolts (not shown)
- Eight M3 30 mm bolts (not shown)
- 16 M3 nuts (not shown)

Let's start putting it together:

1. Using the 10 mm M3 bolts and nuts, attach each wheel mount (**D**) to the chassis (**E**) so that the head of the bolt sinks flat into the wheel mount (**D**). Refer to the following photo for clarification:

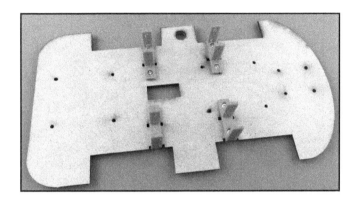

2. Using 30 mm M3 bolts and M3 nuts, mount the motors (**B**) onto the chassis (**E**) by using the wheel mount (**D**). Ensure that the head of the bolt is sunk flat. Refer to the following photo for clarification:

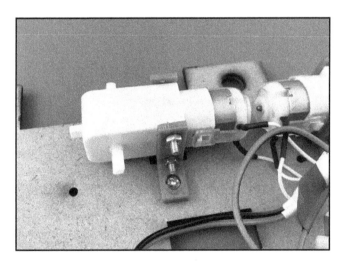

3. Alternatively, you may use part **C** instead of part **D** to mount the wheels. See the following photo for clarification:

4. Attach the wheels (**A**) to the motors (**B**):

# Step 7 – Wiring up the motors

Next, we will attach the motor drive plate assembly and wire up the wheel motors:

1. Start by securing the DC motor plate assembly from step 5 to the top of the chassis using four M3 10 mm bolts. Be sure to thread the wires from the wheel motors through the central hole. The tail light LEDs should go to the back of the robot car. See the following photo for clarification:

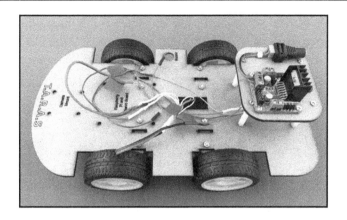

2. Install the wires from the wheel motors into terminal blocks OUT1, OUT2, OUT3, and OUT4 on the motor driver board. The right wires should be connected to OUT1 and OUT2 and the left wires should be connected to OUT3 and OUT4. At this point, it does not matter which of the right wires goes to OUT1 or OUT2 (or left wires regarding OUT3 and OUT4). See the following photo for clarification:

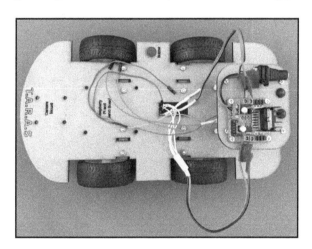

# Step 8 – Attaching the camera mount, Raspberry Pi, and Adafruit servo board

The robot car is starting to look like a robot car. In this step, we will attach the camera mount (or the head of T.A.R.A.S) and Raspberry Pi.

We will start with Raspberry Pi. This is where we must be a little creative in how we mount Raspberry Pi and the Adafruit servo board to the chassis. The Adafruit servo board is an amazing little board, but the kit lacks the standoffs needed to keep part of the board from touching Raspberry Pi. I found it difficult to put an M3 bolt through the mounting holes on the board. My solution was to use 30 mm of female-to-male standoff to attach Raspberry Pi to the chassis and a 10 mm female-to-female standoff to separate Raspberry Pi from the Adafruit servo board.

The following is a photo of Raspberry Pi with some standoffs I gathered:

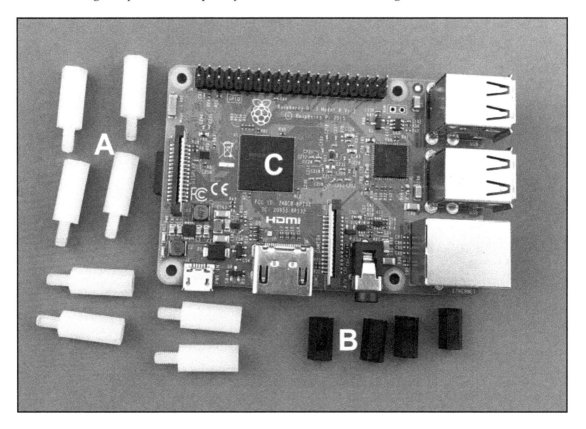

Here are the components in the above image:

- **A**: 15 mm female-to-male nylon standoff
- **B**: 10 mm female-to-female nylon standoff
- **C**: Raspberry Pi

To create this circuit do the following:

1. Create four 30 mm female-to-male standoffs by screwing one end of **A** into another. Screw the **B** standoffs onto the **A** standoffs through Raspberry Pi (see the following photo for clarification):

2. Secure Raspberry Pi to the chassis using four 10 mm M3 bolts:

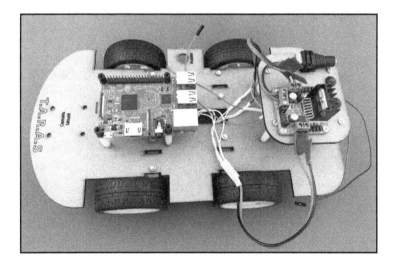

Now, let's attach the camera mount, hook up the camera, and install the Adafruit servo board:

1. Attach the camera mount to the front of the chassis using four 10 mm M3 screws and M3 nuts (see the following photo for clarification):

2. Insert the ribbon cable from the camera module through the appropriate opening of the Adafruit servo board (see the following photo for clarification):

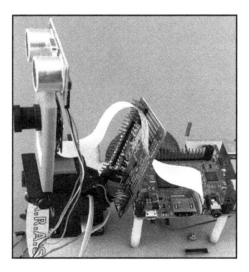

3. Secure the Adafruit servo board onto Raspberry Pi:

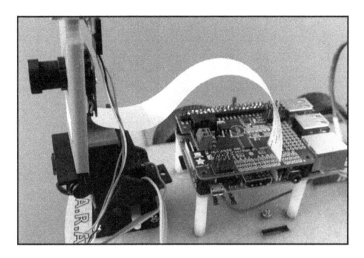

# Step 9 – Attaching the buzzer and voltage divider

The final components to install on the chassis are the buzzer and voltage divider. We need the voltage divider so that we can supply 3.3V to the Raspberry Pi from the echo pin of the distance sensor. For the buzzer, we are using an active buzzer.

An active buzzer omits a sound when a DC voltage is applied to it. Passive buzzers require an AC voltage. More coding is required for a passive buzzer. Passive buzzers are more like little speakers and, as such, you can control the sound coming from them.

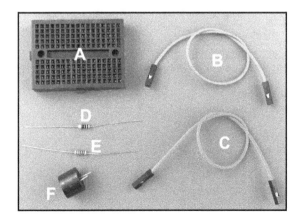

The following are the components that are needed to complete this step:

- **A**: Mini breadboard
- **B**: Brown female-to female jumper wire
- **C**: Red female-to-female jumper wire
- **D**: 470 Ohm resistor
- **E**: 330 Ohm resistor
- **F**: Active buzzer

Follow the below steps to complete the circuit :

1. To create a voltage divider, place the 330 Ohm (**E**) and 470 Ohm (**D**) resistors in series on the breadboard (**A**):

2. Connect the red jumper (**C**) to the positive terminal of the buzzer and the brown jumper (**B**) to the other terminal:

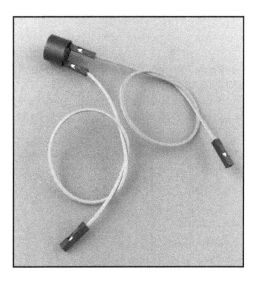

3. Install the buzzer (**F**) in the appropriate hole on the chassis. Using double-sided foam tape, attach the mini breadboard (**A**) to the front of the chassis (see the following photo for clarification):

# Step 10 – Wiring up T.A.R.A.S

Now for the part you have been waiting for: hooking up all the wires! OK, maybe sorting through a rat's nest of wires to make sense of them is not your idea of a good time. However, with a little patience this step, will be over before you know it.

Referring to the following wiring diagram, connect all the wires to their appropriate places. The power and motor connections to the motor driver board are not included in our wiring diagram as we took care of that in step 7,Wiring up the motors. I have taken care to group wire colors by their uses. Please note that the wiring diagram is not to scale:

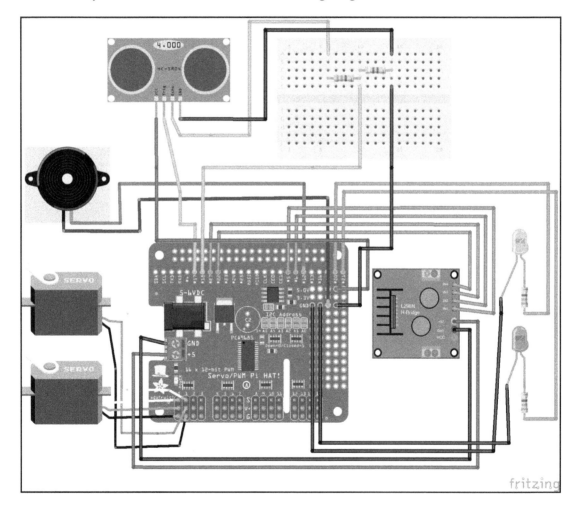

To wire up T.A.R.A.S, perform the following connections:

- Pin five from Servo HAT to In1 on the L298N (motor board)
- Pin six from Servo HAT to In2 on the L298N (motor board)
- Pin 27 from Servo HAT to In3 on the L298N (motor board)
- Pin 22 from Servo HAT to In4 on the L298N (motor board)
- Trig from HC-SR04 (distance sensor) to pin 17 on Servo HAT
- Echo from HC-SR04 (distance sensor) to the left-hand side of the 330 Ohm resistor on the mini breadboard
- VCC from HC-SR04 (distance sensor) to 5 Volts on Servo HAT
- Output from the voltage divider to pin 18 on Servo HAT
- GND from HC-SR04 to the right-hand side of the 470 Ohm resistor on the mini breadboard
- GND from the mini breadboard to the GND on Servo HAT
- +5V from the Servo HAT power terminal (left of the HAT) to +5V on the motor driver board (use a thicker wire)
- GND from the Servo HAT power terminal (left of the HAT) to the GND on the motor driver board (use a thicker wire)
- Servo from the bottom of the camera mount (pan) to servo zero on Servo HAT
- Servo from the middle of the camera mount (tilt) to servo one on Servo HAT
- Red wire from green tail light to pin 20 on the Servo HAT
- Brown wire from green tail light to GND on Servo HAT
- Red wire from red tail light to pin 21 on Servo HAT
- Brown wire on red tail light to GND on Servo HAT
- Red wire from active buzzer to pin 12 on Servo HAT
- Brown wire from active buzzer to GND on Servo HAT

To power up T.A.R.A.S, we will use two portable power supplies. For Raspberry Pi, we will use a standard USB portable power pack. For the motor driver board and Servo HAT, we will use a rechargeable 7.4V battery. To install the batteries, do the following:

1. The following are the two batteries we will be using for our robot car. The one on the left is for Raspberry Pi and uses a USB-to-micro-USB connector. The one on the right is the motor driver board and uses a standard DC jack:

2. Apply peel-and-stick velcro strips to both batteries and to the chassis and put the batteries into place on the chassis:

3. After some much-needed grooming (cleaning up the wires), T.A.R.A.S is ready to go:

# Learning how to control the robot car

In `Chapter 14`, *Controlling the Robot Car Using Python*, we will start writing code to control T.A.R.A.S. Before we jump into the code, it's a good idea to look at how we may set up Raspberry Pi to access the interfaces that are needed. We should install the libraries we need to use to create the control code.

# Configuring our Raspberry Pi

To ensure that we have the inferences that we require enabled for the robot car, do the following:

1. Navigate to **Application Menu** | **Preferences** | **Raspberry Pi Configuration**
2. Click on the **Interfaces** tab

3. Enable **Camera**, **SSH**, and **I2C**. You may need to restart your Raspberry Pi:

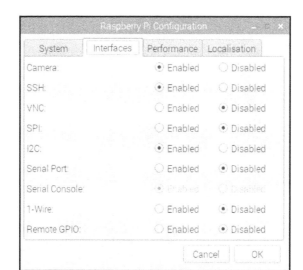

 If you haven't changed the default password for the `pi` user, you may get a warning about it after you enable **SSH**. It's a good idea to change the password from the default. You may change it under the **System** tab in the **Raspberry Pi Configuration** tool.

# Python library for Adafruit Servo HAT

In order to access the Adafruit Servo HAT, you must download and install the library:

1. `git` is used to download the Adafruit Servo HAT library from the internet. Open up a Terminal in Raspbian and type the following:

```
sudo apt-get install -y git build-essential python-dev
```

2. If `git` is already installed, you will get a message indicating that. If not, proceed to install `git`.

3. Type the following into the Terminal to download the library:

```
git clone
https://github.com/adafruit/Adafruit_Python_PCA9685.git
```

4. Type the following to change directories:

    **cd Adafruit_Python_PCA9685**

5. Install the library with the following command:

    **sudo python3 setup.py install**

6. The library has been installed successfully to **Tools | Manage Packages** in Thonny. You should see it listed:

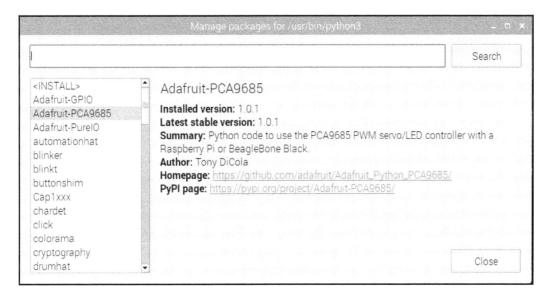

# Summary

In this chapter, we built our robot car, T.A.R.A.S. We started by outlining the parts and then proceeded to put it all together. If you have never built a robot before, then congratulations! You've officially entered the world of robotics. Where you take it from here is up to you.

For the rest of this book, we will be programming T.A.R.A.S to perform tasks. In Chapter 14, *Controlling the Robot Car Using Python*, T.A.R.A.S will be called upon to engage in a secret mission.

# Questions

1. True or false? T.A.R.A.S stands for Technically Advanced Robots Are Superior.
2. What is the difference between an active buzzer and a passive one?
3. True or false? T.A.R.A.S has cameras for eyes.
4. What does the motor driver board do?
5. What is the purpose of the Adafruit Servo HAT?
6. How long should it take to 3D print a wheel brace?
7. What is the purpose of a robot face?
8. True or false? Velcro strips are a great way to secure batteries onto the chassis.

# 14
# Controlling the Robot Car Using Python

In Chapter 13, *Introducing the Raspberry Pi Robot Car*, we built our T.A.R.A.S robot car. At the end of the chapter, we discussed how we could control T.A.R.A.S through code. In this chapter, we will start writing code to do just that.

We will start out by writing simple Python code, and then utilize the GPIO Zero library to make the car wheels move forward, move the servo motors holding the camera, and light up the LEDs at the back of the robot car.

We will then organize our code using classes, before enhancing it further, as we send T.A.R.A.S off on a secret security mission.

The following topics will be covered in this chapter:

- Taking a look at the Python code
- Modifying the robot car Python code
- Enhancing the code

# Knowledge required to complete this chapter

If you have jumped to this chapter without going through the projects in the previous chapters, let me outline the skills you need to complete the following projects. We will, of course, have to know how to get around the Raspbian OS in order to find our **Integrated Development Environment** (**IDE**).

After you have finished programming T.A.R.A.S, you may be inclined to take your new skills and compete against other people building Raspberry Pi robots. Pi Wars (`https://piwars.org/`) is such a place to do just that. Pi Wars is an international robotics competition that takes place in Cambridge in the UK. Up to 76 teams compete in challenge-based robotics competitions over the course of a weekend. Even though it is called Pi Wars, you can rest assured that you will not come back with a box of broken parts, as each of the competitions are non-destructive challenges. Check out `https://piwars.org/`, or search for Pi Wars videos on YouTube for more information.

As well, a working knowledge of Python is needed, as we will be doing all our coding in this chapter in Python. Since I like to use an object-oriented approach as much as I can, some knowledge of **Object-Oriented Programming** (**OOP**) will help you to benefit more from this chapter as well.

# Project overview

In this chapter, we will program T.A.R.A.S to dance around the table and take photographs. The projects in this chapter should take a few hours to complete.

# Getting started

To complete this project, the following will be required:

- A Raspberry Pi Model 3 (2015 model or newer)
- A USB power supply
- A computer monitor
- A USB keyboard
- A USB mouse
- A completed T.A.R.A.S robot car kit (see `Chapter 13`, *Introducing the Raspberry Pi Robot Car*)

# Taking a look at the Python code

In a way, our robot car project is like an overview of the code we've done in previous chapters. Through the use of Python and the amazing GPIO Zero library, we are able to read sensory data from the GPIO and control output devices by writing to GPIO pins. In the following steps, we will start with very simple Python code and the GPIO Zero library. If you have completed some of the earlier projects in the book, the code will seem quite familiar to you.

# Controlling the drive wheels of the robot car

Let's see if we can make T.A.R.A.S move a little. We will start by writing some basic code to move the robot car back and forth:

1. Open up Thonny from **Application Menu** | **Programming** | **Thonny Python IDE**
2. Click on the **New** icon to create a new file
3. Type the following code into the file:

```
from gpiozero import Robot
from time import sleep

robot = Robot(left=(5,6), right=(22,27))
robot.forward(0.2)
sleep(0.5)
robot.backward(0.2)
sleep(0.5)
robot.stop()
```

4. Save the file as motor-test.py
5. Run the code

You should see the robot car move forward for 0.5 seconds, before moving backward for the same amount of time. If there was nothing in the way, the robot car should have returned to the same position it started from. The code is pretty self-explanatory; however, we will go over it now.

We start off by importing the libraries we need: `Robot` and `sleep`. After that, we instantiate a `Robot` object, called `robot`, and configure it to have the `5` and `6` pins for the left-hand side motors, and `22` and `27` for the right-hand side motors. After that, we move the robot forward at a speed of `0.2`. In order for the robot to go faster, we increase this value. After a short delay, we return the robot back to its original position with the `robot.backward(0.2)` command.

One thing to take note of is the way the motors spin, and keep spinning, until they are stopped with the `robot.stop()` command.

> If you found that the motors did not move the way they should, it is because of the wiring. Try experimenting with the wiring and changing the pin numbers for the `Robot` object (`left=(5,6)`, `right=(22,27)`. It may take a few tries to get it right.

# Moving the servos on the robot car

We will now test the servo motors. To do this, we will pan the robot camera mount (the robot's head) from right to left:

1. Open up Thonny from **Application Menu** | **Programming** | **Thonny Python IDE**
2. Click on the **New** icon to create a new file
3. Type the following code into the file:

```
import Adafruit_PCA9685
from time import sleep

pwm = Adafruit_PCA9685.PCA9685()
servo_min = 150
servo_max = 600

while True:
    pwm.set_pwm(0, 0, servo_min)
    sleep(5)
    pwm.set_pwm(0, 0, servo_max)
    sleep(5)
```

4. Save the file as `servo-test.py`
5. Run the code

You should see the robot head move all the way to the right, wait for 5 seconds, and then move all the way to the left.

In the code, we start by importing the `Adafruit_PCA9685` library. After importing the `sleep` function, we then create a `PCA9685` object that we call `pwm`. This is, of course, an object built with code from Adafruit to support the HAT. We then set the minimum and maximum values that the servo can move, with `servo_min` and `servo_max` respectively.

 If you are not getting the results you expect, experiment with the `servo_min` and `servo_max` values. We touch a bit on servos in `Chapter` 5, *Controlling a Servo with Python*.

# Taking a picture

You may remember using the Raspberry Pi camera from previous chapters; in particular, `Chapter 9`, *Building a Home Security Dashboard*, where we used it to take a picture for our security application. Since T.A.R.A.S will be our trusty security agent, it makes sense for it to have the ability to take pictures. Let's write some code to test out that the camera is working on our robot car:

1. Open up Thonny from **Application Menu** | **Programming** | **Thonny Python IDE**
2. Click on the **New** icon to create a new file
3. Enter the following code:

```
from picamera import PiCamera
import time

camera = PiCamera()
camera.capture("/home/pi/image-" + time.ctime() + ".png")
```

4. Save the file as `camera-test.py`
5. Run the code

If everything is set up correctly, you should see an image file in your `/home/pi` directory, with the name `image`, followed by today's date.

# Making a beep noise

Our security agent is limited to making a noise in order to alert us and scare away potential intruders. In this section, we will test the active buzzer installed on T.A.R.A.S.

 The old British police whistle was one of the earliest and trusted pieces of equipment that police officers of the past had to defend themselves. With its unique sound, the police whistle allowed officers to communicate with each other. Despite the fact that police whistles are no longer in use, its legacy has left its impact on society, such that the term 'Whistle Blower' is used to this day to refer to someone exposing hidden injustices or corruption.

1. Open up Thonny from **Application Menu** | **Programming** | **Thonny Python IDE**
2. Click on the **New** icon to create a new file
3. Type the following code into the file:

```
from gpiozero import Buzzer
from time import sleep

buzzer = Buzzer(12)
buzzer.on()
sleep(5)
buzzer.off()
```

4. Save the file as `buzzer-test.py`
5. Run the code

You should hear the buzzer sound for 5 seconds, before shutting off.

# Making the LEDs blink

On the back of T.A.R.A.S, we have installed two LEDs (preferably, one red one and one green one). We have used simple GPIO Zero library commands to blink LEDs before, so that shouldn't be a challenge for us. Let's take this a step further, and create code that we can use to encapsulate LED blinking patterns:

1. Open up Thonny from **Application Menu** | **Programming** | **Thonny Python IDE**
2. Click on the **New** icon to create a new file

3. Type the following code:

```
from gpiozero import LEDBoard
from time import sleep

class TailLights:
    led_lights = LEDBoard(red=21, green=20)
    def __init__(self):
        self.led_lights.on()
        sleep(0.25)
        self.led_lights.off()
        sleep(0.25)
    def blink_red(self, num, duration):
        for x in range(num):
            self.led_lights.red.on()
            sleep(duration)
            self.led_lights.red.off()
            sleep(duration)
    def blink_green(self, num, duration):
        for x in range(num):
            self.led_lights.green.on()
            sleep(duration)
            self.led_lights.green.off()
            sleep(duration)
    def blink_alternating(self, num, duration):
        for x in range(num):
            self.led_lights.red.off()
            self.led_lights.green.on()
            sleep(duration)
            self.led_lights.red.on()
            self.led_lights.green.off()
            sleep(duration)
        self.led_lights.red.off()
    def blink_together(self, num, duration):
        for x in range(num):
            self.led_lights.on()
            sleep(duration)
            self.led_lights.off()
            sleep(duration)
    def alarm(self, num):
        for x in range(num):
            self.blink_alternating(2, 0.25)
            self.blink_together(2, 0.5)

if __name__=="__main__":

    tail_lights = TailLights()
    tail_lights.alarm(20)
```

4. Save the file as `TailLights.py`

5. Run the code

You should see a 20-second long, blinking display from the LEDs. Of note in our code, however, is the use of the `LEDBoard` class from the GPIO Zero library, as follows:

```
led_lights = LEDBoard(red=21, green=20)
```

In this code, we instantiate an object, called `led_lights`, from the `LEDBoard` class, and configure it with the values of `red` and `green`, pointing to the `21` and `20` GPIO pins respectively. By using `LEDBoard`, we are able to control the LEDs separately or as one unit. The `blink_together` method controls the LEDs as one unit, as follows:

```
def blink_together(self, num, duration):
        for x in range(num):
            self.led_lights.on()
            sleep(duration)
            self.led_lights.off()
            sleep(duration)
```

Our code is rather self explanatory; however, there are few other things we should point out. When we initialize the `TailLights` object, we give the LEDs a short blink to signify that the object has been initialized. This allows for troubleshooting later on; although, if we feel that the code is redundant, then we can remove it later instead:

```
def __init__(self):
        self.led_lights.on()
        sleep(0.25)
        self.led_lights.off()
        sleep(0.25)
```

Keeping the initialization code in place may come in handy though when we want to ensure that our LEDs have not been disconnected (after all, who hasn't disconnected something when trying to connect something else?). To do this from the shell, type the following code:

```
import TailLights
tail_lights = TailLights.TailLights()
```

You should see the LEDs blink for half a second.

# Modifying the robot car Python code

Now that we have tested the motors, servos, camera, and LEDs, it's time to modify the code into classes to give it more unity. In this section, we will make T.A.R.A.S dance.

## Move the wheels

Let's start by encapsulating the code that moves the wheels on the robot car:

1. Open up Thonny from **Application Menu | Programming | Thonny Python IDE**
2. Click on the **New** icon to create a new file
3. Type the following code into the file:

```python
from gpiozero import Robot
from time import sleep

class RobotWheels:
    robot = Robot(left=(5, 6), right=(22, 27))
    def __init__(self):
        pass
    def move_forward(self):
        self.robot.forward(0.2)
    def move_backwards(self):
        self.robot.backward(0.2)
    def turn_right(self):
        self.robot.right(0.2)
    def turn_left(self):
        self.robot.left(0.2)
    def dance(self):
        self.move_forward()
        sleep(0.5)
        self.stop()
        self.move_backwards()
        sleep(0.5)
        self.stop()
        self.turn_right()
        sleep(0.5)
        self.stop()
        self.turn_left()
        sleep(0.5)
        self.stop()

    def stop(self):
        self.robot.stop()
```

```
if __name__=="__main__":

    robot_wheels = RobotWheels()
    robot_wheels.dance()
```

4. Save the file as `RobotWheels.py`
5. Run the code

You should see T.A.R.A.S do a little dance in front of you. Be sure to keep the wires that connect to T.A.R.A.S loose, so that T.A.R.A.S can do its thing. Who says that robots can't dance?

The code is pretty self explanatory. Of note, though, is the way we call the `move_forward`, `move_backwards`, `turn_left`, and `turn_right` functions from the `dance` method. We could actually parameterize the amount of time between the moves, but that would complicate things a little more than need be. The delay of `0.5` seconds (coupled with the hardcoded speed of `0.2`) seems to be perfect for a dancing robot that does not fall off the desk. Think of it as T.A.R.A.S being on a very crowded dance floor with little room to move.

But wait, there's more. T.A.R.A.S can also move its head, light up, and make some noise. Let's start to add these moves.

# Move the head

Since the camera on T.A.R.A.S is attached to the head, it makes sense to encapsulate the head movements (camera mount servos) with the camera functionality:

1. Open up Thonny from **Application Menu | Programming | Thonny Python IDE**
2. Click on the **New** icon to create a new file
3. Type the following code into the file:

```
from time import sleep
from time import ctime
from picamera import PiCamera
import Adafruit_PCA9685

class RobotCamera:
    pan_min = 150
    pan_centre = 375
    pan_max = 600
    tilt_min = 150
```

```
        tilt_max = 200
        camera = PiCamera()
        pwm = Adafruit_PCA9685.PCA9685()
        def __init__(self):
            self.tilt_up()
        def pan_right(self):
            self.pwm.set_pwm(0, 0, self.pan_min)
            sleep(2)
        def pan_left(self):
            self.pwm.set_pwm(0, 0, self.pan_max)
            sleep(2)
        def pan_mid(self):
            self.pwm.set_pwm(0, 0, self.pan_centre)
            sleep(2)
        def tilt_down(self):
            self.pwm.set_pwm(1, 0, self.tilt_max)
            sleep(2)
        def tilt_up(self):
            self.pwm.set_pwm(1, 0, self.tilt_min)
            sleep(2)
        def take_picture(self):
            sleep(2)
            self.camera.capture("/home/pi/image-" + ctime() + ".png")
        def dance(self):
            self.pan_right()
            self.tilt_down()
            self.tilt_up()
            self.pan_left()
            self.pan_mid()
        def secret_dance(self):
            self.pan_right()
            self.tilt_down()
            self.tilt_up()
            self.pan_left()
            self.pan_mid()
            self.take_picture()

    if __name__=="__main__":

        robot_camera = RobotCamera()
        robot_camera.dance()
```

4. Save the file as RobotCamera.py

5. Run the code

You should see T.A.R.A.S move its head to the right, then down, then up, and then all the way to the left, before returning to the middle and stopping.

Again, we try and write our code so that it is simple to figure out. The `init` method, called when a `RobotCamera` object is instantiated, ensures that T.A.R.A.S has its head up before moving it:

```
def __init__(self):
    self.tilt_up()
```

By calling the `RobotCamera` class, we structure our code to view the servos and movement of the robot car's head as part of operating the camera. Although we don't use the camera in our example, we will be using it soon. The values that are set for the minimum and maximum servo position were determined though trial and error as follows:

```
pan_min = 150
pan_centre = 375
pan_max = 600
tilt_min = 150
tilt_max = 200
```

Play around with these values to make it suit your build of the T.A.R.A.S robot car.

The `dance` and `secret_dance` methods perform a series of moves with the head of the robot car to simulate dancing. They are basically the same method (with the exception of the `take_picture` call at the end) of the `secret_dance` method that takes a picture with the Raspberry Pi camera and stores it in the home directory with a date-based name.

# Make sounds

Now that T.A.R.A.S can move its body and head, it's time to make some noise:

1. Open up Thonny from **Application Menu** | **Programming** | **Thonny Python IDE**
2. Click on the **New** icon to create a new file
3. Type the following code into the file

   ```
   from gpiozero import Buzzer
   from time import sleep

   class RobotBeep:
       buzzer = Buzzer(12)
       notes =
   [[0.5,0.5],[0.5,1],[0.2,0.5],[0.5,0.5],[0.5,1],[0.2,0.5]]
   ```

```
def __init__(self, play_init=False):
    if play_init:
        self.buzzer.on()
        sleep(0.1)
        self.buzzer.off()
        sleep(1)
def play_song(self):
    for note in self.notes:
        self.buzzer.on()
        sleep(note[0])
        self.buzzer.off()
        sleep(note[1])

if __name__=="__main__":

    robot_beep = RobotBeep(True)
```

4. Save the file as `RobotBeep.py`
5. Run the code

You should hear a short beep coming from the active buzzer on T.A.R.A.S. This seems like a lot of code just to do that, doesn't it? Ah, but wait until the next section, when we take full advantage of the `RobotBeep` class.

The `init` function of `RobotBeep` allow us to turn on and off the initial beep that is heard once the class is instantiated. This is good for testing that our buzzer actually works, which we do by passing `True` to the class when we are creating the `robot_beep` object:

```
robot_beep = RobotBeep(True)
```

The `notes` list and `play_song` methods perform the actual magic of the class. The list is actually a list of lists, as each value represents the time the buzzer plays or rests:

```
for note in self.notes:
    self.buzzer.on()
    sleep(note[0])
    self.buzzer.off()
    sleep(note[1])
```

Cycling through the `notes` list, look at the `note` variable. We use the first element as the length of time for which to keep the buzzer on, and the second element as the amount of time to rest before turning the buzzer back on. In other words, the first element determines the length of the note, and the second the space between that note and the next note. The `notes` list and `play_song` method give T.A.R.A.S the ability to sing (albeit without a melody).

We will use the `play_song` method in our next section.

# Enhancing the code

It's a cold, dark, and dreary December night. Not much is known about our adversaries, but we do know that they like to dance. T.A.R.A.S has been assigned to a local dance club located deep into enemy territory. All of the persons of interest are there on this night. Your mission, should you choose to accept it, is to write a program to have T.A.R.A.S take secret photos at the club. However, it must not look like T.A.R.A.S is taking photos. T.A.R.A.S has to dance! If our adversaries found out that T.A.R.A.S was taking photos, that would be bad. Really bad! Think C3PO in the Empire Strikes Back bad.

## Stitching our code together

So, we have the ability to make T.A.R.A.S move its head and body, make sounds, light up, and take pictures. Let's put all of this together so that we may complete the mission:

1. Open up Thonny from **Application Menu** | **Programming** | **Thonny Python IDE**
2. Click on the **New** icon to create a new file
3. Type the following into the file:

```python
from RobotWheels import RobotWheels
from RobotBeep import RobotBeep
from TailLights import TailLights
from RobotCamera import RobotCamera

class RobotDance:
    light_show = [2,1,4,5,3,1]
    def __init__(self):
        self.robot_wheels = RobotWheels()
        self.robot_beep = RobotBeep()
        self.tail_lights = TailLights()
        self.robot_camera = RobotCamera()
```

```
def lets_dance_incognito(self):
    for tail_light_repetition in self.light_show:
        self.robot_wheels.dance()
        self.robot_beep.play_song()
        self.tail_lights.alarm(tail_light_repetition)
        self.robot_camera.secret_dance()

if __name__=="__main__":

    robot_dance = RobotDance()
    robot_dance.lets_dance_incognito()
```

4. Save the file as `RobotDance.py`
5. Run the code

You should see T.A.R.A.S perform a series of moves before secretly taking a picture. If you check the Raspberry Pi `home` folder after the dance is done, you should see six new photos.

Something of note in our code is the use of the list called `light_show`. We use this list in two ways. First, the values stored in the list are passed to the `alarm` method of the `TailLights` object that we instantiate in our `RobotDance` class. We do this with the `tail_light_repetition` variable in the `lets_dance_incognito` method, as shown here:

```
def lets_dance_incognito(self):
    for tail_light_repetition in self.light_show:
        self.robot_wheels.dance()
        self.robot_beep.play_song()
        self.tail_lights.alarm(tail_light_repetition)
        self.robot_camera.secret_dance()
```

As you can see in the previous code, the variable of the `TailLights` class for the `alarm` method is named `tail_lights`. This will cause the LEDs to go through their sequence a number of times, based on the value of `tail_light_repetition`. For example, when the value of 2 is passed into the `alarm` method (the first value in the `light_show` list), the LED sequence will be performed twice.

We run the `lets_dance_incognito` method six times. This is based on the number of values in the `light_show` list. This is the second way in which we use `light_show`. In order to increase or decrease the number of times that T.A.R.A.S performs the dance, we can either add or subtract some numbers from the `light_show` list.

As we are calling the `secret_dance` method on the `RobotCamera` object named `robot_camera`, for each value in the `light_show` list (in this case, six), we should have six photos in our home directory with date-based names after the dance is done.

After T.A.R.A.S performs its dance, check the home directory for pictures T.A.R.A.S took during the dance. Mission accomplished!

# Summary

By the end of this chapter, you should be familiar with controlling a Raspberry Pi-powered robot with Python code. We started off by simply getting the various components on the robot car to work using simple code. After we were satisfied that the robot car does indeed move using our Python commands, we encapsulated the code in classes in order to make it easier to work with. This resulted in the `RobotDance` class, that contained calls to classes, which, in turn, encapsulated the control code for our robot. This allowed us to use the `RobotDance` class as a black box, abstracting away control code, and allowing us to focus on the task of designing dance steps for T.A.R.A.S.

In `Chapter 15`, *Connecting Sensory Inputs from the Robot Car to the Web*, we will pull sensory information from T.A.R.A.S (the distance sensor values) and publish it to the web, before unleashing T.A.R.A.S from the wires on the desktop and setting it free.

# Questions

1. True or false? The `LEDBoard` object allows us to control many LEDs at the same time.
2. True or false? The notes list on the `RobotCamera` object is used to move the camera mount.
3. True or false? The adversaries in our fictional story love to dance.
4. What is the difference between the `dance` and `secret_dance` methods?
5. What is the name of the `gpiozero` library for robots?
6. What is the term, inspired by the old police whistle, given to the act of exposing crime?
7. True or false? Encapsulating control code is a meaningless and unnecessary step.
8. What is the purpose of the `TailLights` class?
9. Which class and method would we use to turn the robot car to the right?
10. What is the purpose of the `RobotCamera` class?

# Further reading

One of the best reference books for learning GPIO Zero is the GPIO Zero PDF document itself. Google search for GPIO Zero PDF, and then download and read it.

# 15
# Connecting Sensory Inputs from the Robot Car to the Web

In order to make our robot car, T.A.R.A.S, a true IoT **thing**, we have to connect T.A.R.A.S to the internet. In this chapter, we will start the transformation from desktop robot to internet robot by connecting the distance sensor from T.A.R.A.S to the web.

The following topics will be covered in this chapter:

- Identifying the sensor on the robot car
- Reading robot car sensory data with Python
- Publishing robot car sensory data to the cloud

## Knowledge required to complete this chapter

To complete this chapter, you should have built a T.A.R.A.S robot car, as described in detail in `Chapter 13`, *Introducing the Raspberry Pi Robot Car*. As with the other chapters in this book, a working knowledge of Python is required, as well as a basic understanding of object-oriented programming.

# Project overview

The project in this chapter will involve sending sensory distance data from T.A.R.A.S to the internet. We will create an online dashboard using ThingsBoard, which will display this distance information on an analogue gauge.

This project should take a couple of hours to complete.

# Getting started

To complete this project, the following will be required:

- A Raspberry Pi Model 3 (2015 model or newer)
- A USB power supply
- A computer monitor
- A USB keyboard
- A USB mouse
- A completed T.A.R.A.S robot car kit (see `Chapter 13`, *Introducing the Raspberry Pi Robot Car*)

# Identifying the sensor on the robot car

Throughout the course of the book, we have used a few input sensors. We have also published data from these sensors to the web. T.A.R.A.S. uses a distance sensor to detect objects close by, as can be seen in the following picture:

Looking at T.A.R.A.S for the first time, you would be forgiven for not knowing where the distance sensor is located. On T.A.R.A.S, and many other robots, this sensor is located in the eyes.

The following is a photo of the HC-SR04 distance sensor—the one used on T.A.R.A.S:

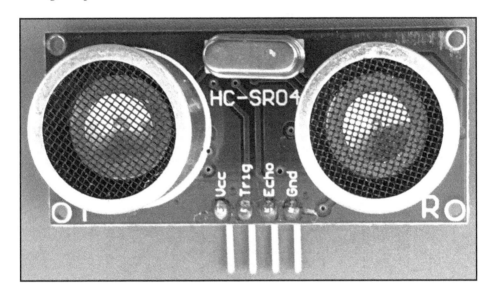

 If you do a Google image search for HC-SR04 on robots, you will see many, many robots that use this sensor. It is a very popular choice due to its low cost and wide availability, as well as its handy resemblance to eyes.

# Taking a closer look at the HC-SR04

As mentioned, the HC-SR04 is a very popular sensor. It is easy to program, and is available from multiple vendors on www.aliexpress.com. The HC-SR04 provides measurements from 2 cm to 400 cm, and is accurate to within 3 mm.

The GPIO Zero library makes it easy to read data from the HC-SR04. The following diagram is a wiring diagram for using this sensor with the Raspberry Pi:

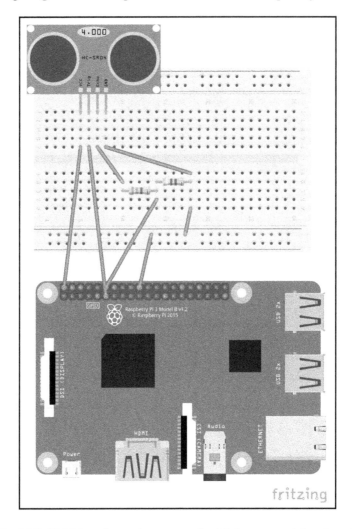

As you can see, the HC-SR04 has four pins, two of which are used for the signal input and output. The wiring diagram is a subdiagram of the one we used to wire up T.A.R.A.S in `Chapter 13`, *Introducing the Raspberry Pi Robot Car*. The connections are as follows:

- Trig from HC-SR04 (distance sensor) to pin 17 on the Raspberry Pi
- Echo from HC-SR04 (distance sensor) to the left side of the 330 Ohm resistor on the breadboard

- VCC from HC-SR04 (distance sensor) to 5V on the Raspberry Pi
- Output from voltage divider to pin 18 on the Raspberry Pi
- GND from HC-SR04 to the right side of the 470 Ohm resistor on the breadboard

The trig, or trigger, is the input of the HC-SR04, and works with 5V or 3.3V. The Echo pin is the output, and is designed to work with 5V. Since this is a little too much for our Raspberry Pi to handle, we use a voltage divider circuit to reduce the voltage to 3.3V.

We could have added further sensors to T.A.R.A.S to make it more advanced, including line-tracking sensors, temperature sensors, light sensors, and PID sensors. The line-tracking sensor is of particular interest, as a simple line could provide T.A.R.A.S with a route to follow during its security patrol duties—a very useful addition. As the design is already complicated enough, I will leave it to you to add this functionality if you choose.

The following diagram outlines how a line-tracking sensor works:

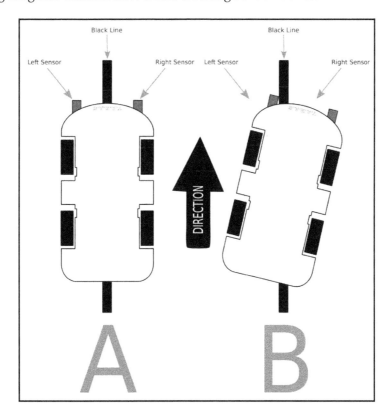

In the diagram, you will see two sensors at the front of the robot car. When the robot car veers off to the side, one of the sensors picks it up. In the previous example, the car in position **B** has veered to the right. The left sensor picks this up, and the program makes corrections by turning the robot car to the left until it returns to position **A**.

# Reading robot car sensory data with Python

Although we have covered this before, it's a good idea to familiarize (or re-familiarize) ourselves with the programming of the HC-SR04:

1. Open up Thonny from **Application Menu** | **Programming** | **Thonny Python IDE**.
2. Click **New** to create a new file.
3. Type the following:

```
from gpiozero import DistanceSensor
from time import sleep

distance_sensor = DistanceSensor(echo=18, trigger=17)

while True:
    print('Distance: ', distance_sensor.distance*100)
    sleep(1)
```

4. Save the file as `distance-sensor-test.py`.
5. Run the code.
6. Place your hand in front of the distance sensor. You should see the following in the shell (depending on how far your hand is from the distance sensor):

```
Distance: 5.05452024001
```

7. As you move your hand closer to, or farther away from, the distance sensor, the value will change. This code is pretty self explanatory. The `distance_sensor = DistanceSensor(echo=18, trigger=17)` line sets up a `distance_sensor` object of class type `DistanceSensor`, with the appropriate pin definitions. We retrieve the distance an object is from the HC-SR04 every time we call the `distance` method of `distance_sensor`. To convert the value to centimeters, we multiply it by 100.

Now that we are able to retrieve values from the distance sensor, let's modify the code to make it more object-oriented friendly:

1. Open up Thonny from **Application Menu** | **Programming** | **Thonny Python IDE**
2. Click **New** to create a new file
3. Type the following:

```
from gpiozero import DistanceSensor
from time import sleep

class RobotEyes:
    distance_sensor = DistanceSensor(echo=18, trigger=17)
    def get_distance(self):
        return self.distance_sensor.distance*100
if __name__=="__main__":

    robot_eyes = RobotEyes()
    while True:
        print('Distance: ', robot_eyes.get_distance())
        sleep(1)
```

4. Save the file as `RobotEyes.py`
5. Run the code

The code should run in exactly the same way as before. The only thing we did was to wrap it up in a class in order to abstract it. This will make things easier as we write more code. We won't have to remember which pins the HC-SR04 is connected to, and we actually don't need to know that it is a distance sensor that we are getting data from. This code makes more sense visually than the previous code.

# Publishing robot car sensory data to the cloud

In `Chapter 10`, *Publishing to Web Services*, we set up a ThingsBoard account for publishing sensory data. If you have not already done so, set up an account at `www.ThingsBoard.io` (refer to `Chapter 10`, *Publishing to Web Services*, for instructions on how to do this).

# Create a ThingsBoard device

To publish our distance sensor data to ThingsBoard, we first need to create a ThingsBoard Device:

1. Log in to your account at `https://demo.thingsboard.io/login`
2. Click on **Devices**, and then the large orange + sign at the bottom-right corner of the screen:

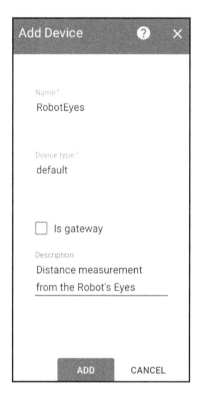

3. Type in `RobotEyes` for the **Name**, leave the **Device type** as `default`, and put in a meaningful description under **Description**
4. Click **ADD**
5. Click on `RobotEyes` to get a menu sliding out from the right
6. Click **COPY ACCESS TOKEN** to copy the token onto your clipboard
7. Paste the token into a text file

For our code, we will be using the MQTT protocol. If the Paho MQTT library has not been installed on your Raspberry Pi, do the following:

1. Open a Terminal application from the Raspberry Pi main toolbar
2. Type `sudo pip3 install pho-mqtt`

You should see the library install.

Now it's time to write the code that will publish the sensory data of T.A.R.A.S to the web. We will modify our `RobotEyes` class:

1. Open up Thonny from **Application Menu** | **Programming** | **Thonny Python IDE**
2. Click **New** to create a new file
3. Type the following:

```python
from gpiozero import DistanceSensor
from time import sleep
import paho.mqtt.client as mqtt
import json

class RobotEyes:
    distance_sensor = DistanceSensor(echo=18, trigger=17)
    host = 'demo.thingsboard.io'
    access_token='<<access token>>'
    def get_distance(self):
        return self.distance_sensor.distance*100
    def publish_distance(self):
        distance = self.get_distance()
        sensor_data = {'distance': 0}
        sensor_data['distance'] = distance
        client = mqtt.Client()
        client.username_pw_set(self.access_token)
        client.connect(self.host, 1883, 20)
        client.publish('v1/devices/me/telemetry',
            json.dumps(sensor_data), 1)
        client.disconnect()
if __name__=="__main__":
    robot_eyes = RobotEyes()
    while True:
        print('Distance: ', robot_eyes.get_distance())
        robot_eyes.publish_distance()
        sleep(5)
```

4. Be sure to paste the access token from the text file to the `access_token` variable

5. Save the file as `RobotEyesIOT.py`

6. Run the code

You should see the `distance` value in the shell, just as you did before. However, when you go to ThingsBoard and click on **Latest Telemetry**, you should see the same value, as follows:

What we have accomplished here, just as in `Chapter 10`, *Publishing to Web Services*, is the successful transmission of our distance sensor information to the internet. We can now see how close an object is to our robot car from anywhere in the world. In the previous screenshot, we can see that there is *something* 3.801 cm away.

Once again, we've written the code to be as self-explanatory as possible. However, we should point out the `publish_distance` method of the class:

```
def publish_distance(self):
 distance = self.get_distance()
 sensor_data = {'distance': 0}
 sensor_data['distance'] = distance
 client = mqtt.Client()
 client.username_pw_set(self.access_token)
 client.connect(self.host, 1883, 20)
 client.publish('v1/devices/me/telemetry',
 json.dumps((sensor_data), 1)
 client.disconnect()
```

In this method, we start by creating a variable called `distance`, which we populate with the actual distance information from our class `get_distance` method. A Python dictionary object called `sensor_data` is created, and is used to store the `distance` value. From there, we create an MQTT client object called `client`. We set the password to the `access_token` we copied from ThingsBoard, and then connect using standard ThingsBoard boilerplate code.

The `client.publish` method sends our `sensor_data` to ThingsBoard through a `json.dumps` method. We then disconnect from `client` to close the connection.

Now, let's create a dashboard widget using our distance sensory data:

1. In ThingsBoard, click **Latest Telemetry**, and check the box in the list next to the `distance` value:

2. Click **SHOW ON WIDGET**
3. Under **Current bundle**, select `Analogue gauges` from the drop-down menu, as follows:

4. Select the last widget:

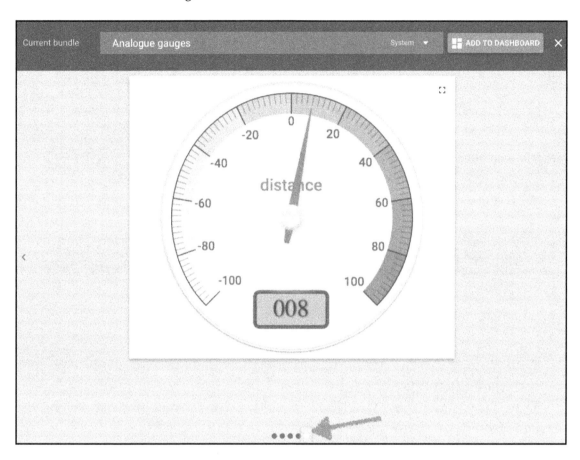

5. Click **ADD TO DASHBOARD** at the top

6. Create a new dashboard called `RobotEyes`, and check the **Open dashboard** box:

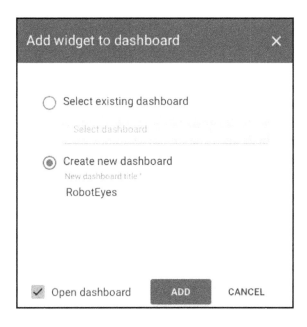

7. Click **ADD**
8. Congratulations! We now have created an IoT dashboard widget for the sensory distance information from T.A.R.A.S. With this, we can go fullscreen and view the information easily:

# Summary

In this chapter, we turned T.A.R.A.S into a true IoT thing by publishing the distance data—the distance from the eyes of T.A.R.A.S to any object within its view—to the internet. By encapsulating our code into a class called `RobotEyes`, we can forget that we are dealing with a distance sensor and just focus on the eyes of T.A.R.A.S as behaving sonar-like.

Through the use of the demo platform in ThingsBoard, we are able to write code that sends the distance information from T.A.R.A.S to a dashboard widget for display. If we really wanted to be creative, we could connect an actual analogue device via a servo and display the distance information that way (as we did in `Chapter 6`, *Working with the Servo Control Code to Control an Analog Device*). In `Chapter 16`, *Controlling the Robot Car with Web Service Calls*, we will take things a step further and start to control T.A.R.A.S from the internet.

# Questions

1. Why do we use a voltage divider circuit when connecting the HC-SR04 to the Raspberry Pi?
2. True or false? T.A.R.A.S has eyes that see through the use of sonar.
3. What is a device in ThingsBoard?
4. True or false? Our class, `RobotEyes`, encapsulates the Raspberry Pi camera module used on T.A.R.A.S.
5. What does the `RobotEyes.publish_distance` method do?
6. True or false? The library that we require to work with MQTT comes pre-installed with Raspbian.
7. Why do we name our class `RobotEyes`, and not `RobotDistanceSensor`?
8. True or false? Encapsulating boilerplate code in a class makes the code much more difficult to work with.
9. True or false? The GPIO Zero library does not have support for distance sensors.
10. What is the difference between `RobotEyes.py` and `RobotEyesIOT.py`?

# Further reading

A good source of guidance for the ThingsBoard platform is its own website. Go to `www.thingsboard.io/docs/guides` to find more information.

# 16
# Controlling the Robot Car with Web Service Calls

One day, driverless cars will dominate our streets and highways. Although the sensory information and control algorithms will be located in the car itself, we will have the ability (and it will possibly be a legislative requirement) to control the cars from elsewhere. Controlling driverless cars will require sensory information from the car to be sent to a control station in the form of speed, GPS location, and so on. Conversely, information from the control station will be sent to the car in the form of traffic and directions.

In this chapter, we will explore both the sending of sensory information from T.A.R.A.S and the receiving of control information by T.A.R.A.S.

The following topics will be covered in this chapter:

- Reading the robot car's data from the cloud
- Using a Python program to control a robot car through the cloud

## Knowledge required to complete this chapter

To complete this chapter, you should have a completed T.A.R.A.S robot car, as described in detail in `Chapter 13`, *Introducing the Raspberry Pi Robot Car*. As with our other chapters in this book, a working knowledge of Python is required, as well as a basic understanding of object-oriented programming.

# Project overview

The projects in this chapter will involve communicating with T.A.R.A.S through the internet. We will take a deeper look at the dashboard analogue dial that we created in Chapter 15, *Connecting Sensory Inputs from the Robot Car to the Web*, before we create switches on the dashboard that control T.A.R.A.S. These projects should take about 2 hours to complete.

# Technical requirements

To complete this project, the following will be required:

- A Raspberry Pi Model 3 (2015 model or newer)
- A USB power supply
- A computer monitor
- A USB keyboard
- A USB mouse
- A completed T.A.R.A.S robot car kit (see Chapter 13, *Introducing the Raspberry Pi Robot Car*)

# Reading the robot car's data from the cloud

In Chapter 15, *Connecting Sensory Inputs from the Robot Car to the Web*, we were able to send the distance sensory data to the cloud using the website https://thingsboard.io/. We ended by showing an analogue meter displaying the distance value. In this section, we will dig a little deeper into the analogue widget by customizing it.

## Changing the look of the distance gauge

This is how we change the look of the distance gauge:

1. Log into your ThingsBoard account
2. Click on **DASHBOARDS**
3. Click on the **ROBOTEYES** title

4. Click on the orange pencil icon in the bottom-right corner of the screen
5. You will notice that the **distance** analogue dial has changed (see the following screenshot)
6. For one thing, there are three new icons located at the top-right corner of the dial
7. At the bottom-right corner, the color has changed to light gray as well
8. You may resize the widget by hovering your mouse over the bottom-right corner
9. You may also move the widget around the dashboard
10. The **X** in the top-right corner allows you to remove this widget from the dashboard
11. The icon with the underlined arrow allows you to download the widget as a `.json` file. This file may be used to import the widget into another dashboard on ThingsBoard
12. Clicking on the pencil icon on the widget produces a menu that slides out from the right-hand side:

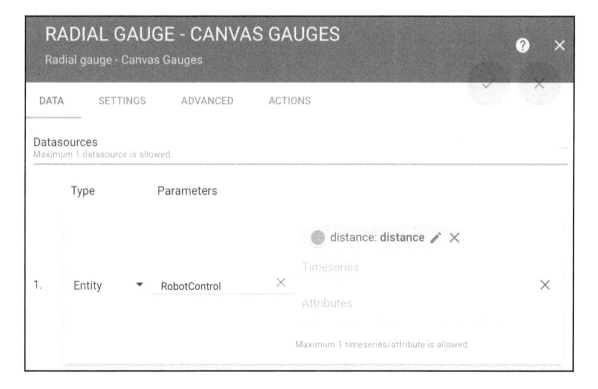

13. As you can see in the previous screenshot, the menu options are **DATA**, **SETTINGS**, **ADVANCED**, and **ACTION**. The default is **DATA**
14. Click on the **SETTINGS** tab
15. Under the **Title**, change the name to RobotEyes:

16. Click on the **Display title** check box
17. Click on the white circle under **Background color**:

18. You will see the color selection dialog:

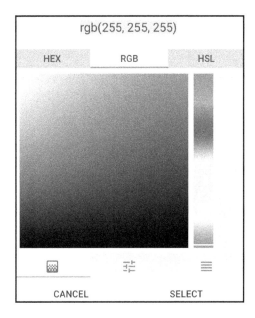

19. Change the top to `rgb(50,87,126)`
20. Click on the orange checkbox to accept the changes
21. You will notice the **distance** gauge has a few cosmetic changes (see the following screenshot):

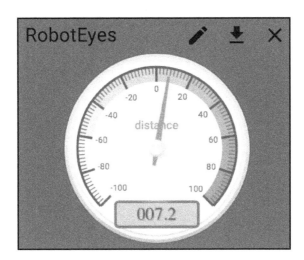

# Changing the range on the distance gauge

Looking at the distance analogue gauge, it's pretty obvious that having negative numbers doesn't make a lot of sense for our application. Let's make the range `0` to `100`:

1. Click on the pencil icon on the widget
2. Click on the **ADVANCED** tab

3. Change the **Minimum value** to 0 and the **Maximum value** to 100:

4. Click on the orange checkbox in the top-right corner to accept the changes to the widget
5. Close the **ROBOTEYES** dialog
6. Click on the orange checkbox in the bottom-right corner to accept the changes to the dashboard
7. You will notice that the distance analogue gauge now shows a range of 0 to 100:

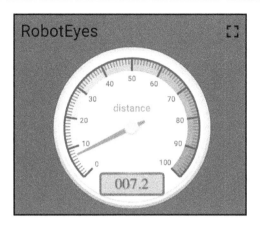

# Viewing the dashboard outside of your account

For our final trick, we will display our dashboard outside of our account (we did this in `Chapter 10`, *Publishing to Web Services*, as well). This also allow us to send our dashboard to a friend. So, why would we want to view our dashboard outside of the account? At the core of the Internet of Things is the concept that we may take information from one place and show it somewhere else, maybe somewhere on the other side of the world. By making our dashboard accessible outside of our account, we allow dashboards to be set up anywhere without the need to share our account information. Picture a large computer screen somewhere in the world, where a small section of the screen shows our dashboard. Showing distance information from T.A.R.A.S may not be of great interest to many, but the concept is what is important.

To share our dashboard, do the following:

1. In the ThingsBoard app, click on the **DASHBOARDS** option
2. Click on the middle icon under the **RobotEyes** dashboard:

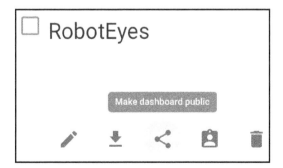

3. You will see a dialog similar to the following (the URL has been partially blurred):

4. Click on the icon beside the URL to copy the URL to the clipboard
5. To test out the URL, paste it into a completely different browser on your computer (or email it to a friend and have them open it)
6. You should be able to see the dashboard with our distance analogue gauge

# Using a Python program to control a robot car through the cloud

Being able to see sensory data in a dashboard is pretty impressive. However, what if we wanted to actually control something from our dashboard? In this section, we will do just that. We will start by constructing a simple switch to control an LED on T.A.R.A.S. We will then expand on this and have T.A.R.A.S do its dance from a push of a button over the internet.

Let's start by changing the name of the dashboard from `RobotEyes` to `RobotControl`:

1. In the ThingsBoard application, click on the **DASHBOARDS** option
2. Click on the pencil icon under the **RobotEyes** dashboard:

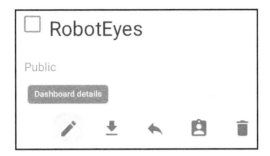

3. Click on the orange pencil icon
4. Change the tile from `RobotEyes` to `RobotControl`:

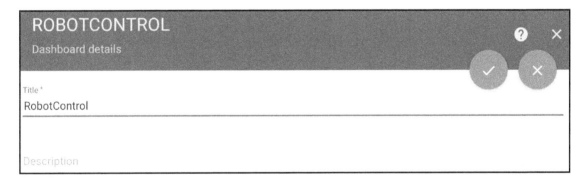

5. Click on the orange check to accept the changes
6. Exit out of the side dialog

Now let's control an LED on T.A.R.A.S from our ThingsBoard dashboard.

# Adding a switch to our dashboard

In order to control an LED, we need to create a switch:

1. Click on the **RobotControl** dashboard
2. Click on the orange pencil icon
3. Click on the + icon
4. Click on the **Create new widget** icon
5. Select **CONTROL WIDGETS** and click on **Switch control**:

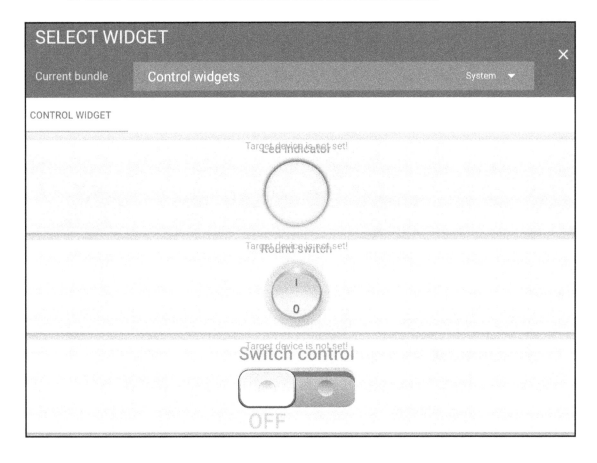

6. Under **Target device**, select **RobotControl**
7. Click on the **SETTINGS** tab:

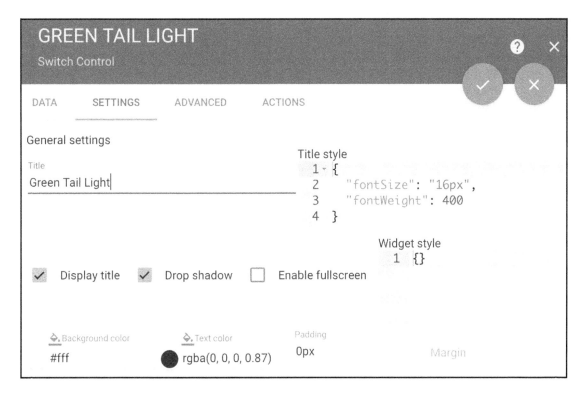

8. Change the title to `Green Tail Light` and click on **Display title**
9. Click on the **ADVANCED** tab
10. Change the **RPC set value method** to `toggleGreenTailLight`:

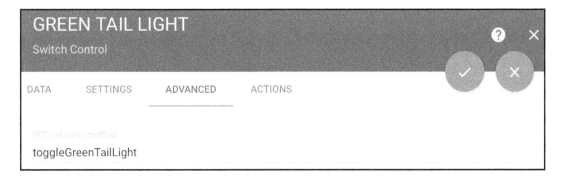

11. Click on the orange check mark icon to accept the changes to the widget
12. Close the side dialog
13. Click on the orange check mark icon to accept the changes to the dashboard

So, what did we just do here? We have added a switch to our dashboard that will publish a method called `toggleGreenTailLight`, which will return a value of either `true` or `false` (the default return values as `this is a switch`).

Now that we have the switch, let's write some code on our Raspberry Pi that will respond to it.

# Controlling the green LED on T.A.R.A.S

To control the green LED on T.A.R.A.S, we will need to write some code to the Raspberry Pi on T.A.R.A.S. We will need the access token for our dashboard (see `Chapter 15`, *Connecting Sensory Inputs from the Robot Car to the Web*, on how to get that):

1. Open up Thonny from **Application Menu** | **Programming** | **Thonny Python IDE**
2. Click on the **New** icon to create a new file
3. Type the following:

```
import paho.mqtt.client as mqtt
from gpiozero import LED
import json

THINGSBOARD_HOST = 'demo.thingsboard.io'
ACCESS_TOKEN = '<<access token>>'
green_led=LED(21)

def on_connect(client, userdata, rc, *extra_params):
    print('Connected with result code ' + str(rc))
    client.subscribe('v1/devices/me/rpc/request/+')

def on_message(client, userdata, msg):
    data = json.loads(msg.payload.decode("utf-8"))
    if data['method'] == 'toggleGreenTailLight':
        if data['params']:
            green_led.on()
        else:
            green_led.off()

client = mqtt.Client()
client.on_connect = on_connect
```

```
client.on_message = on_message
client.username_pw_set(ACCESS_TOKEN)
client.connect(THINGSBOARD_HOST, 1883, 60)

client.loop_forever()
```

4. Save the file as `control-green-led-mqtt.py`
5. Run the code
6. Go back to our ThingsBoard dashboard (if you haven't been using a computer other than the Raspberry Pi on T.A.R.A.S, now is a good time to do so)
7. Click on the switch to turn it on
8. You should see the green LED on T.A.R.A.S turn on and off with the switch

So, what did we just do here? Using boilerplate code taken from the ThingsBoard website, we have built a **Message Querying Telemetry Transport (MQTT)** client that listens to the dashboard and responds whenever the `toggleGreenTailLight` method is received. We accomplish this by subscribing to `'v1/devices/me/rpc/request/+'` in the `on_connect` method. We used MQTT in `Chapter 10`, *Publishing to Web Services*, as well. However, as this code is pretty much just MQTT code, let's look into it a little closer.

MQTT is a lightweight messaging protocol based on a `publisher` and `subscriber` method, perfect for use in the Internet of Things. A good way to understand publishers and subscribers is to relate them to newspapers of the past. The publisher was the entity that produced the newspaper; the subscribers were the people that bought and read the newspaper. The publisher did not know, or even have to know, how many subscribers it had in order to print the newspaper (not taking the cost of publishing into account). Think of the giant newspapers that published every day, not knowing how many people would buy their newspaper. So, the publisher can have many subscribers and, conversely, the subscriber can subscribe to many publishers, as a reader could read many different newspapers.

We start off by importing the libraries we need for the code:

```
import paho.mqtt.client as mqtt
from gpiozero import LED
import json

THINGSBOARD_HOST = 'demo.thingsboard.io'
ACCESS_TOKEN = '<<access token>>'
green_led=LED(21)
```

Of note here are the json and pho.mqtt.client libraries, which are needed for communication to the MQTT server. THINGSBOARD_HOST and ACCESS_TOKEN are standard variables needed to connect to the right server and service. Then, of course, there is the GPIO Zero LED class, which sets the green_led variable to GPIO pin 21 (which happens to be the green taillight on T.A.R.A.S).

The on_connect method prints out connection information and then subscribes to the service that will connect us to rpc methods from our ThingsBoard dashboard:

```
def on_connect(client, userdata, rc, *extra_params):
    print('Connected with result code ' + str(rc))
    client.subscribe('v1/devices/me/rpc/request/+')
```

It is the on_message method that allows us to really modify the code for our purposes:

```
def on_message(client, userdata, msg):
    data = json.loads(msg.payload.decode("utf-8"))
    if data['method'] == 'toggleGreenTailLight':
        if data['params']:
            green_led.on()
        else:
            green_led.off()
```

We first collect the data from our msg variable and convert it to a json file using the json.loads method. The method declaration, on_message(client, userdata, msg), is again standard boilerplate code from the ThingsBoard website. We are really only concerned with getting the msg value.

The first if statement, if data['method'] == 'toggleGreenTailLight', checks our msg for the toggleGreenTailLight method we set up with our switch on the ThingsBoard dashboard. Once we know that msg contains this method, we extract the other key-value pair in data, using if data['params'] to check for a True value. So, in other words, the json file we get back calling the on_message method will look something like {'params': True, 'method': 'toggleGreenTailLight'}. This is basically a Python dictionary of two key-value pairs. This may seem confusing, but the easiest way to think about it would be to imagine this as a json version of a method (toggleGreenTailLight) with a return value (True).

One way to really understand what is going on is to put a `print` statement to `print data` inside of the `on_message` method, just after `data = json.loads(msg.payload.decode("utf-8"))`. Hence, the method would look something like the following:

```
def on_message(client, userdata, msg):
    data = json.loads(msg.payload.decode("utf-8"))
    print(data)
    .
    .
    .
```

When the value returned from `params` is `True`, we simply turn on the LED using standard GPIO Zero code. We turn the LED off when the value returned from `params` is not `True` (or `False`, as there are only two values possible).

Seeing the LED turn on and off by using the internet is pretty impressive. However, that's not enough. Let's utilize some of the code we used in previous chapters and make T.A.R.A.S dance. This time, we will make it dance using the internet.

# Using the internet to make T.A.R.A.S dance

To make T.A.R.A.S dance again, we are going to need to ensure that the code from `Chapter 14`, *Controlling the Robot Car Using Python*, is in the same directory as the code we are going to write.

We will start by creating a dance switch on our dashboard:

1. Follow the previous steps 1 through 9 under **Adding a switch to our dashboard** to create a switch
2. Change the title to **Dance Switch** and click on **Display title**
3. Click on the **ADVANCED** tab
4. Change the `RPC set value method` to `dance`
5. Click on the orange check mark icon to accept the changes to the widget
6. Close the side dialog
7. Click on the orange check mark icon to accept the changes to the dashboard

Now that we have the switch, let's modify our code:

1. Open up Thonny from **Application Menu** | **Programming** | **Thonny Python IDE**
2. Click on the **New** icon to create a new file
3. Type the following from step 4:

```python
import paho.mqtt.client as mqtt
import json
from RobotDance import RobotDance

THINGSBOARD_HOST = 'demo.thingsboard.io'
ACCESS_TOKEN = '<<access token>>'
robot_dance = RobotDance()

def on_connect(client, userdata, rc, *extra_params):
    print('Connected with result code ' + str(rc))
    client.subscribe('v1/devices/me/rpc/request/+')

def on_message(client, userdata, msg):
    data = json.loads(msg.payload.decode("utf-8"))
    if data['method'] == 'dance':
        if data['params']:
            robot_dance.lets_dance_incognito()
client = mqtt.Client()
client.on_connect = on_connect
client.on_message = on_message
client.username_pw_set(ACCESS_TOKEN)
client.connect(THINGSBOARD_HOST, 1883, 60)

client.loop_forever()
```

4. Save the file as `internet-dance.py`
5. Run the code

Now go to the dashboard and flick on the dance switch (unfortunately, it's a switch and not a button). T.A.R.A.S should start dancing just like it did in `Chapter 14`, *Controlling the Robot Car Using Python*.

So, what did we just do? Well, we took simple code, modified it a bit, and through the power of object-oriented programming, we were able to get T.A.R.A.S to dance without having to change or even go through our old `RobotDance` code (isn't OOP the best thing since whatever you think the best thing is?).

For the MQTT code, all we had to do was add `import` to the `RobotDance` class, take away the redundant GPIO Zero import, take away any reference to the LED (as this would cause conflict), and then modify our `on_message` method to look for `dance` as the method.

The `robot_dance` object of the `RobotDance` class type does all the work. When we call the `lets_dance_incognito` method on this object, it puts into motion the methods used for movement in the `RobotWheels`, `RobotBeep`, `TailLights`, and `RobotCamera` classes. The end result is a way to make T.A.R.A.S dance through the use of a switch on the internet.

# Summary

In this chapter, we looked a bit further into the dashboard analogue gauge we used for distance sensory information. We modified it cosmetically before changing the range and making it available publicly. We then turned our attention to controlling T.A.R.A.S thorough the internet. Through the use of a simple program, we were able to turn on the green LED on T.A.R.A.S. with a dashboard switch. We took this knowledge and modified our code to make T.A.R.A.S dance via another dashboard switch.

In `Chapter 17`, *Building the JavaScript Client*, we will continue with this by writing a JavaScript client to control T.A.R.A.S through the internet.

# Questions

1. What type of information would a driverless car need from a central station?
2. True/false? It is not possible to change the background color of widgets in the ThingsBoard dashboard.
3. How would you change the range on a dashboard analogue gauge?
4. True/false? The information returned from the line `print(data)` cannot be read by humans.
5. Which method from the `RobotDance` class do we call to make T.A.R.A.S dance?
6. True/false? The library that we require to work with `json` data is called `jason`.
7. How do we create a switch on our dashboard?
8. True/false? The green LED on T.A.R.A.S is connected to GPIO pin 14.
9. True/false? A publisher can only have one subscriber.
10. How many key-value pairs are returned from `msg` with the `on_message` method?

# Further reading

As we only briefly touched on ThingsBoard, it is a good idea to check out their documentation at `https://thingsboard.io/docs/guides/`.

# Building the JavaScript Client

# 17

Let's face it. We really wouldn't have an Internet of Things if it wasn't for the internet. JavaScript, along with HTML and CSS, is one of the core technologies of the internet. At the heart of the Internet of Things is the protocol for communicating between devices, MQTT.

In this chapter, we will turn our attention away from Python and focus on using JavaScript to build a JavaScript client to subscribe to a topic on an MQTT server.

The following topics will be covered in this chapter:

- Introducing JavaScript cloud libraries
- Connect to Cloud Services using JavaScript

## Project overview

We will start this chapter by creating a simple JavaScript client that connects to an MQTT Broker (server). We will send a test message to the the MQTT Broker and then have that message return to the same page we created the JavaScript client on. We will then publish a message from Raspberry Pi to our MQTT Broker.

It should take a couple of hours to complete this chapter.

# Getting started

To complete this project, the following will be required:

- Raspberry Pi model 3 (2015 model or newer)
- A USB power supply
- A computer monitor
- A USB keyboard
- A USB mouse
- A separate computer for writing and executing the JavaScript client program

# Introducing JavaScript cloud libraries

Let's start off by providing a background on JavaScript cloud libraries. JavaScript has been around since the dawn of the internet (1995, for argument's sake). It has become a language that can turn a HTML web page into a fully functioning desktop equivalent app. Personally, I find JavaScript to be one of the most useful programming languages out there (besides Python, of course).

 JavaScript was released in 1995 and was designed to work with the most popular web browser at the time, Netscape Navigator. It was originally called livescript, but the name was changed to JavaScript due to the use and support of Java within the Netscape Navigator browser. Despite the similar syntax, Java and JavaScript really have nothing to do with each other—a confusing fact that continues to this day.

# Google Cloud

Through `google-api-javascript-client`, we may access Google Cloud services. Specifically, we may access the Google Compute Engine, which is a component of the Google Cloud platform. With the Google Compute Engine, we may access the infrastructure that runs Gmail, YouTube, the Google search engine, and other Google services through the use of on-demand virtual machines. If this sounds like the type of tech babble that will impress your friends, you may want to dig a little deeper into this JavaScript library. You may find out more about the `google-api-javascript-client` here: `https://cloud.google.com/compute/docs/tutorials/javascript-guide`.

# AWS SDK for JavaScript

The AWS SDK for JavaScript in Node.js provides JavaScript objects for AWS services. These services include Amazon S3, Amazon EC2, Amazon SWF, and DynamoDB. This library uses the Node.js runtime environment. You may find out more about this library here: `https://aws.amazon.com/sdk-for-node-js/`.

 Node.js was released in May of 2009. The original author was Ryan Dhal and it is currently being developed by the company Joyent. Node.js allows for the execution of JavaScript code outside of the browser, thereby making it a JavaScript everywhere technology. This allows JavaScript to be used both on the server side and client side for web applications.

# Eclipse Paho JavaScript client

The Eclipse Paho JavaScript client library is an MQTT browser-based library for JavaScript clients. Paho is itself written in JavaScript and may easily be inserted into a web application project. The Eclipse Paho JavaScript client library uses web sockets to connect to an MQTT Broker. We will be using this library for our projects in this chapter.

# Connecting to cloud services using JavaScript

For our project, we will build a JavaScript client and connect it to an MQTT Broker. We will both **Publish** and **Subscribe** to a **topic** named **test**. We will then write a small simple program on Raspberry Pi to publish to the topic named test. What this code will demonstrate is how easy it is to send and receive messages using MQTT.

Take a look at the following diagram to see what we will accomplish with this project:

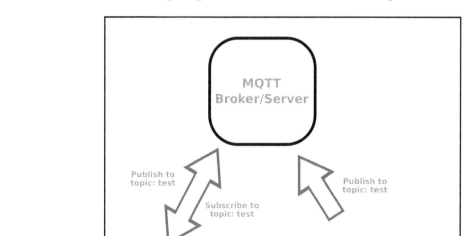

## Setting up a CloudMQTT account

The first step is to set up an MQTT Broker. We may do this by installing one locally using the Mosquitto platform (www.mosquitto.org). What we will do instead is set up a cloud-based MQTT Broker using the website www.cloudmqtt.com.

To set up an account:

1.  In your browser, navigate to www.cloudmqtt.com.
2.  Click on **Log in** at the top-right corner.

3. In the **Create an account** box, type in your email address:

4. You will be sent an email to that email address asking you for confirmation. You can complete the confirmation process by clicking on the **Confirm email** button in the email.

5. You will then be taken to a page where you need to enter a password. Choose a password, confirm it, and then press **Submit**:

6. You will then be taken to the **Instances** page. This is where we will create an MQTT Broker instance to send and publish MQTT messages.

# Setting up an MQTT Broker instance

Now that we have a CloudMQTT account set up, it's time to create an instance to use for our app:

1. From the **Instances** page, click on the big green button stating **Create new instance**.
2. You will see the following page:

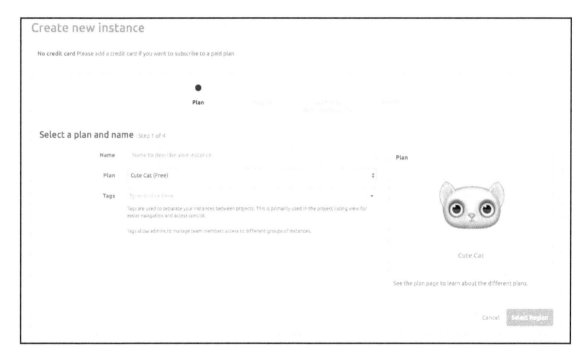

3. In the **Name** box, enter T.A.R.A.S (we will name the MQTT Broker instance this as we will consider this broker part of the T.A.R.A.S robot car).
4. In the **Plan** dropdown, select **Cute Cat** (this is the free option that is good for development purposes).
5. Click on the green **Select Region** button.
6. Based on where you are located in the world, select a region that is close to your geographic location. Since I am located in Canada, I will choose **US-East-1 (Northern Virginia)**:

7. Click on the green **Confirm** button.

8. You will see the **Confirm new instance** page. Review this information before clicking on the green **Confirm instance** button:

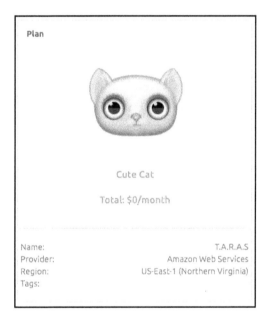

9. You should see a list of **Instances** with the **T.A.R.A.S** instance in the list:

# Writing the JavaScript client code

Here is a screenshot of the T.A.R.A.S instance that I set up on my account. Please note the values in the list. These values are from my instance and yours will be different. We will use these values when writing our JavaScript client:

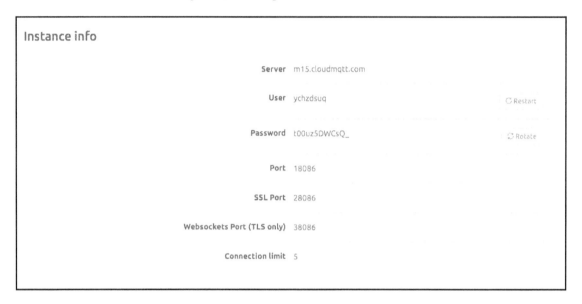

To write our JavaScript client code, we should use a computer other than Raspberry Pi on T.A.R.A.S. You may use whichever OS and HTML editor you desire. I wrote my JavaScript client code using macOS and Visual Studio Code. You will also need the Paho JavaScript library:

1. Navigate to the Eclipse Paho downloads site at `https://projects.eclipse.org/projects/technology.paho/downloads`.
2. Click on the **JavaScript client** link. It will be marked with the name `JavaScript client`, followed by a version number. At the time of writing, the version was 1.03.
3. The JavaScript client library will download as a ZIP file with `paho.javascript-1.0.3`. Unzip the file.
4. We will need a folder on our computer to use as a projects folder. Create a new folder on your computer and name it `MQTT HTML Client`.
5. Create a subfolder called `scripts` inside the `MQTT HTML Client` folder.
6. Drag and drop the unzipped `paho.javascript-1.0.3` folder into the `MQTT HTML Client` folder.

7. The directory structure inside of the `MQTT HTML Client` folder should look like the following:

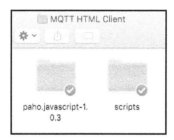

Now, it's time to write the code. We are going to make our code as simple as possible so that we may gain an understanding of how MQTT works with JavaScript. Our client code will consist of two files, an HTML page and a `.js` (JavaScript) file. Let's start by creating the HTML page:

1. Using your favorite HTML editor, create a file called `index.html` and save it to the project root.

2. Your `project` folder should look like the following:

3. Type the following into the `index.html` file:

```html
<!DOCTYPE html>
<html>

<head>
    <title>MQTT Message Client</title>
    <script src="paho.javascript-1.0.3/paho-mqtt.js"
type="text/javascript"></script>
    <script src="scripts/index.js"
type='text/javascript'></script>
```

```
</head>

<body>

    <h2>MQTT Message Client</h2>
    <button onclick="sendTestData()">
        <h4>Send test message</h4>
    </button>

    <button onclick="subscribeTestData()">
        <h4>Subscribe to test</h4>
    </button>

    <div>
        <input type="text" id="messageTxt" value="Waiting for
MQTT message" size=34 />
    </div>

</body>

</html>
```

4. Save the changes to `index.html`.
5. What we have done here is we have created a simple HTML page and imported two JavaScript libraries, the Paho JavaScript library and a file called `index.js`, which we haven't created yet:

```
<script src="paho.javascript-1.0.3/paho-mqtt.js"
type="text/javascript"></script>
<script src="scripts/index.js" type='text/javascript'></script>
```

6. We then need to create two buttons; on the top button, we set the `onclick` method to `sendTestData`. On the bottom button, we set the `onclick` method to `subscribeTestData`. These methods will be created in the JavaScript file we will write. For simplicity's sake, we do not assign ID names to these buttons as we will not be referencing them in our JavaScript code:

```
<button onclick="sendTestData()">
        <h4>Send test Message</h4>
</button>
<button onclick="subscribeTestData()">
        <h4>Subscribe to test</h4>
</button>
```

7. The last element we will create in our `index.html` page is a textbox. We assign an `id` of `messageTxt` and a value of `Waiting for MQTT message` to the text box:

```
<div>
    <input type="text" id="messageTxt" value="Waiting for MQTT
message" size=34 />
</div>
```

8. If we were to load `index.html` into a browser, it would look like as follows:

# Running the code

Before we can run our client code, we need to create the JavaScript file that will provide the functionality we require:

1. Using the HTML editor, create a file called `index.js` and save it to the `scripts` folder in our project directory.

2. Add the following code to `index.js` and save it. Replace the `Server`, `User`, `Password`, and `Websockets Port` with values from your instance (shown as `"m10.cloudmqtt.com"`, `38215`, `"vectydkb"`, and `"ZpiPufitxnnT"`, respectively):

```
function sendTestData() {
    client = new Paho.MQTT.Client
        ("m10.cloudmqtt.com", 38215, "web_" +
                parseInt(Math.random() * 100, 10));

    // set callback handlers
    client.onConnectionLost = onConnectionLost;

    var options = {
        useSSL: true,
        userName: "vectydkb",
        password: "ZpiPufitxnnT",
```

```
            onSuccess: sendTestDataMessage,
            onFailure: doFail
        }

        // connect the client
        client.connect(options);
    }

    // called when the client connects
    function sendTestDataMessage() {
        message = new Paho.MQTT.Message("Hello from JavaScript
                client");
        message.destinationName = "test";
        client.send(message);
    }

    function doFail() {
        alert("Error!");
    }

    // called when the client loses its connection
    function onConnectionLost(responseObject) {
        if (responseObject.errorCode !== 0) {
            alert("onConnectionLost:" +
    responseObject.errorMessage);
        }
    }

    // called when a message arrives
    function onMessageArrived(message) {
        document.getElementById('messageTxt').value =
    message.payloadString;
    }

    function onsubsribeTestDataSuccess() {
        client.subscribe("test");
        alert("Subscribed to test");
    }

    function subscribeTestData() {
        client = new Paho.MQTT.Client
            ("m10.cloudmqtt.com", 38215, "web_" +
                parseInt(Math.random() * 100, 10));

        // set callback handlers
        client.onConnectionLost = onConnectionLost;
        client.onMessageArrived = onMessageArrived;
```

```
var options = {
    useSSL: true,
    userName: "vectydkb",
    password: "ZpiPufitxnnT",
    onSuccess: onsubsribeTestDataSuccess,
    onFailure: doFail
}

// connect the client
client.connect(options);
}
```

3. Run the code by refreshing the browser, where you have `index.html` loaded.
4. Click on the **Subscribe to test** button. You should get pop-up dialog with the message **Subscribed to test**.
5. Close the pop-up dialog.
6. Click on the **Send test message** button.
7. You should see the message `Hello from JavaScript client` in the text box.

Was this some kind of magic we just performed? Well, in a way, it was. We just accomplished subscribing to a topic on our MQTT Broker and then followed that up by publishing to the same topic and then receiving a message in our same JavaScript client. To witness this from the MQTT Broker, do the following:

1. Log in to your CloudMQTT account
2. Click on the **T.A.R.A.S** instance
3. Click on the **WEBSOCKET UI** menu option
4. You should see the following dialog saying that you are connected:

5. In another tab or window on your browser, navigate back to the JavaScript client, `index.html`
6. Click on the **Send test message** button again

7. Navigate back to the CloudMQTT page
8. Under the **Received messages** list, you should see a message:

9. Click on the **Send test message** button a few more times and you should see a list of the same messages under **Received messages**.

# Understanding the JavaScript code

Before we write code for Raspberry Pi, let's take a look at the JavaScript code from `index.js`.

We will look at the subscribe code first. The two methods we use to subscribe to a topic from our MQTT Broker are `subscribeTestData` and `onsubsribeTestDataSuccess`. `subscribeTestData` creates a Paho MQTT client object named `client`. It uses the `client` object to connect to our MQTT Broker by instantiating the object with `Server` and `Websockets Port` values (I've left the values from my account in the code for simplicity's sake):

```
function subscribeTestData() {
    client = new Paho.MQTT.Client
        ("m10.cloudmqtt.com", 38215, "web_" +
                        parseInt(Math.random() * 100, 10));

    // set callback handlers
    client.onConnectionLost = onConnectionLost;
    client.onMessageArrived = onMessageArrived;

    var options = {
        useSSL: true,
        userName: "vectydkb",
        password: "ZpiPufitxnnT",
        onSuccess: onsubsribeTestDataSuccess,
        onFailure: doFail
    }
```

```
    // connect the client
    client.connect(options);
}
```

We then set the callback handlers with `client.onConnectionLost` and
`client.onMessageArrived`. The callback handlers link functions in our JavaScript code
to events from our `client` object. In this case, when the connection to the MQTT Broker is
lost or when a message has arrived from the MQTT Broker. The `options` variable sets the
use of SSL to `true`, sets the `User` and `Password` settings, and then sets the conditions of a
successful connection to the `onsubsribeTestDataSuccess` method and an unsuccessful
connection attempt to the `doFail` method. We then connect to our MQTT broker through
the `client.connect` method by passing in our `options` variable.

The `onsubsribeTestDataSuccess` method is called when there is a successful connection
to the MQTT Broker. It sets the `client` object up to subscribe to the `test` topic. It then
creates an alert with the message `Subscribed to test`:

```
function onsubsribeTestDataSuccess() {
    client.subscribe("test");
    alert("Subscribed to test");
}
```

The `doFail` method is called if the connection to the client is unsuccessful. It simply creates
a pop-up alert with the message `Error!`:

```
function doFail() {
    alert("Error!");
}
```

Now that we understand the code to subscribe to the `test` topic, let's take a look at the
code that publishes to the `test` topic.

The `sendTestData` function is very similar to the `subscribeTestData` function:

```
function sendTestData() {
    client = new Paho.MQTT.Client
        ("m10.cloudmqtt.com", 38215, "web_" + parseInt(Math.random() * 100,
10));

    // set callback handlers
    client.onConnectionLost = onConnectionLost;

    var options = {
        useSSL: true,
        userName: "vectydkb",
        password: "ZpiPufitxnnT",
```

```
        onSuccess: sendTestDataMessage,
        onFailure: doFail
    }

    // connect the client
    client.connect(options);
}
```

A Paho MQTT client object named `client` is created with the same parameters that were used in the `subscribeTestData` function. The only callback handler set is `onConnectionLost`. We do not set `onMessageArrived` as we are sending a message and not receiving one. The `options` variable is set with the same values that were used in the `subscribeTestData` function, with the exception of `onSuccess`, which we assign to the `sendTestDataMessage` function.

The `sendTestDataMessage` function creates a new Paho MQTT Message object with the `Hello from JavaScript client` value and names it `message`. The `destinationName` is the topic we are creating the message for and it is set to the `test` value. We then send off the message with `client.send`:

```
function sendTestDataMessage() {
    message = new Paho.MQTT.Message("Hello from JavaScript client");
    message.destinationName = "test";
    client.send(message);
}
```

The `onConnectionLost` function is used for both subscribe and publish and simply creates an alert popup with an error message taken from the JavaScript response object:

```
// called when the client loses its connection
function onConnectionLost(responseObject) {
    if (responseObject.errorCode !== 0) {
        alert("onConnectionLost:" + responseObject.errorMessage);
    }
}
```

Now that we have our JavaScript client subscribing and publishing to our MQTT Broker, let's get Raspberry Pi in on it.

# Publishing MQTT messages from our Raspberry Pi

Let's return to our Raspberry Pi (if you have been using another computer) and write some code to communicate with our MQTT Broker:

1. Open up Thonny from **Application Menu** | **Programming** | **Thonny Python IDE**.
2. Click on the **New** icon to create a new file.
3. Type the following into the file:

```
import paho.mqtt.client as mqtt
from time import sleep

mqttc = mqtt.Client()
mqttc.username_pw_set("vectydkb", "ZpiPufitxnnT")
mqttc.connect('m10.cloudmqtt.com', 18215)

while True:
    try:
        mqttc.publish("test", "Hello from Raspberry Pi")
    except:
        print("Could not send message!")
    sleep(10)
```

4. Save the file as `CloudMQTT-example.py` and run it.
5. Navigate back to the CloudMQTT page. You should see messages coming from the Raspberry Pi:

6. Navigate to our JavaScript client, `index.html`. You should see the message `Hello from the Raspberry Pi` in the textbox (if you do not see the message, refresh the page and click on **Subscribe to test** again):

The Raspberry Pi Python code was deliberately kept simple so that the concepts may be understood. We start the code by importing the libraries we need. Then, we create an MQTT client object we call `mqttc`. The username and password are set using the `username_pw_set` method. We then connect to the MQTT Broker using the `connect` method by passing in the `Server` and `Port` values (we use `Port` instead of `Websockets Port` for the Python client). Inside a continuous loop, we publish to the MQTT Broker through the `publish` method by passing in the topic, `test`, and the message `Hello from Raspberry Pi`.

# Summary

In this chapter, we explored JavaScript libraries before using JavaScript to create an MQTT client. We set up a cloud-based MQTT Broker and were able to publish and subscribe to messages using both our JavaScript client and a Python program on our Raspberry Pi.

In `Chapter 18`, *Putting It All Together*, we will expand on what we have learned in this chapter and build a JavaScript client that can control T.A.R.A.S over the internet.

# Questions

1. Which program (platform) may we use to install an MQTT Broker locally?
2. True or false? JavaScript and Java are the same technologies.
3. True or false? We may use JavaScript to create an MQTT client.
4. Which Google services may we access using the `google-api-javascript-client` library?
5. True or false? MQTT is a protocol used in the Internet of Things.
6. What does the JavaScript Node.js technology allow you to do?
7. True or false? Python may be used in developing an MQTT client.
8. True or false? We may add functionality from an outside JavaScript library to our web page by using the script tag.
9. How do we set the username and password for our MQTT client in our JavaScript code?
10. True or false? We may view our published messages inside the Cloud MQTT app.

# Further reading

For further information on using a cloud-based MQTT Broker, consult the CloudMQTT documentation at `https://www.cloudmqtt.com/docs.html`.

# 18
# Putting It All Together

For our final act, we will get T.A.R.A.S to respond to control signals sent using MQTT from a JavaScript client. We will do this by modifying the code we have wrote up to this point. If you have been reading this book from the start, thank you for your perseverance. It has been a long journey to get here. We have finally made it. By the end of this chapter, we will have finished building the ultimate in IoT devices, an internet-controlled robot car.

Buckle up (pun intended)—it's time to take T.A.R.A.S to the next level.

In this chapter we will cover following topics:

- Build a JavaScript client to connect to our Raspberry Pi
- JavaScript client to access our Robot Car's sensory data
- Enhance our JavaScript client to control our Robot Car

# Project overview

In this chapter, we will connect T.A.R.A.S to an MQTT Broker. Through the MQTT messages, we will control the movement of T.A.R.A.S as well as read from the distance sensor on T.A.R.A.S. The following is a diagram of what we are going to build:

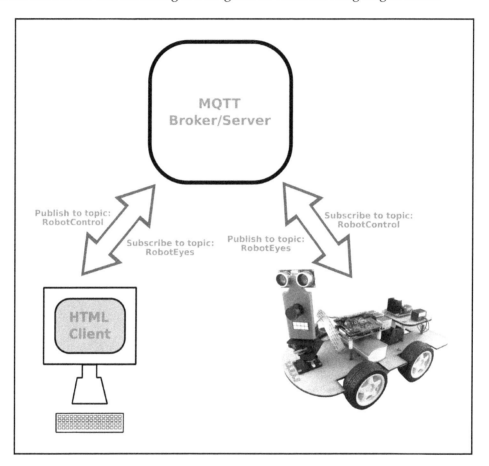

We will start off by writing the HTML JavaScript Client (shown as **HTML Client** in the diagram) and use it to send and receive MQTT messages. We will then turn our attention to writing code on T.A.R.A.S to send and receive messages from the same MQTT Broker. We will use these messages to control T.A.R.A.S using a browser. Finally, we will livestream video from T.A.R.A.S using a browser as well.

This project should take half a day to complete.

# Getting started

To complete this project, the following will be required:

- A Raspberry Pi model 3 (2015 model or newer)
- A USB power supply
- A computer monitor
- A USB keyboard
- A USB mouse
- A T.A.R.A.S robot car

# Building a JavaScript client to connect to our Raspberry Pi

The following is a screenshot of the HTML JavaScript client we will build to control T.A.R.A.S over the network. The HTML JavaScript client won't win any design awards, but it will serve as an excellent learning platform for sending robot control information over the internet:

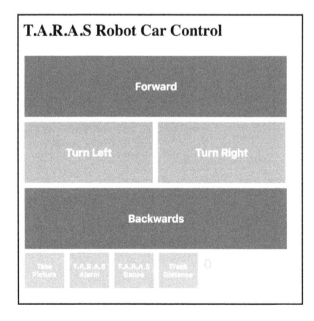

The big purple buttons are used to send `Forward` and `Backwards` commands to T.A.R.A.S. The smaller green buttons send `Turn Left` and `Turn Right` control information to T.A.R.A.S. The small silver buttons at the bottom allow us to take a picture using the camera from T.A.R.A.S, set off an alarm on T.A.R.A.S, and make T.A.R.A.S dance. The `Track Distance` button connects the HTML JavaScript client to distance information coming from T.A.R.A.S.

We will track control information using the dashboard in CloudMQTT before we build a Python MQTT client for our Raspberry Pi.

# Writing the HTML code

We will start by writing the HTML code for our HTML JavaScript client. You may use a computer other than the Raspberry Pi:

1. Create a `project` folder on your computer and call it `HTML JavaScript Client`
2. Copy the Paho JavaScript library from `Chapter 17`, *Building the JavaScript Client*, into the `project` folder
3. Using your favorite HTML editor, create a file called `index.html` and save it inside the folder you created in *step 1*
4. Type the following into `index.html` and save it again:

```html
<html>
    <head>
        <title>T.A.R.A.S Robot Car Control</title>
        <script src="paho.javascript-1.0.3/paho-mqtt.js"
                        type="text/javascript"></script>
        <script src="scripts/index.js"
                        type='text/javascript'></script>
        <link rel="stylesheet" href="styles/styles.css">
    </head>
    <body>
        <h2>T.A.R.A.S Robot Car Control</h2>
        <div>
            <button onclick="moveForward()"
                            class="big_button">
                <h4>Forward</h4>
            </button>
        </div>
        <div>
            <button onclick="turnLeft()"
                            class="small_button">
```

```
                <h4>Turn Left</h4>
            </button>
            <button onclick="turnRight()"
                            class="small_button">
                <h4>Turn Right</h4>
            </button>
        </div>
        <div>
            <button onclick="moveBackward()"
                            class="big_button">
                <h4>Backwards</h4>
            </button>
        </div>
        <div>
            <button onclick="takePicture()"
                            class="distance_button">
                <h4>Take Picture</h4>
            </button>
            <button onclick="TARASAlarm()"
                            class="distance_button">
                <h4>T.A.R.A.S Alarm</h4>
            </button>
            <button onclick="makeTARASDance()"
                            class="distance_button">
                <h4>T.A.R.A.S Dance</h4>
            </button>
            <button onclick="subscribeDistanceData()"
                            class="distance_button">
                <h4>Track Distance</h4>
            </button>
            <input type="text" id="messageTxt" value="0"
                            size=34 class="distance" />
        </div>
    </body>
</html>
```

Before we can view `index.html` in a browser, we must create a `.css` file for the styles. We will also create a folder for our JavaScript file:

1.  In your `project` folder, create a new folder and call it `styles`
2.  Create another folder in the `project` folder and call it `scripts`

3. Your `project` directory should look the same as the following:

4. Inside the `styles` folder, create a file called `styles.css` using an HTML editor
5. Type the following into the `styles.css` file and save it:

```
.big_button {
    background-color: rgb(86, 76, 175);
    border: none;
    color: white;
    padding: 15px 32px;
    text-align: center;
    text-decoration: none;
    display: inline-block;
    font-size: 16px;
    margin: 4px 2px;
    cursor: pointer;
    width: 400px;
}
.small_button {
    background-color: rgb(140, 175, 76);
    border: none;
    color: white;
    padding: 15px 32px;
    text-align: center;
    text-decoration: none;
    display: inline-block;
    font-size: 16px;
    margin: 4px 2px;
    cursor: pointer;
    width: 195px;
}
.distance_button {
    background-color: rgb(192, 192, 192);
```

```
            border: none;
            color: white;
            padding: 1px 1px;
            text-align: center;
            text-decoration: none;
            display: inline-block;
            font-size: 10px;
            margin: 2px 2px;
            cursor: pointer;
            width: 60px;
        }
        .distance {
            background-color: rgb(255, 255, 255);
            border: none;
            color: rgb(192,192,192);
            padding: 1px 1px;
            text-align: top;
            text-decoration: none;
            display: inline-block;
            font-size: 20px;
            margin: 2px 2px;
            cursor: pointer;
            width: 300px;
        }
```

6. Open up a browser and navigate to the `index.html` file in the `project` folder
7. You should see the T.A.R.A.S robot car control dashboard

Before we add the JavaScript code, let's take a look at what we just wrote. We will start off by importing the resources we need. We will need the Paho MQTT library, an `index.js` file (which we haven't wrote yet), and our `styles.css` file:

```
<script src="paho.javascript-1.0.3/paho-mqtt.js"
                        type="text/javascript"></script>
<script src="scripts/index.js"
                        type='text/javascript'></script>
<link rel="stylesheet" href="styles/styles.css">
```

We will then create a series of buttons which we will tie to functions in our soon-to-be-written `index.js` JavaScript file:

```
<div>
    <button onclick="moveForward()" class="big_button">
        <h4>Forward</h4>
    </button>
</div>
```

Since our buttons are pretty much similar, we will only discuss the first one. The first button is tied to the `moveForward` function in our JavaScript file through the `onclick` property. The style of the button is set by assigning `class` to `big_button`. We use the first button to move T.A.R.A.S forward.

# Writing the JavaScript code to communicate with our MQTT Broker

Now that we have our HTML and CSS files, let's create the JavaScript file that will make the magic of MQTT happen:

1. Inside the `scripts` folder, create a file called `index.js` using an HTML editor.
2. Type the following into the `index.js` file and save it:

```
function moveForward() {
    client = new Paho.MQTT.Client("m10.cloudmqtt.com", 38215,
"web_" + parseInt(Math.random() * 100, 10));

    // set callback handlers
    client.onConnectionLost = onConnectionLost;
    var options = {
        useSSL: true,
        userName: "vectydkb",
        password: "ZpiPufitxnnT",
        onSuccess: sendMoveForwardMessage,
        onFailure: doFail
    }

    // connect the client
    client.connect(options);
}

// called when the client connects
function sendMoveForwardMessage() {
    message = new Paho.MQTT.Message("Forward");
    message.destinationName = "RobotControl";
    client.send(message);
}

function moveBackward() {
    client = new Paho.MQTT.Client("m10.cloudmqtt.com", 38215,
"web_" + parseInt(Math.random() * 100, 10));

    // set callback handlers
```

```
        client.onConnectionLost = onConnectionLost;
        var options = {
            useSSL: true,
            userName: "vectydkb",
            password: "ZpiPufitxnnT",
            onSuccess: sendMoveBackwardMessage,
            onFailure: doFail
        }

        // connect the client
        client.connect(options);
    }


// called when the client connects
function sendMoveBackwardMessage() {
    message = new Paho.MQTT.Message("Backward");
    message.destinationName = "RobotControl";
    client.send(message);
}

function turnLeft() {
    client = new Paho.MQTT.Client("m10.cloudmqtt.com", 38215,
"web_" + parseInt(Math.random() * 100, 10));

    // set callback handlers
    client.onConnectionLost = onConnectionLost;
    var options = {
        useSSL: true,
        userName: "vectydkb",
        password: "ZpiPufitxnnT",
        onSuccess: sendTurnLeftMessage,
        onFailure: doFail
    }

    // connect the client
    client.connect(options);
}

// called when the client connects
function sendTurnLeftMessage() {
    message = new Paho.MQTT.Message("Left");
    message.destinationName = "RobotControl";
    client.send(message);
}

function turnRight() {
    client = new Paho.MQTT.Client("m10.cloudmqtt.com", 38215,
"web_" + parseInt(Math.random() * 100, 10));
```

```
        // set callback handlers
        client.onConnectionLost = onConnectionLost;
        var options = {
            useSSL: true,
            userName: "vectydkb",
            password: "ZpiPufitxnnT",
            onSuccess: sendTurnRightMessage,
            onFailure: doFail
        }

        // connect the client
        client.connect(options);
}

// called when the client connects
function sendTurnRightMessage() {
    message = new Paho.MQTT.Message("Right");
    message.destinationName = "RobotControl";
    client.send(message);
}

function takePicture() {
    client = new Paho.MQTT.Client("m10.cloudmqtt.com", 38215,
"web_" + parseInt(Math.random() * 100, 10));

    // set callback handlers
    client.onConnectionLost = onConnectionLost;
    var options = {
        useSSL: true,
        userName: "vectydkb",
        password: "ZpiPufitxnnT",
        onSuccess: sendTakePictureMessage,
        onFailure: doFail
    }

    // connect the client
    client.connect(options);
}

// called when the client connects
function sendTakePictureMessage() {
    message = new Paho.MQTT.Message("Picture");
    message.destinationName = "RobotControl";
    client.send(message);
}

function TARASAlarm() {
    client = new Paho.MQTT.Client("m10.cloudmqtt.com", 38215,
```

```
"web_" + parseInt(Math.random() * 100, 10));

    // set callback handlers
    client.onConnectionLost = onConnectionLost;
    var options = {
        useSSL: true,
        userName: "vectydkb",
        password: "ZpiPufitxnnT",
        onSuccess: sendTARASAlarmMessage,
        onFailure: doFail
    }

    // connect the client
    client.connect(options);
}

// called when the client connects
function sendTARASAlarmMessage() {
    message = new Paho.MQTT.Message("Alarm");
    message.destinationName = "RobotControl";
    client.send(message);
}

function makeTARASDance() {
    client = new Paho.MQTT.Client("m10.cloudmqtt.com", 38215,
"web_" + parseInt(Math.random() * 100, 10));

    // set callback handlers
    client.onConnectionLost = onConnectionLost;
    var options = {
        useSSL: true,
        userName: "vectydkb",
        password: "ZpiPufitxnnT",
        onSuccess: makeTARASDanceMessage,
        onFailure: doFail
    }

    // connect the client
    client.connect(options);
}

// called when the client connects
function makeTARASDanceMessage() {
    message = new Paho.MQTT.Message("Dance");
    message.destinationName = "RobotControl";
    client.send(message);
}
```

```
function doFail() {
    alert("Error!");
}

// called when the client loses its connection
function onConnectionLost(responseObject) {
    if (responseObject.errorCode !== 0) {
        alert("onConnectionLost:" +
responseObject.errorMessage);
    }
}

// called when a message arrives
function onMessageArrived(message) {
    document.getElementById('messageTxt').value =
message.payloadString;
}

function onsubsribeDistanceDataSuccess() {
    client.subscribe("distance");
    alert("Subscribed to distance data");
}

function subscribeDistanceData() {
    client = new Paho.MQTT.Client("m10.cloudmqtt.com", 38215,
"web_" + parseInt(Math.random() * 100, 10));

    // set callback handlers
    client.onConnectionLost = onConnectionLost;
    client.onMessageArrived = onMessageArrived;
    var options = {
        useSSL: true,
        userName: "vectydkb",
        password: "ZpiPufitxnnT",
        onSuccess: onsubsribeDistanceDataSuccess,
        onFailure: doFail
    }

    // connect the client
    client.connect(options);
}
```

3. I have left the values of my CloudMQTT instance in the code. Just as we did in Chapter 17, *Building the JavaScript Client,* replace those values with the ones from your instance (Server, Websockets Port, userName, password).

4. Navigate back to `index.html` in your browser and refresh the page.

5. We now have our HTML JavaScript client in place. What we have essentially done is modify the `index.js` code from `Chapter 17`, *Building the JavaScript Client*, so that we may send control messages to our MQTT Broker and ultimately our robot car:

```
function moveForward() {
    client = new Paho.MQTT.Client("m10.cloudmqtt.com",
38215, "web_" + parseInt(Math.random() * 100, 10));

    // set callback handlers
    client.onConnectionLost = onConnectionLost;
    var options = {
        useSSL: true,
        userName: "vectydkb",
        password: "ZpiPufitxnnT",
        onSuccess: sendMoveForwardMessage,
        onFailure: doFail
    }

    // connect the client
    client.connect(options);
}

// called when the client connects
function sendMoveForwardMessage() {
    message = new Paho.MQTT.Message("Forward");
    message.destinationName = "RobotControl";
    client.send(message);
}
```

We have changed the code in the previous example. The `moveForward` function creates a Paho MQTT Client named `client` with `Server` and `Websockets Port` connection information taken from our CloudMQTT instance. A callback handler to handle when the connection is lost is set to the `onConnectionLost` function. The `options` variable is created using our `userName` and `password` information, which was taken from our CloudMQTT instance. We set a successful connection to the MQTT Broker to the `sendMoveForwardMessage` function. We then connect to our client by passing in the `options` variable.

The `sendMoveForwardMessage` function creates a new Paho MQTT message called `Forward`. This message is then assigned to the `RobotControl` topic and sent using our Paho MQTT Client object, `client`.

Functions to send messages to move backwards, turn right, turn left, take a picture, set off an alarm, and dance are written in a similar way to the `moveForward` function.

Now that we have the HTML JavaScript client for controlling T.A.R.A.S over the web built, let's test it out using the `WEBSOCKETS UI` page on our CloudMQTT instance:

1. Navigate back to your CloudMQTT account.
2. Select the instance where you obtained the server, user, password, and web sockets port connection information (in `Chapter 17`, *Building the JavaScript Client*, we created the instance called `T.A.R.A.S`).
3. Click on the **WEBSOCKETS UI** menu option on the left-hand side. You should get a notice on the right-hand side indicating a successful connection.
4. Navigate back to `index.html` and click on the **Forward** button.
5. Now, navigate back to your CloudMQTT instance. You should see a new message in the `Received messages` list:

Congratulations! You have just connected a HTML JavaScript client to an MQTT Broker and sent a message. We will now develop another client on another device using a completely different programming language and then use that client to subscribe to the messages coming from our HTML JavaScript client.

# Creating a JavaScript client to access our robot car's sensory data

The `index.js` file we created contains functions that subscribe our HTML JavaScript client to the `distance` topic:

```
function subscribeDistanceData() {
    client = new Paho.MQTT.Client("m10.cloudmqtt.com", 38215, "web_" +
parseInt(Math.random() * 100, 10));
```

```
    // set callback handlers
    client.onConnectionLost = onConnectionLost;
    client.onMessageArrived = onMessageArrived;
    var options = {
        useSSL: true,
        userName: "vectydkb",
        password: "ZpiPufitxnnT",
        onSuccess: onsubsribeDistanceDataSuccess,
        onFailure: doFail
    }

    // connect the client
    client.connect(options);
}

function onsubsribeDistanceDataSuccess() {
    client.subscribe("distance");
    alert("Subscribed to distance data");
}
```

Similar to the code we wrote in Chapter 17, *Building the JavaScript Client*, the subscribeDistanceData function creates a Paho MQTT Client with the connection information from our CloudMQTT instance. Upon successful connection, the onsubscribeDistanceDataSuccess function is called, which subscribes client to the distance topic.

An alert is also created, telling us that the HTML JavaScript client is now subscribed to the distance topic.

# Writing the code for T.A.R.A.S

We will now turn our attention back to our Raspberry Pi robot car and write Python code to communicate with our MQTT Broker and ultimately our HTML JavaScript client. The following code should be run directly from T.A.R.A.S. If you'd like to run T.A.R.A.S without tethers, use the USB power supply to power the Raspberry Pi and disconnect the HDMI cable once the following program is run:

1. Open up Thonny from **Application Menu** I **Programming** I **Thonny Python IDE**.
2. Click on the **New** icon to create a new file.

3. Type the following code into the file:

```
import paho.mqtt.client as mqtt
from time import sleep
from RobotDance import RobotDance
from RobotWheels import RobotWheels
from RobotBeep import RobotBeep
from RobotCamera import RobotCamera
from gpiozero import DistanceSensor

distance_sensor = DistanceSensor(echo=18, trigger=17)
def on_message(client, userdata, message):
    command = message.payload.decode("utf-8")
    if command == "Forward":
        move_forward()
    elif command == "Backward":
        move_backward()
    elif command == "Left":
        turn_left()
    elif command == "Right":
        turn_right()
    elif command == "Picture":
        take_picture()
    elif command == "Alarm":
        sound_alarm()
    elif command == "Dance":
        robot_dance()
def move_forward():
    robotWheels = RobotWheels()
    robotWheels.move_forward()
    sleep(1)
    print("Moved forward")
    robotWheels.stop()
    watchMode()
def move_backward():
    robotWheels = RobotWheels()
    robotWheels.move_backwards()
    sleep(1)
    print("Moved backwards")
    robotWheels.stop()
    watchMode()
def turn_left():
    robotWheels = RobotWheels()
    robotWheels.turn_left()
    sleep(1)
    print("Turned left")
    robotWheels.stop()
    watchMode()
```

```
def turn_right():
    robotWheels = RobotWheels()
    robotWheels.turn_right()
    print("Turned right")
    robotWheels.stop()
    watchMode()
def take_picture():
    robotCamera = RobotCamera()
    robotCamera.take_picture()
    watchMode()
def sound_alarm():
    robotBeep = RobotBeep()
    robotBeep.play_song()
def robot_dance():
    robotDance = RobotDance()
    robotDance.lets_dance_incognito()
    print("Finished dancing now back to work")
    watchMode()

def watchMode():
    print("Watching.....")
    mqttc = mqtt.Client()
    mqttc.username_pw_set("vectydkb", "ZpiPufitxnnT")
    mqttc.connect('m10.cloudmqtt.com', 18215)
    mqttc.on_message = on_message
    mqttc.subscribe("RobotControl")

    while True:
        distance = distance_sensor.distance*100
        mqttc.loop()
        mqttc.publish("distance", distance)
        sleep(2)
watchMode()
```

4. Save the file as MQTT-RobotControl.py.
5. Run the code from Thonny.
6. Navigate to the HTML JavaScript client and click on the **Forward** button:

7. T.A.R.A.S should move forward for one second and then stop.

8. The small grey buttons at the bottom allow you to perform various tasks with T.A.R.A.S:

9. Explore the functionality of each of these buttons by clicking on them. The `Take Picture` button will take a picture and store it in the filesystem, `T.A.R.A.S Alarm` will sound the alarm on T.A.R.A.S, and `T.A.R.A.S Dance` will make T.A.R.A.S dance.

10. To subscribe to the `distance` data coming from the distance sensor on T.A.R.A.S, click on the **Track Distance** button:

11. After clicking on the **Track Distance** button, you should see a popup that tells you that your HTML JavaScript client is now subscribed to the `distance` data:

12. Click **Close** to close out of the popup. You should now see distance data information from T.A.R.A.S displayed beside the **Track Distance** button.

13. As with all the code we have written so far, we write it to be as simple and self-explanatory as possible. At the heart of our code is the `watch_mode` method:

```
def watchMode():
    print("Watching.....")
    mqttc = mqtt.Client()
    mqttc.username_pw_set("vectydkb", "ZpiPufitxnnT")
    mqttc.connect('m10.cloudmqtt.com', 18215)
    mqttc.on_message = on_message
    mqttc.subscribe("RobotControl")
```

```
while True:
    distance = distance_sensor.distance*100
    mqttc.loop()
    mqttc.publish("distance", distance)
    sleep(2)
```

The watch_mode method is the default method in our code. It is called immediately after the code is run and is called whenever another method completes. In watch_mode, we need to create a MQTT client object called mqttc and then use it to connect to our CloudMQTT instance. From there, we set the on_message callback to the on_message method. We then subscribe to the RobotControl topic. The while loop that follows calls the loop method of our MQTT client, mqttc. Since we've set the on_message callback, any time a message is received from the RobotControl topic, the program is taken out of the while loop and the on_message method of our code is executed.

In watch_mode, the distance sensory information is published to the distance topic every 2 seconds. Since our HTML JavaScript client is set up to subscribe to messages on the distance topic, our HTML JavaScript client will update the distance information on the page every two seconds.

# Livestreaming videos from T.A.R.A.S

Amazing as it is to be able to control T.A.R.A.S from the web, it wouldn't be of much use if we couldn't see what what we were doing. Streaming live video from Raspberry Pi is actually quite simple if you install RPi-Cam-Web-Interface on your Raspberry Pi. Let's do that now:

1. If you do not have git installed on your Raspberry Pi, please install it with sudo apt-get install git from a Terminal.
2. Using the Terminal, get the installation files by running the git clone https://github.com/silvanmelchior/RPi_Cam_Web_Interface.git command.
3. Change directories with the cd RPi_Cam_Web_Interface command.
4. Run the installer with the ./install.sh command.

5. You should see the **Configuration Options** screen:

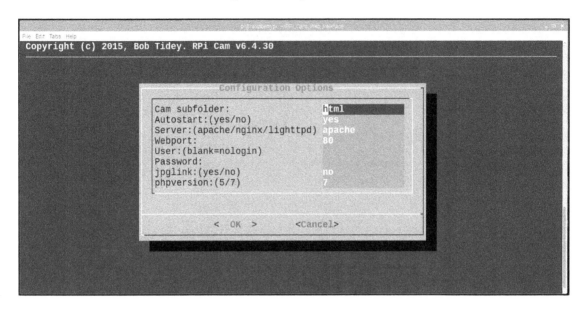

6. Accept all the defaults by hitting *Tab* on your keyboard until the **OK** option is highlighted. Hit *Enter*.
7. Select **Yes** when you see the **Start camera system now** dialog:

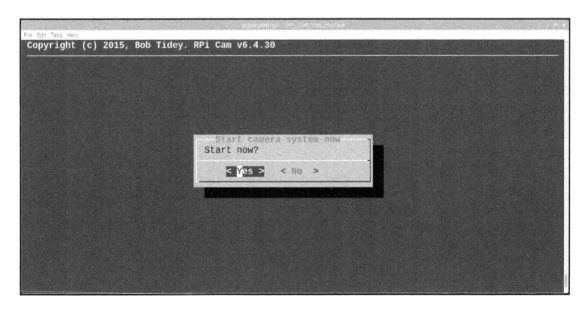

8. We are now ready to livestream video from our Raspberry Pi (T.A.R.A.S). On another computer, open a browser and type in the address `http://<<ip address of your raspberry pi>>/html` (use `ifconfig` on your Raspberry Pi in order to find your IP address; in my case, the URL for video streaming is `http://192.168.0.31/html`).

9. You should now see the video streaming player load into your browser with live video from your Raspberry Pi. The following is a screenshot of the livestream from T.A.R.A.S in my office, looking up at my drones on display:

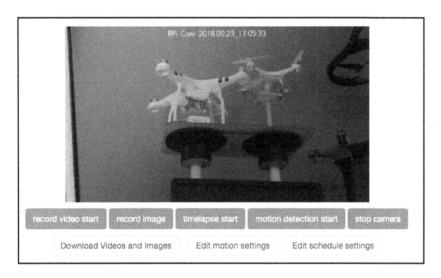

The RPi-Cam-Web-Interface utility is an amazing tool. Take some time to experiment with the various options and functions that are available.

# Enhancing our JavaScript client to control our robot car

As we've mentioned already, our HTML JavaScript client is the most attractive of interfaces. I designed it to be as simple and straightforward as possible in order to explain various concepts. But what if we want to take it to another level? The following is a list of JavaScript libraries that may be used to enhance our HTML JavaScript client.

# Nipple.js

Nipple.js (`https://www.bypeople.com/touch-screen-joystick/`) is a JavaScript touchscreen joystick library that may be used in the control of robots. Nipple.js is basically an onscreen version of pointing stick controls found on some laptops:

If you are creating a JavaScript client for a touchscreen tablet or laptop, Nipple.js may be a good technology to build it on. Incorporating a technology such as Nipple.js into our design would require a fair bit of coding in order to translate the movements into messages that T.A.R.A.S would understand. A simple forward message might not suffice. The message may be something like `Forward-1-Left-2.3` and it would have to be parsed and information taken out to determine how the amount of time to turn the motor and which motors to move.

# HTML5 Gamepad API

Would you like to connect a physical joystick to control our robot car? You may do so with the HTML5 Gamepad API (`https://www.w3.org/TR/gamepad/`). With the HTML5 Gamepad API, you may utilize your standard gaming joystick in web applications you build. Controlling your robot car may be as easy as playing your favorite video game with a HTML5 Gamepad API.

# Johnny-Five

Johnny-Five (`http://johnny-five.io`) is a JavaScript Robotic and IoT platform. It is a completely different platform than what we have developed our robot car on. Now that we have built our robot car from scratch and have coded our control code by hand, we may be interested in trying something new. Johnny-Five may be that next technology you decide to become an expert in.

# Summary

We've have done it! We've reached the end of our Raspberry Pi Internet of Things journey. In this chapter, we brought what we've learned together and created our own HTML JavaScript client that we used to control T.A.R.A.S using a web page. Our use of classes to control T.A.R.A.S made creating the control code relatively easy as we only had to call methods on the classes and not create control code from scratch.

We touched briefly on how easy it is to stream live video from our Raspberry Pi. Although we did all of this to control a robot car over our network, it is not too hard to imagine how we may use what we've learned to build any number of different IoT projects using Raspberry Pi.

We live in a very exciting time. Any one of us may build the next killer app using only our intellect and a few relatively inexpensive electronic components. If anything, I hope that I was able to inspire you to use the amazing Raspberry Pi computer to build your next great project.

For those who are questioning how we may view this as an Internet of Things project when we are only using our local network, please do some research into how you can open up ports on your router to the outside world. This is not a task that should be taken lightly, though, as there are security concerns that you must address whenever you do something like that. Please note, too, however, that your Internet Service Provider may not be giving you a static IP address and thus anything you build to access your network from the outside will break every time your IP address changes (I once built a PHP page that checked my IP address periodically, stored the latest address, and had outside clients which would go to that PHP for the address instead of having it hardcoded).

# Questions

1. Which topic do we publish control-type messages to in our project?
2. True or false? MQTT Broker and MQTT Server are words used to describe the same thing.
3. True or false? T.A.R.A.S publishes and subscribes on the same MQTT topic.
4. What color are the big forward and backwards buttons in our HTML JavaScript client?

5. True or false? Using the HTML JavaScript client, we are able to remotely take a picture using the camera on T.A.R.A.S.

6. What is the name of the MQTT topic we use to subscribe to distance data coming from T.A.R.A.S?

7. True or false? Our HTML JavaScript client incorporates an award-winning UI design.

8. True or false? Using our CloudMQTT account, we are able to view published messages in our instance.

9. What is the name of the technology we use to livestream video from T.A.R.A.S?

10. True or false? Johnny-Five is the name of a new fruit drink created by the Coca-Cola company.

# Further reading

We glossed over the RPi-Cam-Web-Interface web interface briefly when we set up live streaming on T.A.R.A.S. This web interface is quite amazing and a more in-depth understanding of it will only enhance our grasp of all of the things Raspberry Pi is capable of. Please visit `https://elinux.org/RPi-Cam-Web-Interface` for more information.

# Assessments

## Chapter 1

1. What year did the first Raspberry Pi come out?

   A. 2012

2. What upgrades did the Raspberry Pi 3 Model B+ have over the previous version?

   A. Processor upgraded to 1.4 GHz, 5 GHz wireless LAN support, Bluetooth Low Energy.

3. What does NOOBS stand for?

   A. New Out Of the Box Software

4. What is the name of the pre-installed application that allows for creating music with Python code?

   A. Sonic Pi

5. Where is the operating system stored for the Raspberry Pi?

   A. On the microSD card

6. What are the names of the visual programming environments designed for children that comes pre-installed with Raspbian?

   A. Scratch and Scratch 2

7. What is the name of the language used in Mathematica?

   A. Wolfram

8. What is the default username and password for Raspbian?

   A. pi / raspberry

9. What does GPIO stand for?

   A.   General Purpose Input Output

10. What is RetroPie?

    A.   Retro Game emulator

11. True/false? Clicking on the two-folders icon on the main bar loads
    the `home` folder.

    A.   True

12. True/false? The microSD card slot is located at the bottom of the Raspberry Pi.

    A.   True

13. True/false? To shutdown the Raspberry Pi, select **Shutdown** from
    the **Application** menu.

    A.   True

14. True/false? You may only install the Raspbian OS with NOOBS.

    A.   False

15. True/false? Bluetooth low energy refers to people that eat too many blueberries
    and have a hard time waking up in the morning.

    A.   False

# Chapter 2

1. Which operating systems is Thonny available for?

   A.   Linux (Raspbian), macOS and Windows

2. How do we enter Python 2 from the Terminal command line?

   A.   By typing in the command `python`.

3. Which tool in Thonny do we use to view what is inside an object?

   A.   Object inspector

4. Give two reasons why we use an object in our weather example code?

   A.  Keeps the code clean and prepares us for using classes later on.

5. What is the advantage of adding a method called the `getCity` to `CurrentWeather` class?

   A.  We are able to create classes with more generic names.

6. What language is IDLE written in?

   A.  Python

7. What are the two steps taken in order to print the current date and time?

   A.  Import `datetime` from `datetime`, print `datetime.now()`.

8. How did we compensate in our code for wind speed directions that are represented by only one letter?

   A.  By setting the `wind_dir_str_len` with an `if` statement.

9. What does the `if __name__ =="__main__"` statement do?

   A.  Allows for testing the class.

10. What does IDLE stand for?

   A.  Integrated Development and Learning Environment

# Chapter 3

1. What is the name of the Python package that allows you access to the Raspberry Pi camera module?

   A.  picamera

2. True/false? A Raspberry Pi with code written by students was deployed on the international space station.

   A.  True

3. What sensors are included with Sense HAT?

   A.  Accelerometer, temperature sensor, magnetometer, barometric pressure sensor, humidity sensor, gyroscope.

4. True/false? We do not need to buy a Raspberry Pi Sense HAT for development, as an emulator of this HAT exists in Raspbian.

   A.  True

5. How many ground pins are there on the GPIO?

   A.  8

6. True/false? Raspberry Pi's GPIO has pins that supply both 5V and 3.3V.

   A.  True

7. What is a Pibrella?

   A.  Pibrella is a relatively inexpensive Raspberry Pi HAT that makes connecting to the GPIO easy.

8. True/false? You may only use a Pibrella on early Raspberry Pi computers.

   A.  False

9. What does BCM mode mean?

   A.  Used to access GPIO pins through GPIO numbers.

10. True/false? BOARD is the alternative to BCM.

    A.  True

11. What does the Zero in `gpiozero` refer to?

    A.  Zero boilerplate or set up code.

12. True/false? Using Fritzing, we are able to design a GPIO circuit for our Raspberry Pi.

    A.  True

13. What is the default background parameter in the gpiozero LED blink function set to?

    A.  False

14. True/false? It is far easier to use the `gpiozero` library to access the GPIO than the it is to use the `RPi.GPIO` library.

    A.  True

15. What is the Victorian Internet?

    A.  The telegraph and trans-world telegraph cables of the 19th century.

# Chapter 4

1.  What is IBM Watson?

    A.  IBM Watson is a system capable of answering questions posted in natural language.

2.  True/false? Amazon's IoT web services allows access to other cloud based services from Amazon.

    A.  True

3.  True/false? Watson is a champion of the game-show Jeopardy.

    A.  True

4.  True / False? Google has its own global private network.

    A.  True

5.  True/false? We need to change the names of our functions such as `getTemperature` when we introduce web service data.

    A.  False

6.  True/false? It is a good idea to use test code in your classes in order to isolate their functionality.

    A.  True

7. What is the purpose of the `DisplayWeather` class in our code?

   A. To display weather information in the Sense HAT emulator.

8. Which method of the `SenseHat` object do we use to display weather information onto the Sense HAT Emulator?

   A. `show_message`

# Chapter 5

1. True/false? A stepper motor is controlled using an open-loop feedback system.

   A. True

2. What type of electric motor would you use if you were building an electric car?

   A. DC motor

3. True/false? Servo motors are considered a high-performance alternative to stepper motors.

   A. True

4. What controls the angle of the servo motor?

   A. The angle of a servo is determined by pulses passed to the control pin on the servo.

5. True/false? DC motors have shorter response times than stepper motors.

   A. True

6. Which Python package do we use to control our servo?

   A. gpiozero

7. True/false? We are able to control a servo using the Python shell in Thonny.

   A. True

8. What is the command used to move the servo to its maximum position?

   A.  `servo.max()`

9. True/false? We can only move the servo to its minimum, maximum and neutral positions.

   A.  False

10. How do we convert percentage values to corresponding values that the `servo` object understands in our code?

    A.  We multiply the percentage value by 0.02 and then subtract 1.

# Chapter 6

1. True/false? A servo may be used as an IoT device.

   A.  True

2. True/false? Changing the minimum and maximum pulse width values on the `Servo` object modifies the range of the servo.
   A.  True

3. Why do we add a delay before calling the `close()` method of the `Servo` object?

   A.  To delay closing the servo so that it will not be closed prior to being set to its position.

4. True/false? We do not need a `getTemperature()` method in our `WeatherData` class.

   A.  True

5. True/false? A flashing LED on our dashboard indicates a clear and cloudless day.

   A.  False

6. What do we use a pair of shorts on our dashboard to indicate?

   A.  Summer weather

7. Where would you use a regular expression in our code?

   A.  In the `getLEDValue` method.

8. Why do we import `time` in our code?

   A.  To delay closing the connection to the servo

9. True/false? An IoT enabled servo can only be used to indicate weather data.

   A.  False

# Chapter 7

1. True/false? It's CherryPi not CherryPy.

   A. False

2. True/false? CherryPy is used by Netflix.

   A. True

3. How do we tell CherryPy that we want to expose a method?

   A. By using the `@cherrypy.expose decorator`

4. True/false? CherryPy requires many lines of boilerplate code.

   A. False

5. True/false? The default port used by CherryPy is `8888`.

   A. False

6. Why do we add a margin to our `col` CSS class?

   A. So that the rounded boxes do not touch each other

7. Which Bootstrap component do we use as our content container?

   A. Card

8. True/false? In our example, it is sunny and hot in London.

   A. False

# Chapter 8

1.  What is the difference between an active buzzer and a passive buzzer?

    A. An active buzzer has an internal oscillator and will make a sound when a direct current, or DC, is applied to it. A passive buzzer requires an alternating current, or AC, in order for it to make a sound.

2.  True/false? We check the `button.is_pressed` parameter to confirm whether or not our push button has been pressed.

    A. True

3.  True/false? We require a voltage divider circuit in order to connect our PIR sensor.

    A. False

4.  What are the three different methods we may use to have our active buzzer beep on and off?

    A. `buzzer.on()` and `buzzer.off()` separated by a delay, `buzzer.toggle()` and `buzzer.beep()`

5.  True/false? Push buttons must connect directly to a circuit in order to be useful.

    A. False

6.  Which `DistanceSensor` parameter do we use to check the distance of an object from the distance sensor?

    A. The distance parameter

7.  Which method from the Sense HAT emulator do we use to print pixels to the screen?

    A. The `set_pixels` method

8.  How would we set up our `MotionSensor` to read from GPIO pin 4?

    A. Connect the positive pin to 5 Volts, the negative pin to GND and the signal pin to GPIO 4

9. True/false? Basic alarm systems are far too complicated to create for our Raspberry Pi.

A. False

10. True/false? The Sense HAT emulator may be used to interact with outside sensors connected to the GPIO.

A. True

# Chapter 9

1. True/false? The DHT11 sensor is a high-priced and highly accurate sensor for temperature and humidity?

A.   False

2. True/false? The DHT11 sensor can detect UV rays from the sun?

A.   False

3. True/false? Code needed to run the DHT11 comes pre-installed with Raspbian?

A.   False

4. How do you set the resolution of the Pi camera module?

A.   Through the `PiCamera resolution` property.

5. How do you set up CherryPy so that it can access local static files?

A.   Through the configuration.

6. How do you set up an automatic refresh for a web page?

A.   `<meta http-equiv="refresh" content="30">`

7. True/false? Through the use of CSS we are able to simulate a flashing LED?

A.   True

8. What is the purpose of the class `SecurityData`?

   A.   To provide data for the dashboard.

9. Who or what did we find as our intruder?

   A.   A dog.

10. If we wanted to be sticklers how would we change our `SecurityData` class?

    A.   We would initialize the `SecurityData` class with the values of the switch and PIR sensor.

# Chapter 10

1. What is the name of the service we used to send text messages from our Raspberry Pi?

   A. Twilio

2. True/false? We use a PIR sensor to read temperature and humidity values?

   A. False

3. How do you create a dashboard in ThingsBoard?

   A. You create a dashboard from a device's telemetry data

4. True/false? We built our enhanced security dashboard by using a sensory dashboard?

   A. True

5. What is the name of the library we use to read temperature and humidity sensory data?

   A. `Adafruit_DHT`

6. True/false? The library that we require to send text messages comes pre-installed with Raspbian?

   A. False

7. When naming classes in our code what do we try to do?

   A. Name them after what they represent

8. True/false? In order to change our environment from the test to live in our enhanced home security dashboard we have to re-write the entire code?

   A. False

9. True/false? The `account_sid` number for our Twilio account is the same for the live environment as it is for the test environment.

   A. True

10. Where do we create a `SecurityDashboardDist` object in our `SecurityDashboardDist.py` code?

    A. Under the section `if __name__=="__main__":`

# Chapter 11

1. How does an RGB LED differ from a regular LED?

   A. The RGB LED is basically three LEDs (red, green, blue) in one unit.

2. True/false? The Blue Dot app is found in the Google Play store.

   A. True

3. What is a common anode?

   A. Some RGB LEDs have a common positive pin (+), and, .s such, are referred to as having a common anode

4. True/false? The three colors inside the RGB LED are red, green and yellow.

   A. False

5. How do you pair the Blue Dot application with the Raspberry Pi?

   A. By using Make Discoverable from the Bluetooth drop-down menu

6. True/false? Bluetooth is a communication technology built for extremely long distances.

   A. False

7. What is the difference between `DoorbellAlarm` and `DoorbellAlarmAdvanced`?

   A. The class property delay used to change the delay time between buzzer rings.

8. True/false? The GPIO Zero library contains a class named `RGBLED`.

   A. True

9. True/false? The Blue Dot app may be used to record swipe gestures.

   A. True

10. What is the difference between the `SimpleDoorbell` and `SecretDoorbell` classes?

    A. `SecretDoorbell` takes advantage of the swiping gestures in the Blue Dot app.

# Chapter 12

1. How does the Blue Dot application connect to our Raspberry Pi?

   A. Through Bluetooth.

2. True/false? Running a message through the Twilio test environment creates a text message sent to your phone.

   A. False

3. What is the name of the service we use to send text messages?

   A. Twilio

4. True/false? We create our `SecretDoorbell` class as a sub class of the `Doorbell` class.

   A. True

5. What are the four Blue Dot gestures we use in our second application?

   A. `swipe.up`, `swipe.down`, `swipe.left`, and `swipe.right`.

6. True/false? Naming a class for what it is makes coding easier.

   A. True

7. What is the difference between `Doorbell` and `SecretDoorbell`?

   A. `SecretDoorbell` allows for secret gestures so that we may know who is at the door.

8. True/false? Josephine's ring pattern involves one long buzzer sound.

   A. True

9. True/false? You need to use an Android phone in order to receive text messages from our applications.

   A. False

10. How should Constance swipe the blue dot so we know it's her at the door?

    A. Constance should swipe the blue dot right.

# Chapter 13

1. True/false? T.A.R.A.S stands for Technically Advanced Robots Are Superior?

   A.   False

2. What is the difference between an active buzzer and a passive one?

   A.   An active buzzer omits a sound when a DC voltage is applied to it. Passive buzzers require an AC voltage. More coding is required for a passive buzzer. Passive buzzers are more like little speakers and, as such, you can control the sound coming from them.

3. True/false? T.A.R.A.S has cameras for eyes?

   A.   False

4. What does the motor driver board do?

   A.   Controls the motors

5. What is the purpose of the Adafruit servo HAT?

   A.   To drive the servos for the camera mount.

6. How long should it take to 3D print a wheel brace?

   A.   30 minutes

7. What is the purpose of a robot face?

   A.   Faces on robots are used as visual cues for humans to pick up on.

8. True/false? Velcro strips are a great way to secure batteries onto the chassis.

   A.   True

# Chapter 14

1. True/false? The `LEDBoard` object allows us to control many LEDs at the same time.

   A. True

2. True/false? The `notes` list on the `RobotCamera` object is used to move the camera mount.

   A. False

3. True/false? The adversaries in our fictional story love to dance.

   A. True

4. What is the difference between the `dance` and `secret_dance` methods?

   A. `secret_dance` takes a picture

5. What is the name of the `gpiozero` library for robots?

   A. Robot

6. What is the police whistle inspired term given to exposing crime?

   A. Whistles blower

7. True/false? Encapsulating control code is a meaningless and unnecessary step.

   A. False

8. What is the purpose of the class `TailLights`?

   A. To encapsulate LED blinking patterns

9. Which class and method would we use to turn the robot car right?

   A. Robot class and `right()` method

10. What is the purpose of the `RobotCamera` class?

    A. To encapsulate the head movements and camera functionality

# Chapter 15

1. Why do we use a voltage divider circuit when connecting the HC-SR04 to the Raspberry Pi?

   A. 5 Volts is too much voltage for our Raspberry Pi to handle

2. True/false? T.A.R.A.S has eyes that see through the use of sonar?

   A. True

3. What is a device in ThingsBoard?

   A. It is a component used in ThingsBoard for publishing MQTT data

4. True/false? Our class `RobotEyes`, encapsulates the Raspberry Pi camera module used on T.A.R.A.S?

   A. False

5. What does the method `RobotEyes.publish_distance` do?

   A. This methods sends distance sensory data to the ThingsBoard dashboard.

6. True/false? The library that we require to work with MQTT comes pre-installed with Raspbian?

   A. False

7. Why do we name our class `RobotEyes` and not `RobotDistanceSensor`?

   A. We do not need to know that the eyes are made up with a distance sensor. This allows us to change the internal workings of the class without having to change the code that the class interacts with.

8. True/false? Encapsulating boilerplate code in a class makes the code much more difficult to work with?

   A. False

9. True/false? The GPIO Zero library does not have support for distance sensors.

   A. False

10. What is the difference between `RobotEyes.py` and `RobotEyesIOT.py`?

    A. `RobotEyesIOT` publishes sensory information to the internet while `RobotEyes` does not.

# Chapter 16

1. What type of information would a driverless car need from a central station?

   A. Traffic and road conditions

2. True/false? It is not possible to change the background color of widgets in the ThingsBoard dashboard?

   A. False

3. How would you change the range on a dashboard analogue gauge?

   A. By changing the minimum value to `0` and the maximum value to `100` under the **Advanced** tab

4. True/false? The information returned from the line `print(data)` cannot be read by humans?

   A. False

5. Which method from the `RobotDance` class do we call to make T.A.R.A.S dance?

   A. `lets_dance_incognito` method

6. True/false? The library that we require to work with `json` data is called `jason`?

   A. False

7. How do we create a switch on our dashboard?

   A. Click on the `RobotControl` dashboard, click on the orange pencil icon, click on the + icon, click on the **Create new widget** icon, select **CONTROL WIDGETS** and click on **Switch control**.

8. True/false? The green LED on T.A.R.A.S is connected to GPIO pin 14.

   A. False

9. True/false? A publisher can only have one subscriber.

   A. False

10. How many key-value pairs are returned from `msg` with the `on_message` method?

    A. Two

# Chapter 17

1. Which program (platform) may we use to install an MQTT Broker locally?

   A.   Mosquitto

2. True/false? JavaScript and Java are the same technologies?

   A.   False

3. True/false? We may use JavaScript to create an MQTT client?

   A.   True

4. Which Google services may we access using the `google-api-javascript-client` library?

   A.   Google Cloud services

5. True/false? MQTT is a protocol used in the Internet of Things?

   A.   True

6. What does the JavaScript Node.js technology allow you to do?

   A.   Allows for the execution of JavaScript outside of the browser.

7. True/false? Python may be used in developing an MQTT client?

   A.   True

8. True/false? We may add functionality from an outside JavaScript library in our webpage by using the script tag.

   A.   True

9. How do we set the username and password for our MQTT client in our JavaScript code?

   A.   Through the instantiation of a `Paho.MQTT.Client`.

10. True/false? We may view our published messages inside the Cloud MQTT app?

   A.   True

# Chapter 18

1. Which topic do we publish control type messages to in our project?

   A.   `RobotControl`

2. True/false? MQTT Broker and MQTT Server are words used to describe the same thing?

   A.   True

3. True/false?  T.A.R.A.S publishes and subscribes on the MQTT same topic?

   A.  False

4. What is the color of the big forward and backwards buttons on our HTML JavaScript client?

   A.   Purple

5. True/false? Using the HTML JavaScript Client we are able to remotely take a picture using the camera on T.A.R.A.S?

   A.   True

6. What is the name of the MQTT topic we use to subscribe to `distance` data coming from T.A.R.A.S?

   A.   `RobotEyes`

7. True/false? Our HTML JavaScript client incorporates an award winning UI design?

   A.   False

8. True/false? Using our CloudMQTT account we are able to view published messages on our instance?

   A.   True

9. What is the name of the technology we use to livestream video from T.A.R.A.S?

   A.   RPi-Cam-Web-Interface

10. True/false? Johnny-Five is the name of a new fruit drink created by the Coca-Cola company?

   A.   At the time of this writing the answer is False.

# Other Books You May Enjoy

If you enjoyed this book, you may be interested in these other books by Packt:

**Practical Internet of Things with JavaScript**

Arvind Ravulavaru

ISBN: 978-1-78829-294-8

- Integrate sensors and actuators with the cloud and control them for your Smart Weather Station.
- Develop your very own Amazon Alexa integrating with your IoT solution
- Define custom rules and execute jobs on certain data events using IFTTT
- Build a simple surveillance solutions using Amazon Recognition & Raspberry Pi 3
- Design a fall detection system and build a notification system for it.
- Use Amazon Rekognition for face detection and face recognition in your Surveillance project

**Enterprise Internet of Things Handbook**
Arvind Ravulavaru

ISBN: 978-1-78883-839-9

- Connect a Temperature and Humidity sensor and see how these two can be managed from various platforms
- Explore the core components of AWS IoT such as AWS Kinesis and AWS IoTRules Engine
- Build a simple analysis dashboard using Azure IoT and Power BI
- Understand the fundamentals of Google IoT and use Google core APIs to build your own dashboard
- Get started and work with the IBM Watson IoT platform
- Integrate Cassandra and Zeppelin with Kaa IoT dashboard
- Review some Machine Learning and AI and get to know more about their implementation in the IoT domain.

# Leave a review - let other readers know what you think

Please share your thoughts on this book with others by leaving a review on the site that you bought it from. If you purchased the book from Amazon, please leave us an honest review on this book's Amazon page. This is vital so that other potential readers can see and use your unbiased opinion to make purchasing decisions, we can understand what our customers think about our products, and our authors can see your feedback on the title that they have worked with Packt to create. It will only take a few minutes of your time, but is valuable to other potential customers, our authors, and Packt. Thank you!

# Index

## A

alarm system
  building 150
Amazon Web Services (AWS) 75
AWS SDK
  about 351
  URL 351

## B

Blue Dot
  about 221, 222, 223
  bluedot library, installing 224
  paring, with Raspberry Pi 224, 225
bluetooth-enabled doorbell, circuit
  completing 229, 230, 231
  RGB LED 226
  RGB LED, testing 226, 227, 228
  wiring up 225
bluetooth-enabled doorbell
  button information, reading with Python 232,
    233, 234
  button state, reading with Bluetooth and Python
    232
  creating 234, 235, 236
  enhancing 242
  project, overview 221
  requisites 222, 243
  secret Bluetooth doorbell, creating 237, 238
  text message, sending when someone is at door
    243
button
  state, reading 136
  using, with GPIO Zero 136

## C

CherryPy
  about 118
  installing 119
  overview 117
  used, for creating home security dashboards
    160, 166, 170
  used, for creating web page 120
circuit
  building 64, 65
  fritzing process 62
  setting up 61
cloud services
  Amazon Web Services IoT 74
  CloudMQTT account, setting up 352, 353
  code, executing 359, 361
  connecting, with JavaScript 351
  Google Cloud platform 77
  IBM Watson platform 76
  JavaScript client code, writing 356, 357, 359
  JavaScript code 362, 364
  Microsoft Azure 78
  MQTT Broker instance, setting up 354, 355
  MQTT messages, publishing from Raspberry Pi
    365, 366
  using, for IoT 74
  Weather Underground 78
cloud-based MQTT Broker
  URL 352
cloud-based services
  sensory data, publishing 192
cloud
  sensory data, publishing 323
command line
  servo, controlling 95, 96, 97

## D

DC motors 90
DHT11
  used, for finding temperature and humidity 160,
  164
doorbell application, with text messaging
  creating 244, 246, 247, 248
  secret doorbell application with text messaging,
    creating 249, 251, 252, 253

## E

Eclipse Paho JavaScript client 351
Electrical Erasable Programmable Read-Only
  Memory (EEPROM) 57

## G

General Purpose Input Output (GPIO) 11
Google Cloud
  about 77, 350
  services 77
  URL 350
GPIO Zero button
  using 138
GPIO Zero buzzer class
  using 147, 150
GPIO zero package 61
GPIO, Raspberry Pi
  accessing 56
  GPIO zero 61
  Pibrella 57
  RPi.GPIO 60
gpiozero
  used, for performing blink function on LED 66

## H

Hardware Added on Top (HAT) 12, 57, 260
HC-SR04 sensor 319, 322
Hello LED
  distance sensor, configuring 153
  modifying, infrared sensor used 152
  upgrading 155
home security dashboard
  30-second refresh time code, changing 181,
    183, 186, 189

  building, with temperature sensor 172, 175, 179
  creating, CherryPy used 160, 166, 171
  overview 159
  Pi camera, using 165
  sensory data, displaying 171
HTML weather dashboard 125
HTML5 Gamepad API
  reference 390

## I

IBM Watson platform 76
infrared motion sensor
  state, reading from 143
infrared sensor
  used, for modifying Hello LED 152
Integrated Development and Learning Environment
  (IDLE) 35
Integrated Development Environment (IDE) 33,
  299
Internet of Things (IoT) 73
IoT analog weather dashboard
  enhancing 110
  graphic, printing 111, 112
  LED, adding 112, 113, 114
  needle, adding 112, 113, 114
  overview 102
  requisites 103

## J

JavaScript client, building
  HTML code, writing 372, 376
  JavaScript code, writing for communication with
    MQTT Broker 376, 381
JavaScript client
  building, for Raspberry Pi connection 371
  code, writing 356, 357, 359
  enhancing, for controlling robot car 389
  HTML5 Gamepad API 390
  Johnny-Five 390
  Nipple.js 390
  used, for accessing robot car's sensory data 382
JavaScript cloud libraries
  about 350
  AWS SDK 351
  Eclipse Paho JavaScript client 351

Google Cloud  350
JavaScript
    used, for connecting to cloud services  351
Johnny-Five
    reference  390

# L

LED
    creating  66
    toggling, with long button press  141, 143

# M

Message Querying Telemetry Transport (MQTT)
    343
Microsoft Azure  78
Mosquitto platform
    URL  352
MQTT Broker instance
    setting up  354, 355
MQTT messages
    publishing, from Raspberry Pi  366

# N

Nipple.js
    reference  390

# O

Object Oriented Programming (OOP)  300

# P

Pi camera
    used, for clicking pictures  165
Pi-specific libraries
    exploring  49
Pibrella  57, 60
PIR sensor  144
pulse width modulation (PWM)  91
Python command line
    using  37, 38, 39, 40
Python libraries, Raspberry Pi
    about  50
    picamera  52
    pillow  53
    sense-emu  54

sense-hat  54
Python program
    class, creating  41
    class, testing  44
    flexible code, creating  45
    flexible code, example  45
    object inspector, using  43
    object, creating  42
    Sense HAT Emulator, using  82, 84
    used, for controlling robot car through cloud  338
    used, for pulling data from cloud  79
    web service, accessing  79, 81, 82
    writing  41
    writing, to control servo  97, 99
python tools
    integrated development and learning
        environment  35
    Terminal, using  34
    Thonny  35, 36
    using, for Raspberry Pi  34
Python
    used, for reading sensory data  322, 323

# R

Raspberry Pi
    Blue Dot, pairing with  224, 225
    DC motors  90
    GPIO, accessing  56
    history  9, 11
    MQTT messages, publishing  365, 366
    NOOBS  13
    OctoPi  13
    operating systems, overview  12
    PiFM radio transmitter  12
    project overview  13
    Python libraries  50
    python tools, using  34
    RetroPie  12
    servo motor, connecting  93
    servo motor, wiring up  88
    servo motors  91, 92
    stepper motors  88
    Stratux  12
    Twilio, installing  207
    Volumio  12

Raspbian OS
  Chromium web browser 22
  home folder 23
  installer, executing 15, 18, 21
  installing 13
  LibreOffice 29
  Mathematica 26
  microSD card, formatting 14
  NOOBS files, copying to microSD RAM 14
  overview 22
  scratch 28
  scratch 2.0 28
  Sonic Pi 27
  terminal 24
RGB LED
  about 226
  testing 226, 227, 228
robot car Python code
  enhancing 312
  head, moving 308, 310
  integrating 312, 313, 314
  modifying 307
  sound, creating 310, 311, 312
  wheels, moving 307, 308
robot car
  Adafruit 16-Channel PWM/Servo HAT, creating
    for Raspberry Pi 260, 262
  Adafruit servo board, attaching 285, 288, 289
  building 260
  buzzer, dividing 289, 291
  camera mount, attaching 285, 288, 289
  controlling 295
  controlling, with Python program through cloud
    338
  dashboard, viewing outside account 337, 338
  data, reading from cloud 332
  DC motor plate, assembling 274, 276, 278, 281
  distance gauge look, modifying 332, 334, 335
  distance gauge range, modifying 335, 336
  green LED, controlling on T.A.R.A.S 342, 344,
    345
  head, attaching 270, 273, 274
  internet, used for creating T.A.R.A.S dance 345
  motors, attaching 282, 284
  motors, writing up 262, 264, 284

parts 258, 259
Python library, for Adafruit Servo HAT 296
Raspberry Pi, attaching 285, 288, 289
Raspberry Pi, configuring 295
sensor, identifying 318
sensory data, publishing to cloud 323
sensory data, reading with Python 322, 323
servo camera mount, assembling 265, 268, 270
switch, adding to dashboard 340, 341, 342
T.A.R.A.S, wiring up 292, 294
voltage divider, attaching 289, 291
wheels. attaching 282, 284
RPi.GPIO package 60

# S

Sense HAT emulator
  using 82, 84, 138
sensor
  identifying, on robot car 318
sensory data, robot car
  code, writing for T.A.R.A.S 383, 386
  JavaScript client, used for accessing 382
  video, livestreaming from T.A.R.A.S 387, 389
sensory data
  displaying, on home security dashboard 171
  publishing, to cloud-based services 192
  publishing, to ThingsBoard 195, 198
  publishing, with MQTT library installation 192
  reading 195, 198
servo
  controlling, with weather data 106
  position, modifying based on weather data 108,
    109, 110
  range, correcting 106, 107
static pages 124
stepper motors 88

# T

T.A.R.A.S robot car
  beep noise, creating 304
  connecting, to MQTT Broker 370
  dance, creating with internet 345
  drive wheels, controlling 301, 302
  green LED, controlling 342, 344, 345
  LEDs, blinking 304, 306

picture, creating 303
Python code 301
servo motors, moving 302, 303
text message transmission
  account, setting up 202
  Twilio account, setting up 203, 206
text message, bluetooth-enabled doorbell
  sending, when someone is at door 243
ThingsBoard
  account, creating 192, 194, 195
  dashboard, creating 198, 200
  dashboard, sharing 201
  device, creating 192, 194, 195, 324, 326, 327, 329
  sensory data, publishing 195, 198
Thonny 35, 36
Twilio account
  home security dashboard, creating 208, 212, 215, 219
  setting up 203, 206
Twilio
  installing, on Raspberry Pi 207
  text, sending through 207, 208

# W

weather data
  accessing, from cloud 103, 105, 106
  Morse code representation 66, 70
  servo position, modifying 108, 109, 110
  servo, controlling 106
Weather Underground 78
web page
  creating, CherryPy used 120
  HTML weather dashboard 125, 130
  static pages 124

CPSIA information can be obtained
at www.ICGtesting.com
Printed in the USA
LVHW012309161019
634419LV00006B/177/P